INTERNATIONAL ORDER IN A
GLOBALIZING WORLD

Global Interdisciplinary Studies Series

Series Editor: Sai Felicia Krishna-Hensel
Interdisciplinary Global Studies Research Initiative,
Center for Business and Economic Development,
Auburn University, Montgomery, USA

The Global Interdisciplinary Studies Series reflects a recognition that globalization is leading to fundamental changes in the world order, creating new imperatives and requiring new ways of understanding the international system. It is increasingly clear that the next century will be characterized by issues that transcend national and cultural boundaries, shaped by competitive forces and features of economic globalization yet to be fully evaluated and understood.

Comparative and comprehensive in concept, this series explores the relationship between transnational and regional issues through the lens of widely applicable interdisciplinary methodologies and analytic models. The series consists of innovative monographs and collections of essays representing the best of contemporary research, designed to transcend disciplinary boundaries in seeking to better understand a globalizing world.

Also in the series

International Order in a Globalizing World

Edited by
YANNIS A. STIVACHTIS
Virginia Polytechnic Institute and State University, USA

Routledge
Taylor & Francis Group

LONDON AND NEW YORK

First published 2007 by Ashgate Publishing

2 Park Square, Milton Park, Abingdon, Oxfordshire OX14 4RN
52 Vanderbilt Avenue, New York, NY 10017

Routledge is an imprint of the Taylor & Francis Group, an informa business

First issued in paperback 2020

British Library Cataloguing in Publication Data
International order in a globalizing world. - (Global
    interdisciplinary studies series)
    1. International relations 2. Peace 3. International
    economic relations 4. Globalization - Political aspects
    I. Stivachtis, Yannis A., 1965-
    327.1'72

Library of Congress Cataloging-in-Publication Data
Stivachtis, Yannis A., 1965-
    International order in a globalizing world / by Yannis A. Stivachtis.
        p. cm. -- (Global interdisciplinary studies series)
    Includes bibliographical references and index.
    ISBN 978-0-7546-4930-4
    1. International relations. 2. Globalization. 3. World politics--1989- I. Title.

    JZ1308.S77 2007
    327.1--dc22

                                                                    2007005510

ISBN 978-0-7546-4930-4 (hbk)
ISBN 978-0-367-60570-4 (pbk)

Contents

List of Contributors

Olivier A.J. Brenninkmeijer, Project Manager at the United Nations Institute for Disarmament Research (UNIDIR) and the University of Geneva and Adjunct Professor of International Relations at the University of Business and International Studies (UBIS).

Xi Chen, Instructor, Government and International Affairs (GIA) Program, School of Public and International Affairs (SPIA), Virginia Tech.

Maria Raquel Freire, Assistant Professor of International Relations, Faculdade de Economia da Universidade de Coimbra (FEUC), Portugal.

Muge Kinacioglu, Visiting Fellow at the European Institute of the London School of Economics and Political Science (LSE).

Constantinos Koliopoulos, Lecturer of International Politics at the Department of International and European Studies, Panteion University, Athens, and Visiting Professor of Strategic Studies at the Hellenic National Defence College and the Hellenic Supreme Joint War College.

Sai Felicia Krishna-Hensel, Director, Interdisciplinary Global Studies Research Initiative, Center for Business and Economic Development, Auburn University Montgomery.

Angela Liberatore, Social Sciences and Humanities Research Unit, European Commission, Research Directorate General.

Scott G. Nelson, Assistant Professor of Political Science at Virginia Polytechnic Institute and State University.

John M. Nomikos, Director of the Research Institute for European and American Studies (RIEAS), Athens, Greece.

Emel G. Oktay, Assistant Professor of International Relations, Hacettepe University, Ankara and Visiting Senior Research Fellow at the Netherlands Institute of International Relations, Clingendael European Studies Programme at The Hague.

Yannis A. Stivachtis, Director of International Studies Program, Virginia Polytechnic Institute and State University and Head of the Politics and International Affairs Research Unit, Athens Institute for Education and Research (ATINER).

Acknowledgments

A great number of people have influenced my thinking about international order, but here I should at least mention Richard Little and Barry Buzan. My intellectual exchange with Andrew Hurrell, Ole Waever, and Daniel Deudney during the ISA Convention at San Diego was particularly useful.

As with every book, this one, too, could not have been written without the help and assistance of many people. First of all, I would like to thank Professor Sai Felicia Krishna-Hensel, the editor of the Ashgate Publishing's Comparative and Interdisciplinary Studies (CIS) Series, for reviewing the book proposal and accepting it as part of the CIS Series. As the editor of the present volume, it is a great honor for me that Professor Krishna-Hensel has accepted to write the concluding remarks. I would like to express my appreciation to the contributors of this volume for managing to submit their chapters on time despite the fact that some of them faced significant time constraints and personal problems. Without their dedication this book could have never been written. Many thanks go to the anonymous volume reviewers for their constructive criticism, comments and suggestions. I am greatly indebted to Amanda Davis for her excellent editorial and formatting work. The completion of this volume could not have been easy without her invaluable assistance. My special thanks go to the Department of Political Science of Virginia Tech and especially to the Head of the Department, Professor Ilja Luciak, for his continuous support and encouragement. I would also like to thank Rachel Saville for the administrative support she provided for without it, it would have been very difficult to deliver the manuscript on time.

Last but not least, I would like to thank everyone at Ashgate Publishing involved in this project. I will begin with Kirstin Howgate, whose in-depth market knowledge and suggestions have been a blessing for this volume. A special thank you goes to Donna Hamer and Carolyn Court for taking care of the legal aspects of the publication. But the manuscript could not have reached the reviewers and their comments could not have reached the book editor without the essential assistance of Margaret Younger.

It would be very idealistic to assume that academic books can change the world. I would be equally foolish to assume that the present volume will make international society more peaceful or prediction about the future of international order in a globalizing world a more precise science. However, if the arguments put forward in the following chapters help the reader to comprehend some of the issues related to the current state of world affairs and think more critically about the nature of international order, this volume will have achieved more than we can hope for.

Yannis A. Stivachtis
Blacksburg, Virginia

This volume is dedicated to the Political Science and International Studies students at Virginia Tech who lost their lives on 04-16-07, their friends and colleagues who survived during this tragic event, as well as all the other students in the Department of Political Science and International Studies who stood by them during this difficult time ensuring that there is a warm home for them to come back to.

International Order in a Globalizing World: An Introduction

Yannis A. Stivachtis

The purpose of this volume is to address the question of international order in a globalizing world by examining how major international actors seek to respond to major challenges and perceived threats coming from their external environment.

One of the main problems in assessing the impact of major actors' policies, actions and interaction on international order is to identify areas where such an impact may be seen. This requires the use of a theoretical framework that makes such an observation possible. It appears that the English School of International Relations approach to international order provides the best option for doing so. The English School has always been interested in how order is maintained in international relations. For example, in the first edition of *The Anarchical Society* (1977), Hedley Bull, one of the founders of the English School, sought to examine the nature of order in world politics and investigate how order is maintained in the contemporary international system (Bull 2002). Thirty years later, scholars associated with the English School have shown the continuous relevance of Bull's approach to the study of international relations and have re-examined how the anarchical society functions in a globalized world (Little and Williams 2006).

The present volume will attempt to examine the nature of international order in a globalizing world by focusing on the impact of major actors' policies, actions and interactions on the institutions of international society. However, members of the English School do not agree on what these institutional mechanisms are. In the absence of an agreement among the English School scholars, the contributors to this volume will mainly concentrate on assessing the impact of policies and actions on the five institutions of international society identified by Bull, namely, the balance of power, great power management, diplomacy, war, and international law. The contributors to *The Anarchical Society in a Globalized World* have correctly pointed out that certain differences exist between how the institutions of international society were operating during the Cold War from how they operate today (Little and Williams 2006). The analysis provided by the contributors to this volume will provide an additional assessment of the relevance of these institutions to international order in a globalizing world.

The English School and the Question of Order in International Society

According to Bull (2002, 4), the concept of 'order' refers to an arrangement of social life that promotes certain goals and values. Whatever other goals they pursue, all societies recognize three essential goals that need to be attained (Bull 2002, 4). First, all societies seek to ensure that life will be in some measure secure against violence resulting in death or bodily harm. Second, all societies seek to ensure that promises, once made, will be kept, or that agreements, once undertaken, will be carried out. Third, all societies pursue the goal of ensuring that the possession of things will remain stable to some degree, and will not be subject to challenges that are constant and without limit. These three goals are elementary in the sense they provide the basis for the co-existence of people in a society. They are also universal in the sense that all actual societies appear to take account of them.

Bull defines 'international order' as a pattern of activity that sustains the elementary or primary goals of the 'society of states' or 'international society' (Bull 2002, 8). International order should be distinguished from 'world order', which implies the patterns or dispositions of human activity that sustain the elementary or primary goals of social life among humankind as a whole (Bull 2002, 19). International order is order among states; but states are simply groupings of people, and people may be grouped in such a way that they do not form states at all.

Order between states can take two different forms which are reflected in the distinction that Bull drew between an international system and an international society and which is central to the approach of the English School (Stivachtis 1998). According to Bull (2002, 9) an 'international system' is formed when 'two or more states have sufficient contact between them, and have sufficient impact on one another's decisions, to cause them to behave as parts of a whole'. Initially, Bull (2002, 13) defined the 'international society' as coming into existence when 'a group of states, conscious of certain common interests and common values, form a society in the sense that they conceive themselves to be bound by a common set of rules in their relations with one another, and share in the workings of common institutions'. Later, Bull and Watson (1984, 1) redefined international society as a 'group of states ... which do not merely form a system, in the sense that the behavior of each is necessary factor in the calculations of the others, but also have established by dialogue and consent common rules and institutions for the conduct of their relations, and recognize their common interest in maintaining these arrangements'. At first sight, the two definitions appear to be similar, but they in fact correspond to two different historical forms of international society (Stivachtis 1998, 15). The first corresponds to the European international society whose members shared common culture and values (Wight 1977; Watson 1990; 1987), while the second corresponds to the contemporary global international society, which lacks a common global culture.

From the definitions of 'international system' and 'international society' becomes clear that for an international society to exist, it requires the existence of an international system underpinning it. Thus system and society co-exist. The opposite is not true, however. The existence and operation of an international system does not presuppose or require the existence of an international society.

In international society four goals are elementary or primary (Bull 2002, 16–19). First, there is the goal of preservation of the society of states itself. Second, there is the goal of maintaining the independence or external sovereignty of individual states (although this goal is subordinate to the preservation of the society of states itself). Third, there is the goal of peace. For Bull, the term 'peace' implies absence of war among members of international society as the normal condition of their relationship, to be breached only in special circumstances and according to principles that are generally accepted. In this sense peace is also a goal subordinate to that of preservation of the international society itself. Finally, there is the goal of preserving and protecting the common goals of all social life: limitation of violence, the keeping of promises and the stabilization of possession by rules of property.

Within international society, order is the consequence of a sense of common interests in the elementary goals of social life; rules prescribing behavior that sustains these goals; and institutions that help to make these rules effective (Bull 2002, 63). In international society it is the members of the society themselves (states), which are chiefly responsible for performing the functions of helping to make rules effective. In other words, states make, communicate, administer, interpret, enforce, legitimize and change or adapt the rules to changing circumstances. They do so in the absence of either a supreme government or the degree of solidarity one encounters in primitive stateless societies. In this sense it is states themselves that they are the principal institutions of the society of states.

The Maintenance of Order in International Society

Unlike the neorealist approach that assumes order is achieved via an automatic balancing mechanism (Waltz 1979), the approach of the English School suggests that order is achieved and actively protected through a set of institutional mechanisms. It is worth noting that the idea of international order as reflecting an institutional arrangement has also been developed within the 'American School' of international relations (Krasner 1982; Keohane 1989; Ikenberry 2001). Most English School scholars spend little if any time defining what they mean by 'institutions of international society', concentrating instead on listing and discussing a relatively small number that they take to define the essence of whatever international society they are examining (Buzan 2004, 167). For example, Martin Wight argued (1979, 111) that the institutions of international society are 'according to its nature', which implies that institutions will be different from one type of international society to another.

English School writers make a distinction between the 'primary' and 'secondary' institutions of international society. Although a definition of the concept of 'institution of international society' is lacking, there is a general agreement that the key features of primary institutions of international society are: first, that they are relatively fundamental and durable practices that are evolved more than designed; and second, that they are constitutive of actors and their pattern of legitimate activity in relation to each other. There is also a consensus that the secondary institutions represent bureaucratic organizations, like the United Nations, NATO, the European Union, and so on. They are considered to be secondary in the sense that their function depends on how adequately the primary institutions of international society function.

However, members of the English School do not agree on what these institutional mechanisms are. For example, Wight (1977) identifies various institutions of pre-modern international societies including: messengers, conferences and congresses, trade, diplomatic language, religious sites and festivals. With reference to the modern international society, he identifies diplomacy, alliances, guarantees, war, and neutrality as the primary institutions of international society (Wight 1979, 111–12). Elsewhere, he speaks of arbitration, international law, sovereignty, and balance of power but he does not draw together his various comments on institutions into a coherent discussion (Wight 1977, 110–52).

Bull puts institutions on the map for the English School by identifying five such mechanisms. First, a balance of power that is contrived by states and serves the goal of maintaining the system, preserving the independence of states, and providing the conditions on which other institutions of international order depend. Deterrence is seen as one element in the balance of power mechanism (Bull 2002, 121–26; Vincent 1990). Second, international law that represents a body of rules that binds states and other agents in world politics to one another and is considered to have the status of law (Bull 2002, Chapter 6). Third, diplomacy that reflects states' efforts to influence the behavior of other states through bargaining and the use of various non-military activities (Bull 2002, Chapter 7). Fourth, management by the great powers which have the responsibility to promote international order by pursuing policies which work for, rather than against, it. They manage their relations in the interest of international order by preserving the general balance of power, working to avoid or control crises, seeking to limit or contain war among them, unilaterally exploiting their local preponderance to maintain order, agreeing to respect each other's spheres of influence, and acting jointly in concert when necessary (Bull 2002, Chapter 9). Fifth, war, which is the most problematic mechanism to maintain order, as it can also be viewed as a sign of its breakdown (Bull 2002, Chapter 8). Bull argued that under certain conditions war can be the way for an international society to achieve its own purposes and enforce international law. It is accepted as a necessary means to preserve the balance of power.

As it was mentioned earlier, the relevance and nature of some of these institutions to international order has changed over the course of the last, at least, fifteen years. For example, Richard Little argues (Little and Williams 2006, 118) that the long established order associated with the balance of power has given way to a new form of international order associated with hegemony, unipolarity, and empire which represent the negation of the balance of power, with one state setting the rules and then 'ruling the roost'. However, Little recognizes the possibility that other great powers may seek to establish an 'associative balance of power' to counter-balance the United States. David Armstrong suggests that developments in international law (human rights, humanitarian intervention, war crimes) may signify the passage from the traditional pluralist form of international society to a more solidarist type (Little and Williams 2006, 138). Ian Hall points to the decline of diplomacy as an institution of international society (Little and Williams 2006, 143) and the simultaneous rise of anti-diplomacies reflected in the actions of spies and terrorists (Der Derian 1992 and

1987). Finally, Charles Jones mentions the relative decline in inter-state warfare for maintenance of the balance of power among major powers and the development of international law (Little and Williams 2006, 162). But nothing in the work of these scholars implies the complete irrelevance of any of these institutions to international order in a globalizing world.

Bull's failure both to give a clear definition of primary institutions, and to relate to earlier work, continues into, and in some ways worsens within, the more contemporary English School literature (Buzan 2004, 170). For example, James Mayall considers international law to be a master institution, while Alan James (1978) identifies sovereignty, diplomacy, and international law as the key phenomena indicating the existence of an international society. The emphasis on sovereignty is also shared by Robert Jackson (2000, 1990) who adds diplomacy, colonialism, international law, and war. Finally, Reus-Smit (1997) focuses on international law and multilateralism as the key contemporary institutions of international society. Other notable attempts to identify primary institutions of international society have been undertaken by Holsti (2002), Wheeler (2000), Knudsen (1999), Nardin (1998) and Kratochwil (1989).

Acknowledging the weaknesses of the English School to address comprehensibly the issue of international society's primary institutions, Buzan (2004, 171–72) has undertaken the task to confront the following challenges: first, the urgent need to acknowledge the centrality of primary institutions; to generate consistency in the use and understanding of the concept and to make clear what does and does not count as a primary institution; second, the need to flesh out the wider range of primary institutions; third, because institutions can change, the processes of creation and decay need to be part of the picture; fourth, because not all primary institutions of international society are equal, some sort of hierarchy needs to be introduced; and finally, the need to investigate the functional understanding of primary institutions.

In so doing, Buzan (2004, 181–82) has arrived at the following conclusions. First, primary institutions are durable and recognized patterns of shared practices rooted in values held commonly by the members of interstate societies, and embodying a mix of norms, rules and principles. Second, in order to count as a primary institution, such practices must play a constitutive role in relation to both the pieces/players and the rules of the game. Although durable, primary institutions are neither permanent nor fixed. Changes in the practices within an institution may be a sign of vigor, adaptation or of decline. However, one needs to distinguish between changes *in* and changes *of* primary institutions.

With reference to the contemporary international society, Buzan (2004, 187) identifies the following master primary institutions (the derivative primary institutions are placed in parentheses): sovereignty (non-intervention; international law), territoriality (boundaries), diplomacy (bilateralism, multilateralism), great power management (alliances, war, balance of power), equality of people (human rights, humanitarian intervention), market (trade liberalization, financial liberalization, hegemonic stability), nationalism (self-determination, popular sovereignty, democracy), and environmental stewardship (species survival, climate stability). It is with reference to these institutions that the present paper will later attempt to examine the implications of US Foreign Policy for international order.

But if among the elementary goals of international society is the goal of preservation of the society of states itself as well as the maintenance of the independence or external sovereignty of its individual member states, then how does hegemony fit into the picture? Does hegemony imply that international society ceases to exist? Does the US bid for hegemony mean the end of international society?

Hegemony and International Society

A significant change since the first edition of Bull's *The Anarchical Society* is the shift to unipolarity after the end of the Cold War. The implications of the shift to a unipolar system for Bull's international society approach are mixed. In his discussion of the balance of power mechanism, Bull (2002, 101) defines hegemony as 'a state of affairs such that no one power is in a position of preponderance where it can lay down the law to others'. Adam Watson (1992, 15), also identifies 'hegemony' with a state of affairs where some power or authority in a system is able to lay down the law about the operation of the system, that is to determine to some extent the external relations between member states, while leaving them domestically independent. Some scholars like to reserve the term 'hegemony' for the exercise of this authority by a single power. For Watson, the difficulty with this approach is that in fact the authority can be exercised either by a powerful state or by a group of such states.

At first sight, Bull's and Watson's statements would imply that a shift to unipolarity would reflect a complete failure of the balance of power institution. Indeed, the shift has created new challenges for what Bull argued are the mechanisms that preserve international order. After all, the preservation of the various rules and norms that uphold the international order depends on the ability of the society of states to punish any one state that might break the rules. Thus, global US hegemony sets a strong realist challenge to the Grotian thinking of the English School. A powerful state now exists in the system that, presumably, can use its power to do whatever it wants. However, as Watson argues (1992, 15), hegemony is not a dictatorial fiat but it involves continual dialogue between the hegemonic authority and the other states, and a sense on both sides of the balance of expediency. In fact, Watson considers hegemony as one of the forms international society can take along a spectrum that ranges from independence to empire. This means that hegemony does not imply the end of international society but a change of its form. However, hegemony does have important implications for the function of the primary institutions of international society. Therefore, the huge power disparity between the US and the rest of international society's members creates a strong temptation to act unilaterally, and such action is bound to have consequences for the function of the primary institutions (master and derivative) of international society.

Bull discusses only briefly this danger of trying to maintain international order in a unipolar world. However, at the same time he also questions the assertion that a generally preponderant state will always be a menace to the survival of the system of states. He suggests that states that have their own internal checks on the power of rulers may be capable of international virtue (Bull 2002, 101). Bull also argues that at the end of the day, the main function of the balance of power mechanism is to preserve the system of states itself. A stable balance allows for the development of other institutions to manage international order. He does not pass final judgment on the question of whether a power distribution involving global preponderance can also serve this function (Bull 2002, 107). Given this question, it becomes even more intriguing to examine the behavior of the US as a hegemonic state and study its contribution to preserving or weakening the international order.

Ironically, a condition of hegemony brings out more clearly the socially constructed nature of international order. Because there is only one hegemon in the system, it is clearer than before that whatever order or balance is formed will not be automatic, as neorealists argue, but rather contrived as Bull suggests. Indeed, Robert Gilpin (1981) has proposed that hegemonic systems are the most prevalent, and that in such systems the dominant state creates a certain order in its image by designing a set of rights and rules that govern or, at least, influence the interaction among states. Although Gilpin (1981, 29–38) discusses three forms of 'control' in the international system, his third type of governance of the system, its rights and rules, resembles Bull's mechanisms for preserving the society of states. Whereas in a balance of power system the influence of rights and rules may be less conspicuous, in a unipolar system it is easier to see the extent to which the nature of the international order is shaped and molded by the interests and normative agenda of the powerful state in the system. It is clearly not an automatic process.

It is important to stress once more that though a unipolar hegemonic system clearly poses challenges to the viability of the society of states (Reus-Smit 2004), the two concepts are not inevitably opposed to each other. Bull suggests that the function of the balance of power is to prevent the system from being transformed by conquest into a universal empire as well as to provide the conditions within which other institutions of international order can operate. Although the current power distribution is clearly not what Bull had in mind, we can still apply the logic of the argument that links certain power distributions to the maintenance of the basic goals of international society.

Book Structure

The book is divided into three parts and ten chapters. The first part discusses the perspectives of major international actors regarding international order and examines how their policies and interactions affect it. In Chapter 1, Olivier Brenninkmeijer examines the way the United Nations (UN) currently seeks to achieve international peace and security through business and civil society partnerships. He argues that in a globalizing world no single international actor, be it a national government, an international organization, a non-governmental organization or a multinational company, can manage international complex issues or provide solutions to transnational problems on its own. Brenninkmeijer suggests that international actors need to work together not only to address shared concerns and manage common interests, but also to ensure that all affected parties accept the decisions made as legitimate. Although his analysis points to a more solidarist type of international society, the author claims that states have the ability to reduce the capacity of any non-governmental actor to mobilize support and, therefore, they will remain the most powerful actors in international relations even if some national governments are considered to be failing or weak. He concludes that although globalization makes the collaboration among various international actors an imperative, thereby privileging diplomacy and international law, international order and stability will continue to be based on the function of the balance of power and great powers management.

In Chapter 2, Yannis Stivachtis explores the implications of US Foreign Policy for international order. The author challenges the idea that the orientation of US Foreign Policy is absolutely tied to a particular administration and argues that it is necessary to examine the societal roots of US Foreign Policy in order to comprehend its complexity and future orientation. After discussing the post-Cold War US Foreign Policy dilemmas, Stivachtis examines four competing American visions regarding the goals and means of US Foreign Policy: the Hamiltonian, the Wilsonian, the Jeffersonian and the Jacksonian. He then discusses how recent changes in the American society have led to the revival of and changes in these traditions and analyzes what this means for contemporary US Foreign Policy. Focusing on Buzan's, rather than on Bull's, taxonomy of international society's institutions, the author concludes that although all primary institutions of international society will be affected by US Foreign Policy, great power management is the institution that one should expect the US impact to be the greatest. But due to the interdependence among international society's primary institutions, this impact will also be considerable on the institutions of sovereignty, diplomacy, nationalism and equality of people.

In Chapter 3, Maria Raquel Freire discusses the place of Russia in the post-Cold War international order and explores whether and how it affects and is affected by the dynamics of the transatlantic relationship. By analysing the Russian policies in the post-Cold War setting, Freire finds the Russian course to be ambivalent. She argues that the Russian national interest is modeled and readjusted according to opportunities and constraints, and regional power projection is conditioned by the need for collaboration with other major powers, while assuring new ingredients of competition will not be added to this already complex game. Her analysis points to the conclusion that international order will be based primarily on the balance of power and great power management and less on diplomacy, international law, and war.

In Chapter 4, Xi Chen explores the changes in China's foreign and security policy since the establishment of the Peoples Republic of China (PRC) and investigates China's ever changing perception of its national security and interests and their implication for international order in general, and China's relations with the US and its Asian neighbours in particular. Xi Chen discusses two opposing views regarding the possible impact of Chinese Foreign Policy on international order. According to the first view, China's emergence as a regional hegemon in East Asia is the most serious threat the US might face in the twenty-first century. China's challenge of American hegemony most certainly would have a considerable impact on international order. On then other hand, it is argued that China has begun to take a less confrontational and more constructive approach towards regional and international affairs and consequently Chinese Foreign Policy will contribute to a more stable international order. Xi Chen sides with the second view and argues that China will pursue multilateral cooperation both at the regional and global levels.

She also suggests that Chinese Foreign Policy will emphasize the need for states to safeguard their national sovereignty and territorial integrity and that China will build and actively participate in coalitions aimed at counter-balancing American or any other hegemony that may undermine its sovereignty and territorial integrity. Following Chen's analysis one may conclude that from the various institutions of international society, Chinese Foreign Policy will have the greatest impact on diplomacy, sovereignty, the balance of power and great powers management.

The second part of the book focuses on the transatlantic dimension of international order. Since transatlantic relations were considered to be one of the fundamental pillars of international order in the post-World War II era, this part seeks to investigate the nature of current transatlantic relations and their implications for international order in the post-Cold War and post-11 September 2001 world. In Chapter 5, Emel Oktay examines the expanding EU role in geographical areas neighbouring its Member States and its implications for transatlantic relations and international order. She argues that the European Neighbourhood Policy reflects a greater European willingness to be involved in the resolution of conflicts and the spread of peace and prosperity beyond the immediate physical boundaries of Europe. According to Oktay, this policy serves as a useful tool for the EU to project its soft power to a vast area of the world encompassing North Africa, Middle East, Southern Caucasus and the Black Sea region, which could be seen as the EU's enlarged natural sphere of influence. She suggests that through this policy, the EU acquires an additional means of balancing the global dominance of the US, albeit on a limited geographical scale. The author concludes that the current nature of the transatlantic relations and their management will have important implications for international order which is seen to be based more on the balance of power, great power management, diplomacy, and war and less on international law.

In Chapter 6, examining the implications of the European Security and Defence Policy (ESDP) for transatlantic relations and international order, Costantinos Koliopoulos provides the reader with a very different picture. He argues that with the ESDP being overshadowed by NATO, the EU is bound to possess little military muscle for the foreseeable future. This, in turn, is bound to result in correspondingly little international influence for the EU despite the soft power that the latter possesses. Koliopoulos claims that the ESDP can have but a marginal impact on international order. It may provide the Western countries with additional policy options, thus affecting the function of diplomacy. It may conceivably affect the function of war as well, though this is much less likely. However, according to Koliopoulos, when one comes to the institutions of the balance of power and great power management, stark realities emerge in the sense that the EU not only is unable to challenge the hegemony of the US, which implies the absence of a balance of power, but also it does not constitute a power at all. Since the EU represents nothing more than an organization composed by sovereign states, it cannot, according to Koliopoulos, have any effect on great power management as an institution of international society.

In Chapter 7, Angela Liberatore evaluates transatlantic relations with reference to the cases of threat assessment, surveillance technologies, and fundamental rights. These cases are useful illustrations of the relations between security policies on the one hand, and democratic debate, oversight, and rights on the other. She argues that there is a general convergence between the EU and the US with regard to broad features of threat assessment and the resort to surveillance as one of the means to tackle terrorism. At the same time, there is divergence with regard to the stance towards multilateralism, the use of force and the protection of certain fundamental rights. According to Liberatore, a more stable international order can be expected through an increased convergence between the EU and the US. But such an order will only be legitimate if international law and protection of fundamental rights are taken seriously. The author points to the fact that US disregard for international law makes it the least effective institution of international society.

In Chapter 8, John Nomikos discusses transatlantic intelligence cooperation in connection with the global war on terrorism. Nomikos argues that the price of non-cooperation, or partial cooperation, for international order could be enormous. He claims that further terror outrages could have major destabilizing effects in various world regions, sending shockwaves that will affect moderate Islamic regimes and directly affecting national and international economies through rising energy prices. Transatlantic cooperation, however, is not, according to the author, so easy to achieve in practice as it is in theory. Nomikos identifies two problems for this. First, the US' inclination towards unilateralism and the use of military force stands in sharp contrast to EU's commitment to multilateralism and international law; and second, the EU lacks cohesion due to the inclination of its Member States to put national considerations first. Nomikos suggests that the focus of transatlantic intelligence cooperation needs to be on speeding up means of practical exchange on operational matters and not on building elaborate new structures in the EU and the United States. He concludes by proposing the use of NATO military intelligence capabilities to deal with global terrorism.

The last part of the book discusses three major normative issues in contemporary international politics: preemption, legitimacy, and democratization. In Chapter 9, Muge Kinacioglu examines the normative development of self-defence and preemption doctrines and discusses the implications for international order. Kinacioglu argues that because of the current dominance of the US in the international system and its unilateral policies, the existing system of states can hardly be conceived as at 'balance'. In such a state, according to Kinacioglu, one might expect a growing endeavour by other powers to countervail US dominance. She argues that the exercise of pre-emptive action without proper application of the key elements of the customary international law would deeply impair the rules laid down by the society of states to confine reasons for which a state can legitimately resort to force, and would bring with it the threat of breakdown of international society itself. She further suggests that arbitrary interpretation of the central principles of international law by the most dominant power in the international system would also severely weaken the role of diplomacy. The author concludes that the possible positive role war can play in international society would also be eliminated by a widespread feeling that the use of force is self-serving. As a result, great powers' effective management of their relations with one another and their consequent contribution to international order would become problematic as well.

In Chapter 10, Scott Nelson addresses the legitimacy–international order nexus and discusses why political theory is important in analysing this relationship. Nelson argues that the quest for international order was, until recently, a challenge stemming from the accelerated flux of a globalizing world. Today, order, according to Nelson, is sought amidst growing regional violence sparked by the US provoked by strikes and threats of asymmetric power. For Nelson, international order is threatened by more fundamental vulnerabilities that lie at the heart of the liberal doctrines that underpin globalization's logics and processes. To get at these vulnerabilities, Nelson discusses two foundational concepts that serve as crucial supports for the discourses and practices of international order, namely legitimacy and democracy. He concludes that the use of political theory to comprehend the complexity, limitations and contradictions surrounding the concepts of democracy and legitimacy is essential for the study and practice of international relations.

In the concluding part of the volume, Sai Felicia Krishna-Hensel provides an insightful account about international order and the necessity for international cooperation in a globalizing world.

References

Bull, Hedley (2002), *The Anarchical Society*, 3rd edition (New York: Columbia University Press).

Bull, Hedley (2000), 'The Grotian Conception of International Society', in *Hedley Bull on International Society*, edited by Kal Alderson and Andrew Hurrell (London: Macmillan).

Bull, Hedley and Watson, Adam (eds) (1984), *The Expansion of International Society* (Oxford: Clarendon Press).

Buzan, Barry (2004), *From International to World Society?* (Cambridge: Cambridge University Press).

Buzan, Barry (1993), 'From International System to International Society: Structural Realism and Regime Theory Meet the English School', *International Organization*, 47: 3, pp. 327–52.

Der Derian, James (1992), *Antidiplomacy: Spies, Terror, Speed and War* (Oxford: Blackwell).

Der Derian, James (1987), *On Diplomacy* (Oxford: Blackwell).

Gilpin, Robert (1981), *War and Change in World Politics* (Cambridge: Cambridge University Press).

Holsti, Kalevi J. (2002), 'The Institutions of International Politics: Continuity, Change, and Transformation', paper presented at the ISA Convention, New Orleans, March.

Ikenberry, John G. (2001), *After Victory: Institutions, Strategic Restraint, and the Rebuilding of Order after Major Wars* (Princeton: Princeton University Press).

Jackson, Robert (2000), *The Global Covenant: Human Contact in a World of States* (Oxford: Oxford University Press).

Jackson, Robert (1990), *Quasi-States: Sovereignty, International Relations and the Third World* (Cambridge: Cambridge University Press).

James, Alan (1978), *Sovereign Statehood: The Basis of International Society* (London: Allen & Unwin).

Keohane, Robert (1995), 'Hobbes' Dilemma and Institutional Change in World Politics: sovereignty in International Society', in Hans-Henrik Holm and Georg Sorensen (eds), *Whose World Order?* (Boulder, CO: Westview Press).

Keohane, Robert (1989), *International Institutions and State Power: Essays in International Relations Theory* (Boulder, CO: Westview Press).

Keohane, Robert (1988), 'International Institutions: Two Approaches', *International Studies Quarterly*, 32: 4, 379–96.

Knudsen, Tonny Brens (1999), 'Humanitarian Intervention and International Society' (ms. 432), Aarhus: Department of Political Science, University of Aarhus.

Kratochwil, Friedrich (1989), *Rules, Norms and Decisions* (Cambridge: Cambridge University Press).

Little, Richard (2003), 'The English School vs American Realism: A Meeting of Minds or Divided by a Common Language', *Review of International Studies*, 29: 443–460.

Little, Richard (2000), 'The English School's Contribution to the Study of International Relations', *European journal of International Relations*, 6: 395–422.

Little, Richard and Williams John (2006), *The Anarchical Society in a Globalized World* (Basingstoke: Palgrave).

Mayall, James (2000), *World Politics: Progress and its Limits* (Cambridge: Polity).

Mayall, James (1990), *Nationalism and International Society* (Cambridge: Cambridge University Press).

Nardin, Terry (1988), 'Legal Positivism as a Theory of International Society', in David R. Mapel and Terry Nardin (eds), *International Society: Diverse Ethical Perspectives* (Princeton: Princeton University Press).

Reus-Smit, Christian (1997), 'The Constituional Structure of International Society and the Nature of Fundamental Institutions', *International Organization*, 51: 4, 555–89.

Stivachtis, Yannis (1998), *The Enlargement of International Society* (New York: St. Martin's Press).

Vincent, John, R. (1990), 'Order in International Politics', in *Order and Violence: Hedley Bull and International Relations*, edited by D.B. Miller and R.J. Vincent (Oxford: Clarendon Press).

Waltz, Kenneth (1979), *Theory of International Politics* (Reading, Mass.: Addision-Wesley).

Watson, Adam (1992), *The Evolution of International Society* (London: Routledge).

Watson, Adam (1990), 'Systems of States', *Review of International Studies*, 16: 2, 99–109.

Wheeler, Nicholas (2000), *Saving Strangers: Humanitarian intervention in International Society* (Oxford: Oxford University Press).

Wight, Martin (1979), *Power Politics*, edited by Hedley Bull and Carsten Holbraad (Leicester: Leicester University Press).

Wight, Martin (1977), *Systems of States*, edited by Hedley Bull (Leicester: Leicester University Press).

PART I
Major International Actors and International Order

Business and Civil Society Partnerships with the United Nations: Public Policy Challenges under the Impact of Globalization and Implications for International Order

Olivier A.J. Brenninkmeijer[1]

In pursuit of its goals, the United Nations has embarked on a course of action that involves the private sector and civil society organizations. This development is due to an increase in demands made on the United Nations (UN) under the impact of the globalization of markets and communications. The most fundamental change in thinking that is taking place today among social and political scientists is that no single actor, be it a national government, an international organization, a non-governmental organization or a multinational company, can manage complex issues or provide solutions to transnational problems on its own.[2] Be it the pollution of a river or the setting of safety standards for disease control at international airports, both national and global problems require solutions that are supported by every actor that has influence over the issue or that is affected by it.[3] The actors may be political institutions, businesses or civil society associations (CSOs) of all sizes and types. They need to work together, not only to address shared concerns or manage common interests, but also to ensure that all affected parties accept the decisions made as legitimate. New forms of networks and partnerships emerge that are increasingly

---

1   This chapter represents the author's views and does not necessarily reflect the views of the United Nations, UNIDIR, or of its sponsors.

2   The expression 'non-governmental organizations' (NGOs) refers to any kind of association that is not directed by a government or public agent. It can be included within the broader expression of 'civil society organizations' (CSO) and both expressions are used here to refer to the same kind of association that is independent from both government and profit-oriented organizations such as businesses. Within this term for CSOs one may also include associations that are social, cultural, philanthropic or religious in nature.

3   The expressions 'civil society' or 'the public' may be difficult to define depending on whether one chooses to include members of governments or not, or whether one accepts that there may be many publics. For the purpose of clarity here, both imply people who act without the direct support or influence from their employers. The public or civil society is expected to be independent in its behaviour or organization from governments and industry.

managed by professionals and mostly among non-governmental and not-for-profit organizations. They address issues with actors from other sectors – national governments, international organizations, businesses and specialized associations.

> Transnational initiatives are a growth area revealing some interesting inventiveness in problem solving that brings together several interested organizations in multiparty alliances to share expertise on a specific issue or concern. Lacking a permanent identity, they represent a new wave of problem specific alliances designed to brainstorm on consensual policy and secure an immediate response (Krishna-Hensel 2006, 18).

Transnational and interdependent partnerships are the direct result of the globalization of communication and the exchange of ideas. In its drive to develop partnerships with civil society organizations and the private sector, the UN follows a trend of global integration of values and expectations, and sets a dynamic in motion that commits its new partners to the values the United Nations embodies. These are in general global peace, economic prosperity, disarmament and sustainable development to ensure a healthy future for generations to come. Broadly, these values have universal approval and are an asset of the UN that can be enhanced through global awareness-raising, education and development. To advance in this work, the United Nations has engaged in developing partnerships with global and local actors in other sectors next to its traditional affiliation with state governments. Economic development and the facilitation of private entrepreneurship are the most important aspects of human development (employment, food production, education, health-care, and so on). It is therefore interesting for the United Nations and other international and regional organizations to partner with the private sector; business and civil society partnerships are one such avenue about which this chapter offers an introduction.

Most interesting is that the global awareness of the fundamental values that the UN is mandated to promote increasingly leads to local and national demands by the general public to have a voice in policy decision-making ranging from human rights to disarmament or from pollution controls to international development aid. The spread of these values is also closely followed by expectations that the values will be adopted and implemented. This has serious consequences for global order in that the legitimacy of decision-makers in all sectors of society is questioned where communities find that their expectations for participation, transparency and legitimacy remain unmet. In light of this global development, this chapter offers a conceptual discussion of globalization and of the recent growth of cross-sector partnerships. Particular attention is given here those partnerships in which the United Nations has become involved or which it has launched together with businesses and civil society organizations. The UN, in fact, is not only one of the prime global actors solicited to become involved in partnerships, but it has also initiated many governance efforts to enhance its ability to fulfil its own objectives.[4] While some positive aspects of cross-sector partnerships will be presented here, this development is not without its challenges. These include serious asymmetries that are reinforced through the effects of globalization as this study outlines below. This

---

4   As the expression is used here, governance refers to the development and maintenance of norms and regulations. It extends the realm of policy debates and decisions on regulation beyond the national borders of sovereign states.

chapter will not, however, provide a historic account of how cross-sector governance methods have arisen or how exactly global public policy is devised through such new networked partnerships.[5] This has been done elsewhere already (for example Reinicke 1998; Tesner 2000; United Nations 2002). Rather, this text highlights how globalization plays a role in this development, how it may influence global order as we know it, and why primary institutions of international society remain vital for the evolution of cross-sector partnerships and global public policy.

Globalization

Cross-sector partnerships are in part a result of globalization. There is a good reason for this. Globalization is a multi-faceted and multi-layered development driven by technology, trade and the exchange of information and ideas among an ever-growing global population. This exchange links up actors in all sectors: government, industry, civil society, trade unions, expert associations, sports clubs, academic institutes, international organizations, and so on. In this increasingly integrated and interconnected environment, policies designed within any sector are increasingly questioned as to their legitimacy or acceptability by people in other sectors who are affected by the decisions taken. With a growing awareness of democratic principles – the dangers posed by the gap between rich and poor, the need to protect human rights and the importance of a healthy natural environment – people everywhere want better governance. Without restating what has already been said about globalization, it is important here to highlight that its effects, especially from commerce and the spread of ideas, continue to influence ever more people in ever different ways – from consumer behaviour to expectations for democratic decision-making – and that this occurs primarily through the spread of images of life-styles and the values they represent. Globalization has contributed to the dissolution of traditional values and has not only made it possible for (foreign) ideas to be adopted in traditional cultures, but this very influence has also contributed to the evaporation of traditional social structures that provided a sense of security and stability. Most of all, this disappearance of traditional structures has caused a loss of confidence in community elites or elders to make decisions in the interest of their villages, towns or communities. Today, the world-wide spread of modern life-style images and choices, values, economic markets, consumer trends, as well as political ideas has changed traditional hierarchies and patterns of loyalty or kinship.

Although globalization is not new, the 20th century was characterized by the greatest growth of global organizations of all kinds. These are the result of ideas on how to capitalize on business opportunities or political ideologies. Before the onset of communications technology, however, truly global agencies existed only in the form of religious organizations and colonial state companies. One difference between these and today's many multinational companies, global partnerships and networks is that the latter are not under the control of any single national government or religious authority. During the 20th century, corporations, alliances,

---

5   The expression 'global public policy' is taken from: Reinicke, H. Wolfgang, (1998).

networks and partnerships have begun to reach everywhere. They may be driven by political ambitions, business interests or non-government and non-profit advocacy campaigns. They can influence almost any community around the world and they include among their members industrial lobby groups, government agencies, multinational corporations, international organizations, civil society organizations, social actors, non-state armed groups that prone violence for political aims, religious bodies, philanthropic initiatives, or scientific associations. They all have one thing in common, their dependence on modern communication technology.

This massive global change is primarily pushed forward by the logic of the capital market and liberal policies permitting almost any form of communication on almost every subject. This has led to a global economic system that is increasingly interdependent and interlocked, especially in highly industrialized societies. Most important with regard to this study is the spread of ideas through communications technology about the quality and legitimacy of policies in state governments, in big business companies and among civil society organizations. This is the first element that contributes to global integration. In this context, the commercial media portrays impressions of democracies that offer two attractive things: they are governed by leaders who have a popular domestic mandate and they are economically better off than most non-democratic countries. While wealth creation and democracy may not have much in common, both do rely on a free flow of information, goods and services across mental and physical barriers. The second element of global integration is the sophistication of international finance and trading freed from territorial constraints. Third is the deepening of interdependence in the form of regional industrial networks and free trade arrangements. Finally, the fourth element is the end of the bi-polar competitive system that characterized the Cold War. It temporarily froze globalization in countries ruled by autocratic regimes (and still does so in a number of countries).[6]

For the purpose of this study, the change that is most important is the facility with which groups of all sizes and types can influence policies on issues such as security, poverty reduction, education, healthcare, economic growth or employment. Previously, only a few statesmen and business leaders could influence policy debates at home or abroad and thereby affect the lives of people on a massive scale. This was primarily through alliances between politics and industry. Historical examples abound such as of dictators manipulating citizens and industry, large government-run corporatist strategies to colonize populations and exploit natural resources, or the control over the principal export revenues of natural or agricultural resources in 'banana republics'. The biggest change, however, is that because of modern communication technology and its easy availability all over the world, not only government-business alliances can amass power or influence over others. Groups of people working via a network to advance a common interest now have this ability as well. They do not need to be in pre-established positions of authority or power within hierarchical government or industry structures. Instead, they can amass influence through their number and their skillful use (or exploitation) of communications technology.[7] The implications of this network-influence capacity, or as one might call

---

6　Points 2 and 3 borrowed from: Marshall, Don D. (1996), p. 894.

7　One might add here that great mobilizing skills have proven effective before without modern telecommunications. For example the French Revolution, the creation of the Soviet

it, 'mobilization and interface capacity', is immense and still little understood today.[8] What is certain is that this will be an important element in the study of international relations for the foreseeable future.

Networking to mobilize support and develop interface capacity on a global scale is possible in any society where people can share values and pursue common objectives. Networks around the world stimulate the formation of multiple relationships that feed on, learn from, or profit from each other. They become powerful dynamics that can mobilize support for value-laden debates or for new consumer trends. Indeed:

> Web based information can be an effective mechanism for mobilizing public participation in global governance and cooperation by eliciting an organized and informed response to a wide range of issues, as well as providing the means for instant feedback. [...] The involvement of individuals and civil society in the policy formulation process is a relatively new development (Krishna-Hensel 2006, 3–4).

Most networks and campaigns aim to influence specific target communities, population groups or market segments. For example, voices may be mobilized to support anti-terror campaigns, to speak up against immigration and the integration of migrants, to call for a ban on landmines, or to boycott products from a company that stands accused of exploiting laborers. Potent are also collective calls to oppose genetically modified foods, to raise fears about the global spread of viral diseases, the increasing use of nano technology, or about the haphazard mix of man-made chemicals from fertilizers, preservatives and pollutants that reappear in the industrialized food chain. Views of what needs to be done to improve human well-being, security or the environment are intimately connected with values, experiences and expectations of well-being.

But, not only perceptions change through the global spread of ideas; expectations do so as well. From the 'top-down', leaders in government and civil society organizations recognize what customer-oriented businesses often understand well – the importance of their constituencies. They must regularly show that they listen to the needs of their supporters, tax-payers, audiences, shareholders and readers or lose their positions. From the 'bottom-up', people expect that they may have a say in how policies are formulated and how social, political and economic leaders make the decisions that affect them. In business, customers can decide not to buy a product and thus send a message of disapproval. Frustration sets in where such participation in decision-making remains impossible or where choices are unavailable. One observer summarized this in the following words: 'the most important political and ideational development of the last three centuries [are]: the

---

Union, the rise of Nazi power in Germany and the communist government of China are among the most famous historical cases where charismatic and demagogic leaders understood the power they could wield over existing governments and industry through effective public mobilization and propaganda.

8 'Interface capacity can be understood as the ability of an organization to work effectively in multi-stakeholder partnerships. This ability depends on the presence of the skills, policies, mechanisms and tools necessary to facilitate partnership work [...] partnerships are a *complement* to established work streams.' From: Witte, Jan Martin and Wolfgang Reinicke, (2005), p. 62.

notion of representative and accountable government; and the debate about human rights' (James 2004, 10). Recognition lies at the base of respect for human rights, while legitimacy, accountability and transparency are aspects of what is often called 'good governance'.

Governance through Cross-Sector Partnerships

The expectation for participation in policy debates is a characteristic of the new governance networks and partnerships. Their very existence is due to the demands made by those who can exercise serious detrimental or constructive influence, namely the stakeholders. These are the individuals or groups that have a potential influence over a decision-making process in government or any organization, including businesses, and they most often represent communities that are affected by the policies under discussion. Once a global or local issue becomes a topic of debate and advocacy among stakeholders, only governance in partnership with them can provide for the necessary legitimacy. Their participation offers them and their respective constituencies an opportunity to feel consulted and recognized. Their input in decisions may not only inspire greater confidence among the stakeholders' respective publics, but also provide for mobilizing and interface capacity. New kinds of cross-sector partnerships often begin with public debates about policies in the media or by non-governmental organizations. They aim to mobilize sufficient support among affected or potentially affected communities to create a voice loud and influential enough to be heard by those who have influence on the policy-making process.

However, this new development of partnerships should not leave the impression that state governments become redundant or that, because of cross-sector governance partnerships, their role as pillars of international order is changing. Rather, the importance of states remains as final arbiters of power and coercion, as well as suppliers of services, educators, standard setters and law enforcers. They continue to do this within the territories under their jurisdiction and beyond through international treaties and agreements. Within national and international organizations and institutions, states have always played this role unilaterally or by delegating authority to international organizations or specialized agencies. Governance, in the context of this study, implies a process within an institutional setting that guides and sets limits for collective activities and decisions by a group. The executive aspect of governance can be carried out through legal enforcement as a state government would, but also through a 'soft' approach by convincing and educating the recipients of the need to follow the given regulations. Another way to get a constituency to follow new regulations is to apply financial incentives, or to build barriers and limits to their activities. An interesting way of putting this is: 'governance can be accomplished by law, norms, markets, and architecture' (Lessig 1999, 88). Cross-sector governance refers to governance across traditional sectoral divisions or, as some writers call it, 'multisectoral public policy networks'.[9]

---

9   The expression 'multisectoral public policy networks' is from: Benner, Thorsten *et al.*, in Held, David (2005), p. 67.

The Participants' Objectives

The types of actors or associations that join and participate in cross-sector partnerships are varied. For the purpose of this study, however, the list is simplified and includes the following: First, state governments and their national, regional, local and also multilateral agencies including international organizations. Second, private industry (individual businesses or companies from one sector), private industry associations (across different sectors) and employers' associations. Third, civil society organizations that form either non-governmental or non-profit organizations of every type, size and shape. Among these, one can include lobby groups formed to promote a single issue, religious associations, charitable and philanthropic organizations or social and scientific associations. The formation of partnerships is usually the result of the interests and needs expressed by the participants. Industry and government may establish formal public-private partnerships for the development of public services, while international organizations may create partnerships to achieve human development objectives or to improve the UN's mobilizing and interface capacity in areas where the organization wishes to increase its activity.

Each party that joins a partnership not only wishes to increase its individual benefit, but can also contribute in practical ways to enhancing the partnership's interface capacity. A national government or an international organization, such as the World Bank or the United Nations, can provide expertise in a needed area, as well as a nation-wide or world-wide government network. Businesses can not only bring their knowledge about a specific market or service into a partnership, but also make logistics available, as well as provide financial support. Finally, civil society organizations can provide intimate knowledge of a specific issue, access to global advocacy movements, contacts with local communities, trust and confidence (legitimacy) from population groups whom they represent, or a neutral third-party position from which to conduct mediation, surveys, research or verification assessments. Together, the various specializations the participants can provide to a partnership offer an added value that no single actor can provide on their own.

Partnerships can be categorized on the basis of their principal objectives as follows: first, advocacy of specific issues of greatest concern; second, promotion and verification of standards and norms; third, developing markets and economies; and fourth, coordinating resources and research.[10] How the partnerships are created and how they operate varies considerably. Some may be simple agreements to achieve a common aim at a specific point in time, while others may be managed by a permanent independent agent or office that oversees the activities within a legally binding public-private partnership. The diversity of partnerships notwithstanding, all these collaborative efforts to govern specific issues have some things in common. These are: (1) each party shares common interests in achieving specific objectives through collaboration; (2) each party has the ability and willingness to see how individual interests can be advanced through this collaborative effort; (3) each party accepts to include stakeholders to ensure legitimacy of the partnership and

---

10 This classification is loosely based on: Witte, Jan Martin *et al.* (2005), p. 8.

of its future activities; and, (4) each party recognizes the utility of the partnership as a vehicle to enhance its position, product or service for the long-term.

To be realistic, it is important to note that partners may not actually share the same interests. Rather, they may see that through their collaboration, they can more readily achieve their individual aims. The heterogeneity of the actors from the different sectors of society makes it impossible to identify shared ideological aims. Although each party may proclaim a supreme long-term interest, such as a reduction of global warming, sustainable development or the elimination of child labour, these are not ambitions that sustain a partner's willingness to collaborate with others on a day-to-day basis. Most likely, each partner recognizes, with 'enlightened self-interest', that cooperation will contribute to long-term benefits for itself and all the stakeholders and partners, and that the actual collaborative effort hinges on technical, systemic and relational capacities.[11] These result from the partnership's ability to facilitate access to resources, maintain networks of customers, stakeholders or financial and political supporters, as well as provide know-how along with technological services. Along with a partnership's capacities and influence also comes awareness that it must somehow contribute to human well-being, however this is defined. Governance is not only supposed to be legitimate and accountable, it must also be 'good'. Arriving at representative and legitimate decisions that reflect the interests of the individual participants' constituencies is a first step. Partnerships must also offer an acceptable degree of transparency for stakeholders to observe how decisions are reached, implemented and verified in light of broad goals for the welfare of a larger community, the global society or the natural environment. For more than ten years now, arguments in favour of long-term consideration for sustainable policies and practices have become part of the objectives and annual reports of a growing number of large and small businesses.[12]

The United Nations is the most important global actor to enter into partnerships with industry and civil society. It embraces partnerships to obtain greater mobilizing capacities and to be able to benefit from the expertise that participants from other sectors can provide. The UN has always collaborated with state governments and other state-run or regional international organizations. However, a change of paradigm is progressively influencing the UN's own workings. This concerns how the UN has gone from simply purchasing what it needs from the private sector (just as any government does through procurements). Instead, businesses that participate in partnerships are not merely suppliers of goods or services (refugee tents, food, vehicles, office and communication equipment), but partners in achieving common objectives based on shared values. Similarly, civil society organizations are not merely recipients of UN services (peacekeeping, food aid, development assistance), but participants through the work of civil society organizations that help in areas where the UN benefits from their activities.

---

11 Terje Tvedt makes this argument regarding NGOs; see his chapter in Rupert Taylor (2004), p. 141.

12 Numerous examples of good practices through innovative stakeholder dialogue forums or cross-sector partnerships are provided in: Holliday, Charles O. Jr. *et al.* (2002).

Since the end of the Cold War, demands on the UN to increase its work around the world have had a significant impact on the organization's ability to provide its services, be it in peace-keeping, food aid, refugee protection, economic development, training or health-care. State governments, the principal financial backers of the UN cannot or will not contribute all the desired funds to match the demands made on the organization. However, most highly industrialized countries do spend considerable sums for international assistance and humanitarian aid, but this is done increasingly through NGOs – whether as an outsourcing and cost-saving strategy, or because they want to see a diversity of actors collaborate to prevent that any single large bureaucratic agency dominates a given field of expertise. One of the reasons why the UN has become engaged in cross-sector partnerships is precisely to capitalize on the expertise that NGOs have developed over the past ten to fifteen years. Other reasons for the UN to collaborate with civil society organizations and business are:

- To obtain greater access to regions and people around the world through networks other than those from a government or its regional and local agents.
- To receive the help and technological support from experts.
- To show that the organization is undertaking structural and substantive reforms as is demanded of the UN by a number of influential member countries.
- To improve its image through adoption of business-like managerial methods instead of maintaining the old image of an inefficient bureaucracy.
- To increase its chances to obtain financing, support and practical help for specific projects such as emergency assistance programs where the UN cannot raise sufficient funds or capacities quickly enough from its traditional resource base.
- To reduce costs by outsourcing some of the work that international civil servants would otherwise do.

Another reason is also that the United Nations benefits from partnerships to promote the values it stands for and to improve its own internal workings by adopting a more business-like 'brand management' and 'social marketing' approach.[13] Thus, 'the United Nations includes business and civil society in order to capitalize on their experience, knowledge and expertise' (Witte and Reinicke 2005, 62).

This begs the question what interests businesses or non-governmental organizations have in collaborating with the United Nations or with other international organizations. No doubt, businesses have an interest in improving their market positions, their corporate image and developing new potential markets. They join partnerships with the United Nations for some of the same reasons as they may develop corporate social responsibility projects or commit funds to philanthropy.

---

13 An example of this turn towards business-style reforms is most clearly provided in the report of the Secretary-General entitled: *Investing in the United Nations: for a stronger Organization worldwide* (7 March 2006), available at: www.un.org/reform/investing-in-un.html.

Primarily, a business's motives are:

- To develop its image of a good corporate citizen (public relations) in a country or around the world to improve its reputation. The same motive may also underlie an attempt to pre-empt a negative press or repair damage done by negative reviews in the past. This is sometimes labeled social risk mitigation or social marketing.
- To obtain or develop access to a new market and/or new production facilities.
- To reduce the risk of entering a new market where the UN can facilitate the business' positioning.
- To better meet national government standards or international norms (safety, pollution, saving rain forests, and so on).
- To capitalize on the good will that emerges if they channel their donations and contributions through networks of willing partners instead of remaining on their own. This 'virtuous' dynamic can be enhanced if activities and benefits are seen to positively affect 'the needy'. In turn, this may influence the opinions of observers, competitors or stakeholders about the given company.
- Closely linked to the above, a company's participation in a multi-stakeholder process for a 'good purpose' will also have a positive impact on the company's own employees who may very well appreciate working for an employer 'who cares about the well-being of others or of the environment'.

Businesses rarely become involved in cross-sector partnerships with the UN or with NGOs merely for philanthropic or public relations (PR) reasons. The new types of partnerships are based on the premise that all members must see a direct interest in joining and at the same time realize their common long-term goal, for instance improved health, higher school attendance rates for children, employment training, micro-finance or emergency assistance preparedness. In this sense, a partnership does not fulfill only one function, it usually engenders broader knowledge transfers, raises awareness, increases capacities, opens up access to resources and frequently even produces spin-offs such as entrepreneurship, creation of new local civil society organizations, the investment by other private or public actors in the same developing market, and so on.

Non-governmental organizations work to advocate a specific value or investigate an issue they consider vital to improve governance or human welfare. It is possible to distinguish six different kinds of non-governmental or civil society organizations. These are activist, lobbyists and campaigners; researchers and analysts; practical and applied workers in the field of action; watch-dogs and issuers of early warnings; network and information hubs; and developers and verifiers of norms and standards (usually in partnership with other public organizations or businesses). NGOs ally with the UN and with industry for a number of reasons that can be listed as follows:

- NGOs work to promote a cause. For this they need access to the target group, environment or object, and partnering with other actors can help them in obtaining this access.

- NGOs want to be seen as doing the *right* thing for the *right* people or issue (for example, employment, environmental protection, preservation of assets, a change in government policy) and a partnership with other actors may offer increased visibility.
- NGOs need to obtain financial backing for their activities and must, therefore, be seen as doing the *right* thing with and for the *right* partners by their various audiences (for example, their donors and the target group).
- NGOs often act as less expensive sub-contractors where state governments or international organizations do not want to employ civil servants. Joining a partnership may improve an NGO's position in this increasingly competitive marketplace.
- NGOs can do the work at the community level for businesses that want to develop their corporate social responsibility activities. Private companies may not want to engage in community social work on their own because of their lack of local knowledge or because they wish to foster local ownership to render their corporate social responsibility (CSR) work more sustainable. NGOs can offer a convenient bridge between business and the community.
- NGOs can act as neutral arbitrators within a partnership between governments and specific communities where issues are politically sensitive. For example, in situations where different communities are in a political dispute and refuse to negotiate with government mediators. A local or international NGO may be seen by all as neutral and 'close to the ground' or in touch with the affected community.
- NGOs may want to advance their cause through the promotion of standards, for example for human rights or environmental protection. To be integrated in a partnership with their targets (international organizations, industry or national governments) can offer them the ideal opportunity to participate in the formulation, implementation and verification of the desired standards.

A major rapprochement from the civil society organizations towards the business community is that the former joins industry in the global competition for media space, audience and support. At the same time, businesses recognize that they must show a concern for long-term human welfare. How else will they survive when market circumstances change in the future, global competition increases, environmental conditions worsen or the social welfare of their client base dictates different patterns in consumer behaviour Those companies that work with foresight to know their customer and supplier base intimately through both CSR and philanthropy, and that helped improve human well-being wherever they also earned a profit, will be better anchored to adapt and reinvent themselves when necessary.[14]

The development of a global market of ideas may imply a shift in thinking, however. Through the growth of civil society activism and NGO sub-contracting, the competition for favourable reviews and support from audiences, customers and donors alike binds both NGOs and businesses to public opinion and, ideally, to its

---

14 A publication that argues this approach to the business of the future is: Benioff, Marc and Karen Southwick (2004).

approval. This is not really new in so far as businesses always needed the approval from their customers or else risk losing market share. The difference now is that the public can exercise influence through advocacy without needing to be a customer. Under the impact of globalization, both NGOs and businesses compete within a market of ideas for public support where communications technology can be used to make or break that support.

Partnerships in Practice

Among the many types of cross-sector partnerships and governance networks, it is possible to distinguish them by the party that initiated the collaborative work. Thus, one can identify networks led by state governments, international organizations, businesses or NGOs. A majority of cross-sector partnerships are either launched by NGOs or by international organizations, in particular by agencies of the United Nations. Private companies and civil society organizations see the United Nations as offering an image that is good for business, with access to high-level networks and public visibility. The UN is generally considered above the squabbles of national political and economic interests and offers a forum where issues can be discussed across sectors and among equals. Indeed, since the creation of the United Nations in 1945, representatives from industry have supported the organization's development.[15] The bi-polar tension during the Cold War reduced the ability by private actors to work with the UN, in particular regarding politically sensitive issues. Now, however, the global institution has begun to work together with businesses and civil society to enhance its work wherever feasible.[16] The now well known United Nations Global Compact is perhaps the best known corporate citizenship initiative. It comprises a global network of more than 2,000 companies from more than 70 countries.[17] Through this Compact, the UN asks companies to support and implement, 'within their sphere of influence', a number of values concerning human rights, labour standards, the environment, and anti-corruption.[18] The Global Compact is successful

---

15 A good historical presentation of the business linkages with the United Nations can be found in: Tesner, Sandrine (2000).

16 There has been plenty of criticism against the United Nations and its effort to involve business in the promotion of the principles of the UN Charter. A business exists to earn a profitable return on its investments. The United Nations, in contrast, operates to develop social goods such as peace, security, human well-being and environmental health. The United Nations invests human and financial capital – mostly paid for through tax-payers' contributions – into projects, services and diplomatic negotiations that do not provide a quantifiable return on investments. Rather, the result is intended to promote, maintain or facilitate the development of the UN's values and principles. These cannot be numerically accounted for, even though they may have positive economic effects such as economic stability, improved employment conditions, the elimination of crippling diseases, or less pollution.

17   http://www.unglobalcompact.org.

18 They are: *Human Rights* – Principle 1: Within their sphere of influence, businesses should support and respect the protection of internationally proclaimed human rights; and Principle 2: make sure that they are not complicit in human rights abuses. *Labour Standards* – Principle 3: Businesses should uphold the freedom of association and the effective recognition

when one considers that it launched a dynamic that is not only attracting more and more international and national companies, but also that it has set in motion a new kind of 'virtuous' competition. Businesses want to join the 'club' to show and prove their good corporate citizenship. Being among the 'good guys' becomes a positive asset in numerous countries where regional Global Compact offices have sprung up for multinational corporations as well as national and smaller businesses. A principal motive for this regional development is that the Compact demands that its subscribers enact the principles *within their sphere of influence*. Large companies that manufacture around the world want to see that their up-stream and down-stream suppliers, buyers and shipping companies also subscribe to the Global Compact's principles.

Criticism about the Global Compact and its operations is mostly based on the view that the UN is unsuited to be involved with the profit-maximizing objective of business when it should concern itself with the highest goals of human well-being. The assumption here may be that business competition is anathema to sustainable development, human health and security. While it is certainly true that some businesses are only too happy to 'blue-wash their profits-seeking behaviour' – blue being the colour of the UN flag – their membership in the Global Compact does place a responsibility on them to work towards the ten principles. The Global Compact does follow-up with the performance of businesses and uses its global public visibility as a form of pressure towards improving good governance in businesses. A criticism that may be acknowledged is that the Global Compact's effectiveness hinges on the business community's self-serving interest in allying with the UN. So long as the UN receives a broadly positive press world-wide, companies will remain partners of the organization. Global competition for favourable support and public opinion is perhaps the key criteria that determines the success of ambitious partnerships such as the Global Compact.

Other United Nations agencies and offices have also developed partnerships across sectors. Some have become formal public-private partnership arrangements while others are informal agreements to share common tasks and benefits for a pre-determined period of time. Most UN agencies now have links with NGOs and the private sector to develop or manage specific objectives, and the majority of these deal with development, poverty relief or humanitarian aid. An example is the public-private partnership for hand-washing in Central America whose aim it is to reduce infectious diseases among children and mothers. Here, UNICEF allied with the private sector soap manufacturers and with USAID.[19] Similar alliances for development and health are being organized by the UN Development Programme (UNDP) through

---

of the right to collective bargaining; Principle 4: the elimination of all forms of forced and compulsory labour; Principle 5: the effective abolition of child labour; and Principle 6: the elimination of discrimination in respect of employment and occupation. *Environment* – Principle 7: Businesses should support a precautionary approach to environmental challenges; Principle 8: undertake initiatives to promote greater environmental responsibility; and Principle 9: encourage the development and diffusion of environmentally friendly technologies. *Anti-corruption* – Principle 10: Businesses should work against all forms of corruption, including extortion and bribery. See further: http://www.unglobalcompact.org/.

19 See further: http://www.globalhandwashing.org.

its Hub for Innovative Partnerships. The organization builds partnerships with local and national government agencies and brings in expertise from the private sector to stimulate entrepreneurship and industrial investment in poverty-stricken and less development communities around the world (UNDP Commission 2004). Another initiative that an international organization launched in partnership with NGOs is the World Commission on Dams. The World Bank and a number of civil society actors and NGOs agreed to develop a number of standards for the protection of affected populations and the environment where the Bank plans to or already finances the construction of hydroelectric dams.[20] An effort that addresses disaster reduction is carried out, for example, by UNEP's Awareness and Preparedness for Emergencies at the Local Level (APELL)[21] and by the UN World Food Programme (WFP) and the TNT mail, courier and logistics company. With the latter's world-wide network and its interest in developing its market position, collaboration with the WFP has offered the company not only an improved image, but also greater customer and employee loyalty. At the same time, WFP can benefit from reliable transportation logistics for its school feeding initiatives and its emergency relief (often in partnership with other UN agencies and NGOs). Similar examples with regard to emergency relief are the 'First on the Ground Initiative' and the 'Ericsson Response' initiative where the WFP and the UN office of the Coordination of Humanitarian Affairs (OCHA) partner with the Swedish telecommunications company Ericsson. The latter set up a network to help coordinate relief programs with the ambition not only to offer help in times when communication infrastructures may have been damaged, but also to develop its position in the global market. Another collaboration effort underway where an international organization works with NGOs and business as well as with national governments is the Organization for Security and Co-operation in Europe (OSCE). Its Long-Term Missions (in Eastern and South-Eastern Europe, the Caucasus and Central Asia), its election monitors, the High Commissioner on National Minorities, and the OSCE Representative on Freedom of the Media are essentially diplomatic initiatives that work through informal networks with NGOs and the private sector.[22] The latter offer expertise and local visibility and legitimacy while the OSCE, as regional international organization, offers the potential for businesses and international NGOs to improve local living conditions, democratic governance and an open media market that then facilitate economic investment and development.

The business sector has also placed a role in developing cross-sector partnerships such as the 'Ericsson Response' mentioned above. Other examples are the Global Leadership Initiative,[23] the Global Environmental Facility, the World Business Council for Sustainable Development,[24] and the ResponAbility Social Investment Services.[25] Most industry-led partnerships originate following

---

20 http://www.dams.org.
21 http://www.uneptie.org/pc/apell.
22 http://www.osce.org.
23 http://www.globalleadershipinitiative.org.
24 http://www.wbcsd.ch.
25 http://www.responsAbility.ch.

corporate social responsibility programs or are tied to these by including actors from other sectors to improve the environmental, social or humanitarian contributions that businesses can make. CSR often also includes philanthropic initiatives that provide for cross-fertilization through education, development aid, and so on (cf. Benioff 2004). A world-wide CSR campaign that has proven successful was created by *NIKE* corporation in partnership with NGOs to ensure that its sporting goods and apparel are manufactured by employees working in decent conditions (Zadek 2004, 125–132). Here, CSR and partnerships were implemented to rebuild a corporate image that had seriously been damaged by accusations of sweat-shop manufacturing. CSR is not only a strategy to manage the reputation of a brand or the image of a company, it is also a social risk mitigation and crisis prevention tool.[26] The logic here is that greater involvement in local communities for the improvement of human well-being will help a business understand its customer base, its employees and its local market much better and thereby improve its ability to fend off negative criticism or damaging campaigns. NGOs have also played an important part in developing partnerships and networks with actors in industry, government and international organizations. For example, take the now well-known Kimberley Process to curb the international sale of diamonds that stem from war zones,[27] the Coalition for Environmentally Responsible Economies,[28] and the Social Accountability International.[29] NGOs may be seen by businesses as good partners to ensure that a company's up-stream or down-stream suppliers are working in accordance with acceptable standards. For example, textile companies have become far more aware in recent years of the need to support labour safety and health standards or avoid buying from factories where child labour is used.[30]

Challenges To Global Partnerships

While new coalitions of partners may agree on methods of governance, the work and the public policy that emerges from their collaboration is not without its challenges. These include asymmetrical tensions that influence each partnership in different ways and can be listed as follows: complexity and interdependence; territory; speed of adaptation and innovation; international norms; and finally, capacity, recognition and visibility.[31] All actors in cross-sectoral public policy

---

26 See further: Kytle, Beth and John G. Ruggie (2005).

27 http://www.globalwitness.org.

28 http://www.ceres.org/coalitionandcompanies.

29 www.sa-intl.org.

30 Reporting and third-party verification is often carried out by NGOs in partnership with the businesses and local governments concerned. See further, for example: the Worldwide Responsible Apparel Production <www.wrapapparel.org>; the Fair Labor Association <www.fairlabor.org>; the Worker Rights Consortium <www.workersrights.org>; or the the Fair Wear Foundation <www.fairwear.nl>.

31 The notion of asymmetrical challenges to global public policy and the first four ones mentioned here are borrowed from Wolfgang H. Reinicke's lectures at the Executive Seminar,

partnerships are to varying degrees affected by these asymmetries. Other challenges comprise issues such as the concept of state sovereignty, democratic oversight or public accountability.

The first asymmetry is complexity and relates to (1) the human capacity for information absorption (the ability to 'take it all in'), (2) the multi-cultural aspect of any global partnership, and (3) the remoteness of consequences. What civil servants in international organizations know from experience is how difficult it can become to achieve collective decision-making or arrive at results through negotiations in partnership with actors from vastly different cultures. Differences in decision-making among actors are not merely of a social or cultural nature, but also relate to work ethics, business culture, communications styles, and so on. This challenge is as old as human society but, with the emergence of cross-sector global partnerships, it has become far more important. Every analyst of negotiation methods knows that the larger a group of participants in a decision-making process, and the more diverse their interests are, the more complex the process becomes and the more time it usually takes to reach commonly agreed-to decisions. The other challenge of complexity is a technical one. The question is how to oversee and control streams of information, services and products that interact with each other or are dependent on each other. For example, the development of communications infrastructure facilitates the transfer of information over various routes and technologies which all depend on external elements, issues and conditions.[32] Weaknesses in any system become most apparent in times of crisis when unexpectedly, a local system breaks down and unleashes a reaction across other networks, channels, pipelines or grids.[33] What is more, due to globalization, actions on one side of the world may have consequences on the other. There is a geographical as well as a time-related element to this complexity asymmetry that reduces mobilization and interface capacities. For example, a national government, global NGOs or a multinational corporation in one country can severely affect the lives of thousands of people elsewhere on the planet without the effect being visible or recognized in that same country. Complexity is precisely this: causes and effects are no longer close in time and space, and the human mental capacity to oversee or follow-up has reached its limits. Complex issues become remote as they depend on the input from people around the world that must not only be coordinated, but also be synchronized with interdependent electronic communication or control systems. The result of complexity is that concerned stakeholders may not be able to mobilize sufficient support to overcome this asymmetry because the issue is too difficult to present to a broader public (Senge, *et al.* 2005, 208–209).

Hertie School of Governance, Berlin (28 August and 2 September 2005); as well as from his article (2004), p. 18.

32 See, for example, studies done on an integrative approach to risk governance by the International Risk Governance Council (www.irgc.org).

33 Attempts to prevent information black-outs for businesses that rely on communications include the laying of special fibre-optic cables dedicated to the back-up storage of data that users can pay for in advance as a type of insurance. See for example: 'Bankrupt telco cable used for transatlantic disaster recovery project' in: ComputerWeekly. com, 23 June 2006.

The second asymmetry mentioned above, territory, is easier to understand as it refers to countries. It is a challenge because those participants in a partnership that are limited to territory (a national government or its regional or local authorities) have greater difficulty participating in a decision-making process that affects people or territory beyond the national border. In contrast, large civil society organizations and businesses have regional offices around the world and are able to work anywhere. Although governments have policy-making authority, they are unable to control the activities of multinational entities. It is this area where international organizations play an important role carrying national regulations through multilateral agreements to the supra-national or global level.

The third asymmetry mentioned above is that of speed; it concerns the learning process and the time it takes for parties in a partnership to adapt to new demands as a collective. While individual people may be flexible and businesses may adapt rapidly to capitalize on new opportunities, larger organizations, administrations and institutions are usually slow to change. This means that their members who act as parties to a cross-cultural partnership are often unable to adapt to new conditions as quickly as other members in the same group. The asymmetry comes in where NGOs and businesses manage to address a problem or design new standards to facilitate their work, but where governments and international organizations are slow either to incorporate new ideas into the way they work or to pass new laws.

The fourth asymmetry is normative. It concerns the different norms, standards and laws that state governments establish to regulate business, trade, health-care, employment, food safety, education and every other domain under their jurisdiction. The asymmetry relates to universal compliance which does not exist around the world even through regional arrangements provide for trade standards, product standards, safety standards, taxation agreements (to avoid double taxation, for example) or accounting standards. The norms asymmetry is a serious problem where, for example, actors can pick tax havens or permit businesses to emit high pollution where laws are lax. This asymmetry affects those partners in a collective that prefer to stick to standards that suit them best and thus avoid agreeing on common standards for the purpose of their partnership.

The last asymmetry of capacity, recognition and visibility refers to the imbalance that stakeholders experience in their development of networks or partnerships. It concerns the capacities of each participant to mobilize support for their objectives. This has more to do with mobilizing and interface capacities than with structural or technical imbalances such as territorial control, complexity or standards. Directly related to this interface capacity are recognition and visibility. An issue that is of concern to many people around the world may receive global recognition of its importance or danger, but no group of actors is able to develop effective interface capacity. For example, the proliferation of nuclear weapons technology and the enrichment of uranium catch worldwide attention, but there is insufficient interface capacity among actors in all sectors to convince powerful nuclear states to rid themselves of these weapons. This issue, as are many others that touch national defence, is at such a high-level in international politics and in the agendas of powerful capitals, that activists in civil society, business and scientific communities have little influence over them.[34] This asymmetry of capacity, recognition and visibility remains a challenge and one may conclude here that the more critical an issue is to a state government, the less likely it is that it will be taken up by cross-sector partnerships or networks of stakeholders. The same may be said for low-level and highly visible or complex issues. For example, mobilizing capacity is low with regard to complex sociological issues that are well documented, such as international crime prevention and campaigns against terrorism. These issues are not only high-level in the echelons of security priorities of many national governments, but they are also complex and have many causes (poverty, legal loopholes, lack of participation in political decision-making, and so on) and consequences. Then there are issues with repercussions that are much discussed in the public media, such violence in entertainment, health-related stress due to air and noise pollution, addictions to harmful substances, or the proliferation of firearms in ordinary households. These are well documented and affect not just individuals, but also communities and the global society over the long-term. However, these issues are either socially difficult to address or very complex and remain, therefore, of little interest to cross-sector stakeholder mobilization. Similarly, nano technology and the risks it may pose to human well-being is rarely taken up in stakeholder dialogue between governments, industry, civil society and international organizations. The difficulty to raise awareness about this new technology lies in its complexity and its lack of emotive appeal around which interface capacity can be built. The more difficult it is for concerned actors to develop interface capacity by obtaining wide support to bring about change, the less partnerships can be developed for the purpose. Public attention is more easily shifted away from less visible or complex issues to those that are emotive or easily identifiable such as landmines, rainforests, whales, children's health, and others.[35] In contrast to the above, the further removed an issue is from national security policy, or the more easily it can be identified or used to elicit an emotive response, the more likely it is that it will lend itself to public debate across the sectors and among all concerned stakeholders. This challenging asymmetry implies, therefore, that issues for which communities can develop interface and mobilization capacity will always attract attention, but those which are either recognized but inaccessible, or unrecognized and invisible are neglected even if they are important or threatening to human well-being.

---

34 One issue that stands out as an exception and that grabbed the public imagination even though it concerned national security policy was the problem of anti-personnel landmines. Successful NGO-led campaigns led to the Mine Ban Convention that was signed by 100 countries in Ottawa in 1997. This success may be explained by the fact that landmines are not only easily identifiable, but that the majority of their victims are the most innocent whose plight was visibly marketed by the popular media and NGOs in support of their campaigns. Whether other similar weapons systems such as anti-vehicle landmines or cluster bombs will become the target of successful global campaigns remains to be seen and will depend on the interface capacities that concerned actors can mobilize from among influential governments, NGOs and businesses.

35 With regard to the consequences for human well-being and the natural environment from issues that are insufficiently addressed by stakeholders in all sectors, see: Kennedy, Paul (1993), and the yearly publication of the *Human Development Report* by the United Nations Development Program (UNDP) http://hdr.undp.org.

Conclusion

This chapter ends with one certainty, namely that the globalization of ideas, in particular about decision-making in local and global public policy, engenders a growing public demand for legitimacy about decisions made by those in positions of responsibility and authority. This is having a profound effect on national and international public policy, but less so for high-level political and defense policy. While stakeholders do increasingly voice their expectations for participation, for transparency and for good governance in almost all decision-making forums, state governments can choose to remain out of reach in their decision-making for outsiders. They can disregard public opinions and go ahead with a decision, and they can reduce the mobilizing capacities of civil society organizations by tightening laws. A government can give itself license to clamp down on the media, communications, and mobility (travel), and thus reduce the capacity of any non-governmental group (a CSO, a business or even an international organization) to mobilize support. In this sense, states remain (potentially) the most powerful actors in international relations – even though some exceptional circumstances exist where national governments are considered to be failing or weak and where non-governmental actors (militias or businesses) manage to exercise some form of hegemony. To maintain their hold on national and global influence, states must, without a doubt, continually adapt and strengthen their economic competitiveness vis-à-vis other national economies, in part through public mobilization and higher education (soft power). Should some states fail, or should 'push come to shove' (situations of heightened insecurity or catastrophe), states will do all they can to remain the final arbiters of power and coercion.[36] However, this hierarchy of power is not without its challenges for all industrialized states as they are tied to the interdependence that the globalization of trade and information has created. These states rely on other national governments and on non-state actors (businesses, international organizations, professional associations, and so on) for their political stability, their economic resilience and the support and well-being of their populations. They are invariably engaged in efforts to maintain their positions through closer cooperation with others and interdependence in all sectors at the global level. The bases of coexistence and international order at the global level – avoidance of violence and war, the maintenance of agreements according to accepted norms, and the ability for individuals and collectives (partnerships) to have the assurance of their possessions and property – is vital for all forms of cross-sector partnerships as discussed in this chapter.

Business and civil society partnerships with national governments and the United Nations rely on international order and this continues to be based on the primacy of states in international relations. The primary institutions of international society are not only validated with regard to the development of cross-sector partnerships and global public policy, the imperative of these partnerships raises awareness across all sectors of the importance of shared values and goals (security, education, health,

---

36 For example, if a head of state or a ruling party in government decides to enact a war measures or emergency act to counter a perceived threat, there is little that public or industry pressure groups can do to reverse this decision.

environmental protection, sustainable development, and so on). These include the observance of international standards and norms, the legitimacy of decisions made through representative stakeholder diplomacy, as well as the avoidance of violence and war. The multiplication of cross-sector partnerships therefore does not threaten the state as such. While national governments remain the pillars of international order – adopting policies, verifying their implementation, enacting and enforcing the rule of law – their administrations must adjust to new demands posed by the effects of globalization in the same way as businesses, civil society organizations and international organizations must also adapt to the competitive global market of ideas, values and expectation. These challenges offer the opportunity to consider how global public policies are taken up by cross-sector partnerships and how new forms of governance may be at once more effective and legitimate. Collective enterprises that include stakeholders from all relevant sectors – public services, private industry, international organizations, national governments and civil society organizations – are sources of both human ingenuity and public representation. They all have much to contribute to the development of new forms of governance that offer recognition and participation to stakeholders and the communities they represent. One can indeed agree with Kofi Annan that:

> Better governance means greater participation, coupled with accountability. Therefore, the international public domain – including the United Nations – must be opened up further to the participation of the many actors whose contributions are essential to managing the path of globalization. Depending on the issues at hand, this may include civil society organizations, the private sector, parliamentarians, local authorities, scientific associations, educational institutions and many others (Annan 2000, 13).

Globalization is changing the way we manage organizations, make decisions and become aware of ourselves as a part of the relationships we maintain with other people and with our natural environment. Connectedness is the defining feature of the new worldview both in sociological research and in the hard sciences. As concerns this chapter, the most interesting findings can be summarized as follows:

- Decision-making that affects communities or their well-being (their natural environment, their food or water supply, their employment, and so on) is increasingly subject to calls for legitimate, representative and accountable decision-making.
- The forms of governance that do develop upon the meeting of stakeholders and actors from different sectors are the result of both mobilizing capacity and the skilled use of communications technology.
- Because of modern communication technology, groups of people linked through a network can advance values without needing to be in pre-established positions of authority or power. Instead, such groups can amass influence by their numbers and their ability to use communications technology and mobilize supporters.
- While in the past companies needed the approval from their customer base to remain in business, the public that is able to exercise influence on business

today through networking and advocacy do not need to be customers. The larger public can now influence a business's ability to survive.

- The capacity of civil society groups to influence policy-making in national governments or in large businesses leads to the realization that to thrive in a globalized world, both state and private actors have an interest in avoiding isolation or unilateralism and to participate in cross-sector partnerships where they can have a voice in the global public policy environment.
- Stakeholders are more likely to mobilize popular support for their cause if their issue of concern elicits an emotive response from the public, if it can be easily identified and rendered visible, and if it is far removed from the security policy of national governments.
- The greater the challenges of asymmetry (complexity, territory, speed of adaptation, norms, recognition and visibility) are for the development or maintenance of cross-sector partnerships, the less likely that these will be able to influence public policy towards greater legitimacy and good governance.
- New forms of cooperation through partnerships can offer opportunities for all participants to improve their individual standing in society, integrate more effectively in the communities or the markets where they intend to have an influence, and obtain legitimacy for their collective decision-making.
- Cross-sector partnerships provide more than just opportunities for legitimate collective action. Frequently, they also become spaces for innovative problem-solving where people develop synergy to enhance their collective 'interface capacity'. Together, the various specializations that the participants can contribute offer an added value that no single actor can provide on his own.

The most fundamental change in thinking that is taking place under the impact of globalization is that no single actor can provide solutions to global problems on his own. To arrive at new collective decision-making that promotes human well-being for the sustainable future, political, scientific, social and cultural legitimacy as well as good corporate citizenship are not only indispensable, but also expected from NGOs, businesses, state governments and international organizations. Finally, as economic trade and the spread of ideas drive globalization, it only makes sense for the United Nations and other international and regional organizations to partner with the private sector to advance the values of the UN, namely human well-being in a safe, peaceful and healthy global environment.

References

Annan, Kofi (2000), 'Globalization and Governance', in *We the Peoples: The Role of the United Nations in the 21st Century* (New York: United Nations).

Bazerman, Max H. and Watkins, Michael D. (2004), *Predictable Surprises* (Boston, Mass.: Harvard Business School Press).

Benioff, Marc and Karen Southwick (2004), *Compassionate Capitalism: How Corporations can make Doing Good an Integral Part of Doing Well* (Franklin Lakes, N.J.: Career Press).

Benner, Thorsten, Reinicke, Wolfgang H. and Witte, Jan Matin (2005), 'Multisectoral Networks in Global Governance: Towards a Pluralistic System of Accountability', in David Held and Mathias Koenig-Archibugi (eds), *Global Governance and Public Accountability* (Malden, MA.: Blackwell Publishing).

Holliday, Charles O. Jr., Schmidheiny, Stephan and Watts, Philip (2002), *Walking the Talk: The Business Case for Sustainable Development* (San Francisco: Greenleaf Publishers).

James, Harold (2004), 'Is the "Foreign Policy" of companies and NGOs a new phenomenon?' *Sinclair House Debates* (No. 21, Herbert Quandt Foundation, Bad Homburg v.d. Höhe, August).

Kennedy, Paul (1993), *Preparing for the Twenty-First Century* (Harper Collins Publishers).

Krishna-Hensel, Sai Felicia (ed.) (2006), *Global Cooperation: Challenges and Opportunities in the Twenty-First Century* (Aldershot: Ashgate Publishing).

Kytle, Beth and Ruggie, John G. (2005), *Corporate Social Responsibility as Risk Management* (Working Paper Series No. 4, The Kennedy School of Government's CSR Initiative, Harvard University, March).

Lessig, Lawrence (1999), *Code and Other Laws of Cyberspace* (New York: Basic Books).

Marshall, Don D. (1996), 'National Development and the Globalization Discourse: Confronting "Imperative" and "Convergence" Notions', *Third World Quarterly*, 17: 5.

Nye, Joseph S. Jr, and Donahue, John D. (eds) (2000), *Governance in a Globalizing World* (Brookings Institution Press, Washington DC).

Reinicke, H. Wolfgang (2004), 'Business and civil society in global governance', *Beyond the state? 'Foreign Policy' by Companies and NGOs* (Herbert Quandt Foundation, Bad Homburg v.d. Höhe: Sinclair House Debates No. 21, August).

Reinicke, H. Wolfgang (1998), *Global Public Policy: Governing without Government* (Brookings Institution Press, Washington, DC).

Senge, Peter, Scharmer, C. Otto, Jaworski, Joseph and Flowers, Betty Sue (2005), *Presence: Exploring Profound Change in People, Organizations, and Society* (London: Nicholas Brealey Publishing).

Terje Tvedt (2004), 'Development NGOs: Actors in a Global Civil Society or in a New International Social System?' in Rupert Taylor (ed.), *Creating a Better World: Interpreting Global Civil Society* (Bloomfield USA: Kumarian Press, Inc.).

Tesner, Sandrine, and Georg Kell (2000), *The United Nations and Business: A Partnership Recovered* (New York: St. Martin's Press).

UNDP Commission on the Private Sector and Development (2004), *Unleashing Entrepreneurship: Making Business Work for the Poor* (New York: United Nations Development Programme, Report to the Secretary-General of the United Nations).

United Nations (2002), *Building Partnerships: Cooperation between the United Nations System and the Private Sector* (Report commissioned by the UN Global Compact Office, prepared by Jane Nelson, New York).

Witte, Jan Martin and Reinicke, Wolfgang (2005), *Business UNusual: Facilitating United Nations Reform through Partnerships* (New York and Berlin: United Nations Global Compact Office and the Global Public Policy Institute).

Zadek, Simon (2004), 'The Path to Corporate Social Responsibility', *Harvard Business Review* December).

Chapter 2

US Foreign Policy and International Order

Yannis A. Stivachtis[1]

The purpose of this chapter is to assess the implications of United States (US) foreign policy for international order. Galia Press-Barnathan (2003) has correctly pointed out that there is a wide gap in literature on US Foreign Policy between the writings of American scholars (Copeland 2003) and writers of the 'English School' (Buzan 2004; Little 2000, 2003). Indeed, most of the articles published in prominent international relations journals clearly fall within the former category. In this literature, there is either a tendency to discuss US Foreign Policy like it represents a clear-cut response to the unipolar structure of the post-Cold War international system or a heavy focus on the neo-conservative logic of the current US administration.

This has led to four problems. First, there is little discussion about the domestic social forces and factors that underpin US' Foreign Policy goals and orientation. Second, disassociating foreign policy from its societal roots and ignoring the complexity of its making has led to confusion as to whether the George W. Bush Administration follows a Realist or Liberal foreign policy. Third, because these analyses do not relate foreign policy direction to changes within the American society, scholars and analysts work with the assumption that change of administration will automatically lead to change in the direction of US Foreign Policy; especially if the new President comes from the Democratic Party. Finally, there is a tendency to confuse foreign policy management with foreign policy orientation. In other words, scholars and analysts have excluded the possibility that due to changes in the American society, the new President – no matter what his/her personal preferences and political affiliation may be – might be induced to follow his/her predecessor's foreign policy although he/she may manage it in a different – more or less effective – way.

An interesting effort to examine the implications of US Foreign Policy for international order has been undertaken by scholars associated with the 'English School of International Relations' (Sofer 2002; Press-Barnathan 2003). The author will attempt to follow a similar path although his approach will differ in two ways. First, this chapter will discuss US Foreign Policy not as a static phenomenon related to a particular administration but as an evolving and dynamic process that is

1   The author would like to thank Angela Liberatore, Scott Nelson, and John Nomikos for their useful criticism, comments, and suggestions.

influenced and determined by developments in American society. In other words, it will seek to answer the question: what will the implications of US Foreign Policy for International Society be in the period following the George W. Bush Administration? Second, it will attempt to examine the implications of US Foreign Policy for International Order not with reference to the primary institutions of international society presented by Hedley Bull (2002) but to the more sophisticated international society's institutional framework advanced by Barry Buzan (2004).

The approach advocated in this chapter has also been influenced by scholars outside the International Relations discipline. John Lewis Gaddis (2003 and 1990) is one example. He has argued (2003, 171) that US Foreign Policy reflects a long historical dilemma: the choice between international order and international justice, which is directly related to domestic issues. As he puts it (2003, 171), 'Since Americans have never resolved this issue at home – their domestic history has seen many precarious balances struck between the demands of order and justice – it is unrealistic to expect them ever to settle the matter once and for all in their dealings with the outside world'.

John Lukacs (1984) has attempted to explain US Foreign Policy with reference to domestic, social and intellectual developments. He has recently argued (Lukacs 2004, 407) that since Ronald Reagan came to power, US Foreign Policy has reflected a 'resurgent nationalism among the American people: something that most of them were mentally, and spiritually, comfortable with'. He further suggests that to comprehend US Foreign Policy, one needs first to understand its intellectual and ideological origins, which brings one back to the beginnings of the US as a modern state. According to Lukacs (2004, 435), these origins 'reside in the American duality of spirit and mind of which duality American "isolationism" and American "internationalism", or American "exceptionalism" and American "universalism", are only inadequate descriptions'. He also considers the absence of an intellectual tradition – older than the one associated with the Enlightenment – as an additional cause of the American mistaken view of human nature and human affairs (Lukacs 2004, 435).

The last chapter of Lukacs' *A New Republic* creates a link with the work of Walter Russell Mead who has examined the intellectual origins of US Foreign Policy (Mead 2002) as well as the factors that have led to the resurgence of American nationalism since the era of Ronald Reagan (Mead 2004).

Examining the implications of US Foreign Policy for International Society and its institutions, the chapter is divided into four sections. The first section will discuss the 'paradox of American power' and the post-Cold War US Foreign Policy and its dilemmas. The second part will focus on the four competing American visions regarding the goals and means of US Foreign Policy: the Hamiltonian, the Wilsonian, the Jeffersonian and the Jacksonian. The third section will discuss how recent changes in the American society have led to the revival of and changes in these traditions and analyze what this means for contemporary US Foreign Policy. In its final section, the chapter will discuss the implications of US Foreign Policy for International Order by pointing out how it will affect each of the primary institutions of international society as they are identified in Buzan's work.

Post-Cold War US Foreign Policy: Dilemmas and Orientation

Few would deny the fact that a central feature of current international affairs is US' material preponderance. But what exactly should the US do with its strength and how could its actions affect international order? In *Taming American Power*, Stephen Walt (2005, 13) poses a set of very important questions. Should the US seize this 'unipolar moment' to export the ideals of freedom and democracy, use its economic and military strength to deny other states and regimes access to weapons of mass destruction, and take active measures to prevent the emergence of a 'challenger'? Should the US strive for global hegemony or should it be content to lead a multilateral coalition of stable and aspiring democracies? Should US administrations concentrate on building more robust international institutions, strengthening the authority of international law, helping relive global poverty, and preventing gross violations of human rights?

Because these are important questions, American scholars, analysts and policy-makers have been actively debating the strategic options that lie before them (Kristol and Kagan 1996; Ikenberry 2001; Kissinger 2001; Mearsheimer 2001; Nye 2001; Art 2003; Brown 2003; Hirsh 2003; Brzezinski 2004; Jervis 2006). Consensus has proven elusive, however, because the range of options is quite broad and because there has been no single threat or target to concentrate the national mind (Walt 2005, 14). Even the terrorist attacks on 11 September 2001 did not produce long-term unanimity and there is still no national consensus on how terrorism should be fought, or how the US should use its strength to advance either its own interests or the broader welfare of humankind. To this day, how American power should be used remains a hotly contested issue.

A second important feature of current international relations is US' frustrated struggle to translate its material preponderance into desired political outcomes. This is mainly due to the resistance the US faces from both friends and opponents who all view American hegemony as increasingly troubling. Not only is the American position a direct threat to states whose interests and values clash with American ones, but even US' allies now worry about the concentration of military strength in American hands. Over the past years, they have also become increasingly alarmed by the ways that US policy-makers have chosen to use that strength. While Americans debate how they should use their power, the rest of the world is preoccupied with what it can do to tame American power (Walt 2005, 11). This has important implications for international order for its stability depends first, on US actions and other states' or non-state actors' response to them; and second, on the US response to any provocation it may encounter by forces that are interested in challenging the existing international order.

Thus, understanding the nature of power in contemporary world affairs is crucially important both for the US and the future of international order (Stivachtis 2006a and 2006b). As Reus-Smit argues (2004, 3):

> If policy-makers in Washington misunderstand the nature and limits of American strength, miscalculation and misadventure will become the norm, with serious consequences for American security and the pursuit of American national interests. In turn, this would

have significant consequences for international peace and stability. If other states similarly misunderstand the nature of power, and unreflectively equate material might with successful political influence, they will either encourage destabilizing American policies and practices through bandwagoning, or spur accelerated military and strategic competition through balancing, or do both simultaneously.

The end of the Cold War challenged the security assumptions associated with the post-1945 international politics. The distribution of international capabilities was fundamentally altered, raising many questions about the sources of change and about the 'new world order' that would emerge (Fry and O'Hagan 2000). American scholars and analysts offered competing answers to these questions, particularly regarding the implications for the US as the only superpower. Proclamations of a 'unipolar moment' (Krauthammer 1990; Kristol and Kagan 1996) were contrasted with claims of a new multipolarity (Mearsheimer 1990; Waltz 1993) and ideas of 'the end of history' (Fukuyama 1992) were challenged by fears of a 'clash of civilizations' (Huntington 1996). Moreover, concerns about competition from rising powers were countered by arguments about US' enduring 'soft power' (Nye 1990a and 1990b), while democratic peace theory offered a very powerful prescription for US Foreign Policy (Russett 1993).

In practice, after the collapse of the Soviet Union, US leaders saw the strength at their disposal as an opportunity to mold the international environment, to enhance the US position even more, and to extract even greater benefits in the future. In broad terms, US policy-makers have sought to persuade as many countries as possible to embrace their particular vision of a liberal-capitalist world order. As Richard Haas has pointed out (2002 and 2005), the US' overarching objective was to integrate other countries 'into arrangements that will sustain a world consistent with US interests and values and thereby promote peace, prosperity, and justice'. States that welcomed US leadership were rewarded and those that resisted it were ignored or punished.

These broad objectives were pursued by all the post-Cold War American administrations. US presidents and other policy-makers have viewed hegemony as conferring important benefits, such as making other states less likely to threaten the US or its vital interests and giving the US the strength to defend those interests if challenges arise. By dampening great power competition and giving the US the capacity to shape regional balances of power, hegemony has also been seen as contributing to a more tranquil international environment. That tranquility, in turn, has been viewed as fostering global prosperity, because investors and traders can operate more widely when the danger of war is remote. Primacy has also been seen as providing the US with a greater capacity to work for positive ends, such as the advancement of human rights, the alleviation of poverty, the control of weapons of mass destruction, and so on.

In general, both the main goals of US Foreign Policy and the strategies used to achieve these goals did not change fundamentally under the George H.W. Bush and Clinton administrations. Both administrations pursued these objectives by working within the preexisting Cold War order and especially the multilateral institutions created since 1945, while seeking to maximize US influence within these arrangements. Under the pressure of Congress, however, US rhetoric and practice took a unilateralist turn during President Clinton's second-term (Reus-Smit 2004, 29–30). The US Foreign Policy orientation definitely changed once George W. Bush came into power and whose administration has acted mainly under the influence of its neo-conservative members (Callinikos 2003).

According to the neo-conservative conception of power and view of international affairs, the US' material preponderance, coupled with America's universal values, give Washington the means and right to reshape world order. The neo-conservatives advocate an American renaissance and a new century of American hegemony. They seek to awaken American policy-makers, and the American public to the simple fact of American preponderance, to the historical opportunities such primacy provides and to the grave dangers of isolationism or misplaced multilateralism.

In the aftermath of 11 September 2001, the contested field of ideas about US foreign and security policy generated a new discourse of American power and global order reflected in practice in the policies of George W. Bush Administration. According to Reus-Smit (2004,14), 'this new discourse was based on four themes: a celebration of America's material preponderance; a quasi-religious belief in the universality of American values and priorities; a confidence in Washington's capacity to translate its material resources into intended outcomes; and a sense of threat, sufficient to justify institutional adjustment at home and pre-emptive action abroad'. In fact, this discourse represents a curious mixture as ideas of unipolarity and American primacy have been fused into an ideological amalgam with those of democratic peace, the end of history, and the clash of civilizations.

President George W. Bush's approach to foreign policy marked a clear departure from the policies of his predecessors. Although he also sought to achieve the same objectives, his administration was more skeptical of existing international institutions and far more willing to go it alone in foreign affairs. Central to George W. Bush Administration's world-view has been a celebration of American predominance. Convinced that other states would follow if US leadership was clear and uncompromising, and emboldened by a surge of domestic and international support following the terrorist attacks on 11 September 2001, President Bush chose to use American strength and especially its military might to eliminate perceived threats and to promote US ideas around the world.

George W. Bush's basic goals were not radically different from those of his predecessors, but his willingness to use US muscle to achieve them and to act unilaterally was new, and startling. This new approach to foreign policy alarmed many other countries and caused a steady decline in the US image abroad. Most US policy-makers do not fully understand why the rest of the world is worried about US hegemony and alarmed by specific US policies. Thus they underestimate the degree of fear, resentment, and hostility that the US provokes. Those who favor the unilateral exercise of US power sometimes acknowledge that other may not like it, but they quickly conclude that there is nothing that others can do about it. From this perspective, the US is strong enough to take on its remaining opponents and fashion a world that is conductive to US interests and compatible with US ideals, even if forced to act alone. This view also assumes that countries are fully supportive of US Foreign Policy goals either because they genuinely share them or because they know that resistance is futile.

Neo-conservatives call on Americans to embrace the reality of US power and to see it as a unique endowment with the potential to secure vital national interests, while furthering global peace, security and well-being. For example, Condoleezza Rice (2000) criticized many Americans for being 'uncomfortable with the notions of power politics, great powers, and power balances' and argued that Americans had to wake up and recognize that 'Power matters, both the exercise of power by the United States and the ability of others to exercise it'. Rice has attacked Clintonian Foreign Policy for encouraging 'a reflexive appeal instead to notions of international law and norms, and the belief that the support of many states – or even better, of institutions like the United Nations – is essential to the legitimate exercise of power'. She has also argued that President Clinton's Foreign Policy also encouraged a naive neglect of the destabilizing potential of other great powers, which by 'reason of size, geographic position, economic potential, and military strength ... are capable of influencing American welfare for good or ill'.

The importance of power for international order is highlighted in Charles Krauthammer's writings. He claims 'American preeminence is based on the fact that it is the only country with the military, diplomatic, political, and economic assets to be a decisive player in any conflict in whatever part of the world it chooses to involve itself' (Krauthammer 1990, 24). He, therefore, suggests that the US should embrace its power by 'unashamedly laying down the rules of world order and being prepared to enforce them' (Krauthammer 1990, 33).

This view of American power and global responsibility underpins the George W. Bush Administration's foreign and defence policies. As the opening paragraph of the National Security Strategy of the United States indicates (2002, 3), 'the United States possesses unprecedented and unequaled strength and influence in the world. Sustained by faith in the principles of liberty, and the value of a free society, this position comes with unparalleled responsibilities, obligations, and opportunity'. The document declares that Americans 'will work to translate this moment of influence into decades of peace, prosperity, and liberty' (2002, 3) and that they 'will be prepared to act apart when our interests and responsibilities require' (2003, 27). In the preface of the same document, President Bush notes that the 'values of freedom are right and true for every person, in every society – and the duty protecting these values against their enemies is the common calling of all freedom-loving people across the globe and across the ages' (2002, 1). As Robert Kaplan explains (1998, 26), 'the truth is that the benevolent hegemony of the United States is good for a vast majority of the world's population'. The President further warns that US forces 'will be strong enough to dissuade potential adversaries from pursuing a military build-up in the hopes of surpassing, or equaling, the power of the United States' (2002, 27).

Neo-conservatives thus treat power as something actors possess and which flows from material resources as well as ideological and cultural magnetism. Moreover, neo-conservatives treat the use of power as something that is 'moral' when exercised in the pursuit of values one claims to be universal. Christian Reus-Smit (2004) has mounted an excellent critique to this material and imperialist conception of power. He argues (2004, 41) that the neo-conservative theory is deficient in three crucial respects: it assumes that material resources and ideological and cultural characteristics are necessarily 'empowering', that legitimacy can be self-ordained, and that cultural magnetism necessarily delivers political influence and compliance.

But what factors can explain what some may see as a 'schizophrenic' US Foreign Policy following the end of the Cold War? How did the neo-conservative conception of power and ideas about the universal role of the US have come into existence and why have they been so able to influence the majority of the American public? What are the social factors that strengthen and domestically legitimize current US Foreign Policy? Would a presidential change lead to a different US Foreign Policy or would the new President be 'imprisoned' to the demands of the American public?

The Foundations of US Foreign Policy: Competing Visions

Examining US Foreign Policy one should focus on the competing American visions about the role and place of the US within the international society. In his *Special Providence* (2002), Mead has identified four different traditions in the US Foreign Policy: the Hamiltonian, the Wilsonian, the Jeffersonian, and the Jacksonian. According to Mead (2002, 87), these four schools have shaped the US Foreign Policy debate from the eighteenth century to twenty-first. One could quite safely argue that US Foreign Policy will continue to emerge from their collisions and debates far into the future. In his *Power, Terror, Peace, and War* (2004), Mead discusses the revival of these traditions in the post-Cold War era and especially in light of the 11 September events as well as the subsequent wars in Afghanistan and Iraq.

The Hamiltonian Tradition

The Hamiltonian tradition is based on the political ideas of Alexander Hamilton (Chernow 2004; Mitchell 1999). Hamiltonians believe that the US must be able to seek constructive compromises of mutual benefit in its dealings with foreign powers. Hamiltonian thinkers and politicians gradually developed distinctive definitions of American national interests and strategies best adopted to secure them (Mead 2001, Chapter 4).

One of the earliest and most important of these interests is associated with the concept of the 'freedom of the seas'. This involves the freedom of American citizens, goods, and ships to travel wherever they wish in the world in the interests of peaceful trade. To do so, piracy must be suppressed and foreign nations must abide by international law in their treatment of neutral shipping during war. The 'freedom of the seas' is related to the second national interest: the 'open door for American goods'. It is not enough for American ships and goods to have free passage through international waters. American cargoes must also have the same rights and privileges as the cargoes of other nations at the harbors for which they are bound. This leads to satisfaction of another American interest: the need for a free flow of money between the world's principal trading nations. But keeping the world's money markets integrated involves accepting important restraints on domestic economic policy and building a stable international financial system.

In sum, according to the Hamiltonian tradition, the US should be able to contribute to the building of an open international trading and financial system necessary to achieve its national interests. In the post-1945 world, the Hamiltonians sought to base this system – to an unprecedented degree – on the free consent of international society's member states. Hamiltonians would favor strong military forces to protect vital American interests, but in the absence of a direct threat they would prefer to build a global economic system that rests primarily on the free participation of independent states. International law and multilateralism have been the means to achieve this goal. In the post-Cold War era, Hamiltonians have also sought to establish and maintain a global financial and trade system providing support for institutions like the World Trade Organization (WTO), the International Monetary Fund (IMF) and the World Bank.

The Wilsonian Tradition

The Wilsonian tradition in US Foreign Policy is associated with the ideas of President Woodrow Wilson. The Wilsonian philosophy itself is based on the American missionary tradition (Mead 2002, 133). Those who saw an American duty to remake the world in its image spent the nineteenth century seeking action from the US government on three different levels. On the first level came the demand for an active role by the US government in giving American missionaries the right of entry into other countries and providing them with legal protection. Second, it became increasingly important for US diplomacy to protect the lives, property, and other interests of American missionaries. On the third and highest level of activity, missionaries sought to persuade the US government to use its influence to promote what today could be seen as a human rights agenda.

The Wilsonian foreign policy is based on a number of principles (Levin 1968). The first principle is that democracies make better and more reliable partners than monarchies and tyrannies. Non-representative polities are unreliable because public opinion is imperfectly reflected in the government. Democracy guards against one of the most dangerous forms of misrepresentation and misgovernance: the domination of the state by a military elite. Such military states may prefer war to peace because war consolidates military authority and ensures military control over resources. Furthermore, over time, democracies are likely to move toward increasing degrees of moral and political agreement. Democracies are also reliable because they tend to prosper.

As a corollary to their support for democracy around the world, Wilsonians – under missionary influence – became determined opponents of colonialism. Wilsonian beliefs lead to the principle that the support of democracy abroad is not only a moral duty for the US but also a practical imperative as well. Growing American power gave more scope to Wilsonian interventions, and American forces engaged in 'democratic' and 'humanitarian' interventions with increasing regularity.

After the promotion of democracy, the next object of Wilsonian strategic thought is the prevention of war. International law and the limitation of the production, distribution, and use of arms became the main tools of Wilsonian foreign policy in addressing the issue of war.

Wilsonian ideas have conferred a great benefit on US Foreign Policy by aligning it with the major movements of contemporary history: the spread of democracy and the rise to independence and development of increasing portions of the non-European world. Moreover, the Wilsonian presence has provided a strong base of popular support for an active, engaged US Foreign Policy, often enough for policies that serve Hamiltonian ends.

Specifically, a strong common set of concerns draws Wilsonians and Hamiltonians together. Although they often disagree, the two schools are often able to work together on the set of interests and values they have in common. After all, both schools of though look to a stable world order as the ultimate outcome of their activities. The Hamiltonian hope that there will be a worldwide trading and financial system based on international law and enforced by honest and transparent judiciaries in many states closely parallels much of the Wilsonian agenda. Despite their preference for peace, Wilsonians have often joined Hamiltonians in supporting, if necessary, war against states that have challenged international order. Hamiltonians may dislike it when Wilsonians talk about war to make the world safe for democracy but in practice the targets of Wilsonian and Hamiltonian traditions are often the same.

Wilsonianism benefits US Foreign Policy in another important way. Since most great powers have guiding ideologies, Wilsonianism is particularly well-suited for influencing people abroad, especially because it presents itself as reflecting universal values. That is, no races, individuals, countries, or cultures are in principle excluded from the Wilsonian vision of the world of peaceful democracies treating one another with respect. To this end, international law is viewed by Wilsonians as a means to protect poor and weak countries against the rich and strong.

The global triumph of democracy and the rule of law are ambitious goals, and they necessarily involve the US in perpetual quarrels with a number of non-democratic countries, some of which are powerful and important. Given that Wilsonianism cannot be achieved simultaneously everywhere, where should one start? What evils should one eliminate as one prioritizes other causes? How exactly does one build a peaceful, stable, just and democratic world? Wilsonian policy also involves US Foreign Policy in a difficult contradiction. As a global hegemon, the US is a *status quo* power but to the extent it exports Wilsonian values it is a revisionist power as well.

Many Wilsonians wish to redraw the world's territorial and political map to fit nations thereby creating true nation-states. Wilsonians also want to make changes within international boundaries. They want dictatorial regimes to yield power to democratic ones, peacefully if possible, but through violent struggle if there is no other way. Both of these goals – boundaries changes and regime changes – pose great challenges for other countries. Depending on what goals the Wilsonians wish to pursue, Wilsonian policies may attract international support or receive international condemnation. Sometimes Wilsonians have to deal simultaneously with both situations, which bring to the forefront questions of foreign policy management and goal prioritization.

The Jeffersonian Tradition

The Hamiltonian and Wilsonian approaches to US Foreign Policy, no matter how controversial they may be, are relatively easy to understand. The Jeffersonian and Jacksonian schools, however, which more directly spring from idiosyncratic elements of American culture, remain less well known, less well liked and much less well understood. Hamiltonian and Wilsonian values are universalizing and both want the US to build an international order and to make domestic concessions and changes for the sake of that order. Both traditions believe in reciprocity in the sense that if they want the world to become like the US, they also want the US to accommodate better to the rest of the world. Jeffersonians and Jacksonians, however, would be happy if the rest of the world became like the US, though they do not find it likely. They resist, nevertheless, any thought of the US becoming more like the rest of the world.

Both Jeffersonians and Hamiltonians agree that the US is and ought to be a democratic and capitalist republic but they differ on which of the two elements is the more important. Hamiltonians argue that without the prosperity that results from a healthy capitalist economy, democracy cannot endure. But Jeffersonians claim that capitalism cannot flourish unless society itself is healthy and democratic. They have also warned that unchecked operation of capitalism does not always reinforce democracy. Democracy cannot be taken for granted; it must be vigilantly defended.

From this sense of democracy as uniquely precious but achingly vulnerable, the Jeffersonian approach to foreign policy, which is based on the political ideas of President Thomas Jefferson, has developed (Ellis 2001; Randall 1993; Cunningham 1987). According to the Jeffersonian tradition, there are two basic kinds of danger to liberty that might arise from developments in foreign policy (Mead 2002, 184). First, there are those things that foreign countries may do that threaten American liberties directly. For example, foreign countries may invade, devastate, occupy and finally conquer the United States. Second, there are also, perhaps more dangerous, things one may do to oneself as one seeks to defend oneself against others or even as one seeks to advance one's values abroad. Jeffersonians believe that extensive intervention in world politics could corrupt and undermine the Lockean, democratic order that the American people had established at home. Jeffersonians do understand that absolute isolation is impossible. Therefore, the task of the Jeffersonian foreign policy is to manage the unavoidable American involvement in the world with the least possible risk and cost.

War is the first and greatest evil Jeffersonians seek to avoid (Mead 2002, 187). To begin with, war requires secrecy, which is an anathema to the democratic politics envisioned by the Jeffersonians. Wars are not only costly in terms of money and casualties but they also increase the influence of the military establishment on government. Military build ups are seen as putting force in the hands of the central government by strengthening the executive against the legislature. When it becomes politically or morally impossible to ignore provocations or to respond to them with nothing other than verbal protests, Jeffersonians would still not turn to war. Instead, they would prefer to use economic sanctions or other similar instruments to achieve the goals of US Foreign Policy. Unlike the Wilsonian hate for war, which stands more on humanitarian grounds, Jeffersonians oppose to war on political grounds. Wilsonians do not share with Jeffersonians the fear of central authority, but they have worked together to make wars less likely or less horrible though legal means. For example, they both look to arms limits, disarmament agreements, and strict rules of war as ways to achieve these goals and if possible, to reduce the costs of defence in time of peace.

Military build ups are also associated with deficit spending and therefore with increases in the national debt, and they also put force in the hands of the central government. The prospects of debts resulting from wars horrify the Jeffersonians. Consequently, merchants and bankers must be prevented from setting up a monetary aristocracy and the central government should be prevented from growing so powerful that it threatens the freedoms and rights of the federal states and citizens alike. Debt can strengthen the mercantile class and government spending – made possible by that debt – strengthens the central government. According to the Jeffersonian logic, the creditor class can use its wealth to gain effective control of an ever more powerful government.

The constitutional conduct of foreign policy is the second principle of Jeffersonian foreign policy (Mead 2002, 190). Jeffersonians believe that the best policy for the US is limited engagement in world affairs. They see the risks and costs of intervention as so high that only real threats to the nation's existence justify such adventures. They are critical of others' claims that the national interest is endangered by particular crises like the one occurred in Yugoslavia. Jeffersonians define American interests very narrowly in order to have the fewest possible grounds for quarrels with other states. They use the same skepticism to ask where the nation's true security perimeter is to be found. To this end, they often question American troop commitment in Europe and the Far East.

According to Mead (2002, 194), Jeffersonians seek to serve the narrowly defined American interests as economically as possible. This parsimony is about more than saving taxpayers' money. They seek qualitative and quantitative restrictions on US military and diplomatic establishments. Finally, they look into cutting military costs to the lowest possible level and aim to ensure civilian control over military and intelligence institutions.

The Jacksonian Tradition

The Jacksonian tradition in US Foreign Policy is based on the political ideas of President Andrew Jackson (Brands 2005; Remini 1988). Jacksonian foreign policy is usually seen as 'an unhealthy mix of ignorance, isolationism, and irresponsibly trigger-happy cowboy diplomacy' (Mead 2001, 243). Jacksonian philosophy is embraced by large numbers of people who know very little about the wider world (Mead 2002, 244). It is often more of a set of beliefs and emotions than an ideology. According to Mead (2002, 260), although the Jacksonian approach to foreign policy is very controversial, Jacksonian values enjoy wide support within the American society. Jacksonian populism remains the most widespread political philosophy among the American population at large and exercises an enormous influence on US Foreign Policy. It is stronger among the mass of ordinary people than it is among the elite. It is more strongly entrenched in the heartland than either of the two coasts. It has been historically associated with white Protestant males of the lower and middle classes.

Non-Americans have underestimated American determination because they have failed to grasp the structure of Jacksonian opinion and influence. Yet Jacksonian views on foreign affairs are relatively straightforward; once they are understood, US Foreign Policy becomes much less mysterious.

Jacksonian political philosophy provides the basis for what many scholars and practitioners would consider the Realist approach to international affairs. While Jacksonian realists are American rather than Continental realists, of all the American schools of thought, they are closest to the practitioners of classic European realpolitik in their suspicion of Wilsonian and Hamiltonian enthusiasm for international law. In this, they stand with Jeffersonians, deeply suspicious of the global designs found both in Wilsonian and Hamiltonian foreign policy ideas. Jacksonians and Jeffersonians will stand together in opposition to humanitarian interventions or interventions in support of Wilsonian or Hamiltonian world-order initiatives. However, while Jeffersonians espouse a minimalist realism under which the US seeks to define its interests as narrowly as possible and to defend those interests with an absolute minimum force, Jacksonians approach those interests in a very different spirit, one in which honor, concern for reputation, and faith in military institutions play a much greater role.

Jacksonian realism is based on the sharp distinction in popular feeling between the inside of the folk community and the 'dark' world outside (Mead 2002, 248). Jacksonian patriotism is an emotion; not a doctrine. The nation is an extension of the family. Very different rules apply in the outside world. Unlike Wilsonians, who hope ultimately to convert the Hobbesian world of international relations into a Lockean political community, Jacksonians believe that it is natural and inevitable that national politics will work on different principles from those that prevail in international politics. For Jacksonians, the world community that the Wilsonians wish to build is a moral impossibility. To give the money of the American taxpayers to corrupt and incompetent regimes abroad is an anathema. Countries, like families, should take care of their own. Charity should be left to private initiatives and private funds. Jacksonian America is not ungenerous, but it lacks all confidence in the government's ability to administer charity at home and abroad.

Given the moral gap between the folk community and the rest of the world, Jacksonians believe that international life is and will remain both violent and anarchic. Therefore, the US must be vigilant and strongly armed. At times, preventive wars must be fought. There is absolutely nothing wrong with subverting foreign governments or assassinating foreign leaders whose bad intentions are clear. Jacksonians are more likely to charge political leaders with a failure to employ vigorous measures than to worry about the niceties of international law.

Jacksonians believe that there is an honor code in international life and those who live by the code will be treated under it. Specifically, Jacksonians appear to have a particular approach to how wars should be fought and how enemies should be treated. They recognize two kinds of enemy and two kinds of fighting: honorable enemies fight a clean war and are entitled to be opposed in the same way; dishonorable enemies fight dirty wars and in that case rules do not apply. An honorable enemy is one that declares war before beginning combat; recognizes rules of war, honoring traditions, such as the flag of truce; treats civilians in occupied territory with due consideration and refrains from the mistreatment of prisoners of war. But those who violate the code, who commit terrorist acts against innocent civilians in peacetime forfeit its protection and deserve no particular consideration; a fact that explains the Jacksonian approach to the Guatanamo issue or any other case of maltreatment of prisoners who are associated with terrorism or 'dirty' warfare. According to the Jacksonian tradition, the first rule of war is that wars must be fought with all available force. The second rule is that the strategic and tactical objective of American forces is to impose their will on the enemy with as few American casualties as possible.

Many students and scholars of US Foreign Policy dismiss Jacksonians as ignorant isolationists but this misses the complexity of the Jacksonian worldview. Their approach to war is more closely grounded in classical realism than many recognize. Jacksonians do not believe that the US must have an unambiguous moral reason for fighting. In fact, they tend to separate the issue of morality and war more clearly than do many members of the foreign policy establishment. The war in Iraq was a popular one in Jacksonian circles because it contributed to getting rid of Saddam Hussein because he was seen as being capable of eventually threatening the United States. The fact that no extensive ties existed between Al-Qaeda and the Iraqi regime or that no weapons of mass destruction were found did not reduce the popularity of war in the eyes of the Jacksonians. In contrast, the Jacksonians would have had a problem if no actions were taken by the US Administration and Iraq were one day capable of hurting the United States. Getting rid of your enemy before your enemy is able to strike you is perfectly acceptable to Jacksonians; a fact that explains their acceptance of the preemption doctrine. In the absence of a clearly defined threat to the national interest, however, Jacksonian opinion is much less aggressive. It has not, for example, been enthusiastic about the American intervention in the former Yugoslavia despite the atrocities there.

Whatever the theological views of the individual Jacksonians are, their culture believes in original sin, but also partly accepts the Enlightenment's belief in the perfectibility of human nature. Jacksonians believe the Antichrist will get there before Jesus does, and that human history will end in catastrophe and flames, followed by the 'Day of Judgment' (Mead 2002, 248). This has important implications. It deepens the skepticism with which much of the American public receives proposals for foreign aid grants to international financial agencies and developing countries. No matter how much it can be given, it won't create peace on earth. Plans for universal disarmament and world courts are also received with similar skepticism. Jacksonians tend to think none of these things will do any good. In fact they think they may do harm. Linked to the skepticism about human imitations of the 'Kingdom of God' is a deep apprehension about the rise of an evil in world order. In theological terms, this is expressed as a fear of the Antichrist, who is envisaged in Scripture as coming with the appearance of an angel of light – perhaps a charismatic figure who offers what looks like a plan for world peace and order but who is actually a satanic snare.

For most of its history, Jacksonian America believed that the Roman Catholic Church was the chief emissary of Satan on earth (Mead 2002, 249). During the

Cold War, fear of Catholicism has gradually subsided and the Kremlin replaced the Vatican as the principal object of American fears about the forces of evil in the world. Though helpful in sustaining popular support for Cold War strategy, the paranoid streak has proved more difficult to integrate into effective US policy since the Cold War. For example, another chief object of popular concern in post-Cold War America is the Hamiltonian dream of a fully integrated global economy, combined with the Wilsonian dream of global political order. To the Jacksonian, the George H.W. Bush's call for a 'new world order' sounded as a satanic conspiracy being implemented by the pillars of the American establishment (Robertson 1991). The 11 September events, however, have brought into existence a new evil: terrorism and the states that support it, forming an 'axis of evil' that needs to be destroyed.

Another aspect of Jacksonian foreign policy is a deep sense of national honor and a corresponding need to live up to national pride. Honor compels one to undertake some difficult and dirty jobs, however much one would like to avoid them. It is a bad thing to fight an unnecessary war, but it is inexcusable and dishonorable to lose one once it has begun. Reputation is extremely important. It is a question of the respect and dignity one commands in the world at large. Jacksonian opinion is sympathetic to the idea that one's reputation will shape the way others treat one. Therefore, at stake in any crisis is not simply whether one satisfies one's own ideas of what is due one's honor; one's behavior in the crisis and the resolution one obtains must preserve one's reputation, one's prestige – in the world at large. This helps one to understand the US commitment to the democratization and economic reconstruction of Iraq despite the heavy financial and human cost that this endeavor involves.

Convinced that the prime purpose of government is to defend the living standards of the middle class, Jacksonian opinion is instinctively protectionist, seeking trade privileges from foreign exports. They see the preservation of American jobs, even at the cost of some unspecified degree of 'economic efficiency' as the natural and obvious task of the federal government's trade policy. Jacksonians are also skeptical, on both cultural and economic grounds, of the benefits of immigration, which is seen as endangering the cohesion of the folk community and introducing new, low-wage competition for jobs (Huntington 2004).

There are two serious problems that the Jacksonian school perennially poses for US Foreign Policy-makers (Mead 2002, 261). The first problem is the gap between Hamiltonian and Wilsonian promises and Jacksonian performance. The globally oriented, order-building schools see American power as a resource to be expended in pursuit of their far-reaching goals. Many of the commitments they wish to make, the institutions they wish to build, and the social and economic policies they wish to promote do not enjoy Jacksonian support and sometimes they elicit violent Jacksonian disagreement. This puts Hamiltonians and Wilsonians in an awkward position. At best, they are trying to push treaties, laws, and appropriations through a sulky but reluctant Congress. At worst, they find themselves committed to military confrontations without Jacksonian support. Very often, military activities they wish to pursue are multilateral, involving limited warfare or peacekeeping forces. These are often unpopular both inside the military and in the country at large. Caught between their commitments and the manifest unpopularity of the actions required to fulfill them, American policy-makers make an unimpressive show. This is one of the structural problems of the US Foreign Policy, and it is exacerbated by the divided structure of the American government and Senate customs and rules that give a determined opposition many opportunities to block action of which it disapproves.

The second problem is that Jacksonian opinion is slow to focus on a particular foreign policy issue, and slower still to make a long-term commitment to pursue a given policy vigorously. Once that commitment has been made, it is even harder to build Jacksonian sentiment for a change.

These problems cannot be fully solved. They reflect profound differences in outlook and interests in American society. Efforts by policy-makers in the other three schools to finesse these issues often exacerbate the basic problem, which is both cultural and political and reflects class distance between Jacksonian America and the representatives of the other schools (Mead 2001, 262). Attempts to mask Hamiltonian or Wilsonian policies in Jacksonian rhetoric may serve in the short run, but ultimately they can lead to a collapse of popular confidence in an administration and the stiffening of resistance to any and all policies deemed suspect.

Despite some agreements among them, until quite recently these four traditions could be easily distinguished from one another. However, changes in the American society, which, according to Mead (2004, 83), are related to the passage from a Fordist type to a millennial capitalist society have led, on the one hand, to the revival of these traditions and, on the other hand, to important alterations within them as well as a merge between some of them. This has had important implications for the present US Foreign Policy. One may also argue that this revival will continue impacting US Foreign Policy for the years to come irrespective of the preferences and political affiliation of the next American President.

The Revival of the American Foreign Policy Traditions

According to Mead (2004, 83), the ideas and values of the new form of millennial capitalism are becoming increasingly dominant in the Republican Party and, beyond that, in American life. American Revivalists (those who support the shift toward millennial capitalism) believe that the new freedoms and policies they support will lead to a revival of American power and values around the world. The Revivalists are ambitious in foreign policy. They do not wish to contend against the four traditional approaches to US Foreign Policy but to take over all of the four traditions and remake them in the light of American Revival ideas (Mead 2004, 84).

American Revival has its roots in the Hamiltonian tradition, which historically is the group that represents the advanced thinking of the American business elite. The popularity of American Revival ideas among Hamiltonians today reflects the degree to which structural changes in the American economy are driving and shaping the new ideologies now contending for power (Lukacs 2004, Chapter 10). Just as Hamiltonians took the lead in fashioning the Fordist consensus and in translating its ideas into foreign policy, so a new generation of Hamiltonians has played a major role in shaping the new, post-Fordist political economy (Mead 2004, 85) and, as an extension, US Foreign Policy.

The increasingly dominant Revival Hamiltonians reflect a profoundly changed and reenergized American business landscape. Flexibility has become more important for America's cutting-edge businesses than macroeconomic stability (Mead 2004, 86). Support for free trade is one of the few points of continuity between old and new Hamiltonians, but they disagree on whether industrial protection is necessary to support the growth of American industry.

A key aspect of the new Hamiltonian approach to foreign policy is the role of the new high-tech military-industrial complex (Mead 2004, 86). The revolution in military affairs, with its emphasis on a new military that will rely more on advanced weapons systems including space-based systems, is not only a strategy that proponents hope will increase the American advantage over other military powers, it also, advocates claim, makes the defence budget a powerful engine of economic development: government defence spending will, they argue, stimulate new generations of research and development into cutting-edge technologies. Whatever the outcome, the new industrial sectors that will grow up around the military transformation and the civilian spin-offs they will generate will become a major political factor (Brown 2003, 3).

According to Mead (2004, 87), 'confidence' is another difference between Fordist and Revival Hamiltonians. The Fordist-Hamiltonian business establishment of the Cold War era believed that first parts of Western Europe and Japan and then parts of the developing world would overtake the US Revival Hamiltonians have more faith than their predecessors that the unique features of American political economy hold the secret to success, and that if the US remains true to its own values, it will continue to dominate the cutting edge of global technological innovation and economic dynamism. The structural weaknesses of the European economies and the demographic decline of European populations will make Europe a weak competitor. Likewise, the institutional weaknesses and political problems of East and South Asia along with Latin America are seen as reducing US' need to worry about new challenges from those parts of the world (Lucacks 2004, 417).

While the American Revival is transforming some Hamiltonians, the Wilsonian party in US Foreign Policy is being born again. The mainline Protestant denominations that shaped the American Wilsonian tradition of progressive internationalism are losing strength to evangelical and fundamentalist denominations. As a coalition of conservative Christian and Jewish supporters of Israel changed the traditional Republican approach to the Israeli-Palestinian question, the same coalition is developing a new version of the Wilsonian agenda in US international affairs (Mead 2004, 88).

Traditionally, Wilsonianism focused on three ideas: first, that there is a vital linkage between American security and the determined pursuit of American values through foreign policy; second, that rule-based global institutions should play a growing and ultimately decisive role in international life; and third, that questions of value should be addressed in primarily secular terms rather than using the Protestant Christian values message of earlier generations. Revival Wilsonians, whose ranks include the majority of the neoconservative policy intellectuals who have played such an important role in Republican foreign policy debates in recent years, have radically restructured the Wilsonian agenda (Mead 2004, 89). They strengthen the linkage between idealism and security arguing that only a much more aggressive pursuit of American ideological values can deal with the security threats the US now faces. Revival Wilsonians believe that traditional American values are so compelling, so democratically superior, and so widely popular that they can sweep and reshape the world.

Revival Wilsonians are less confident about the role of international institutions. The old Wilsonians believe that international institutions provide a necessary legitimacy and objectivity for exercises of American power in the service of human rights and international values. While embracing the concept of universal human rights, old Wilsonians reject the idea that one nation, however enlightened, can and should serve as the world's judge and enforcer. Old Wilsonians seek to transcend what they see as a narrow and inherently flawed model of American domination for a genuinely consensual, legal, and even militarily supreme international government.

The cultural and historical experiences of sectarian Protestants and persecuted Jews have come together to produce a passionate dissent to the old Wilsonian internationalist orthodoxy (Mead 2004, 90). The non-mainline American Protestant tradition was built on suspicion and rejection of universal institutions like the Catholic Church, and the rejection of the ideal of a single world state is an important part of the theological worldview of contemporary American evangelicalism. On the other hand, modern European Jewry watched the 'world community' stand aside as millions of Jews perished in the holocaust. Since then, it is argued, Jews have watched the UN General Assembly indulge itself in decades of what they see as vicious, one sided, and at some level anti-Semitic attacks on the Jewish state established as a refuge for the victims of persecution. As a result, right-wing American Christians have united with many American Jews not only to defend Israel against its enemies but also against what they see as the deeply flawed and even wicked moral basis of most of the world's elites. Despite argument to the contrary, the alliance between American evangelicals and Orthodox Jews could grow deeper and stronger than many observers believe and this is expected to have significant implications for US Foreign Policy.

For Revival Wilsonians, the US must enforce universal principles and values against institutions and elites that old Wilsonians saw as natural and necessary allies. The alliance of realpolitik with a values-based foreign policy is one of the hallmarks of neoconservative thought and the new Wilsonianism. For neoconservative and Revival Wilsonians generally, the end is so noble that realist means are fully justified. That's why there has been confusion as to whether current US Foreign Policy follows a Realist or an Idealist pattern. It is simply both.

This shift is contributing to the re-energizing of US Foreign Policy. The general tendency of Wilsonian foreign policy is for an active, interventionist United States. A sense of moral duty drives Wilsonians to seek out enemies that more realist thinkers are generally content to leave unmolested. This explains why Realists argued against the Iraq War while the neoconservative Wilsonians pressed for it. In the old Wilsonianism, however, this interventionist impulse was checked by Wilsonian ideas of international law, the morality of nations and a preference for working within international institutions. As the Iraqi case clearly illustrates, Revival Wilsonianism is less inhibited.

The rise of Wilsonian realpolitik is accompanying a trend among Revival Wilsonians to promote specifically Christian rather than liberal secular humanist values in foreign policy (Mead 2004, 91). This is easy to comprehend. Returning to Wilsonianism's nineteenth century roots among missionaries and fervent Protestants, Wilsonian Revivalists are building a strong coalition that binds the Christian right to an assertive long-term strategy of intervention and nation-building abroad. The projection of religious faith and values onto the arena of foreign policy has tremendous appeal and resonance for tens of millions of Americans. The apocalyptic hopes and fears awakened by events in the Middle East and the war on terror reinforce this traditional preoccupation of the American mind at a time when religious interest seems to be growing not only in the United States but also around most of the world.

Moreover, the deinstitutionalization of the Wilsonian project that the Revival Wilsonians propose is popular with many Americans (Mead 2004, 93). Wilsonian human rights and democratic values are much more popular among Americans than Wilsonian institutions. As the Iraqi case has shown, unilateralism in the defence of liberty is more than justified. A principled reference for multilateralism is always a difficult proposition to defend in American politics. For most Americans, multilateralism is a stick minorities use to attack majority policies they oppose in a high-minded and emotionally satisfying way. According to Mead (2004, 93), disentangling the Wilsonian impulse from the obligations of principles of multilateralism is unlikely to hurt the revival Wilsonians and will contribute to the ability of neoconservatives and their allies to push US Foreign Policy in a more activist direction. Although many argue that after the Iraq experience the neoconservative movement may have lost considerable degree of its influence, one should not be so quick to write off Revival Wilsonians.

Mead argues (2004, 95) that it is in the nature of American religion that the religious establishment will seek to shape American foreign policy to reflect its values and that the rise of conservative, Evangelical, Pentecostal, and fundamentalist religious movements, one of the largest and most important cultural developments in the US over the last generation, has laid the foundation for a new kind of religious establishment. As Mead shows, in the recent past, the religious right has felt itself to be standing outside the policy process, especially the foreign policy process. Increasingly, the leaders of the rising religious forces have found themselves on the inside of the process, helping to shape it. To the extent that US Foreign Policy comes to revolve around a struggle with Islamic fundamentalists who believe that they fight a *jihad* (Holy War) against the US, the conservative Protestant religious leadership of the US will play a major role in articulating the values and ideas for which many Americans will be willing to fight. Therefore, the direction of the US Foreign Policy for the years to come will be to a great extent determined by the way international state and non-state actors will decide to deal with the US.

The neoconservative movement – relatively small in numbers, northeastern and socialist in original background, disproportionately Jewish by ethnicity – will probably lose some of its relative power as the Revival Wilsonian camp grows and develops (Mead 2004, 95). According to Mead (2004, 96), the final form of a developed Revival Wilsonianism may lose some of the intellectual rigor that has always been one of the great strengths of the neoconservative movements. It may look more like a religious movement and less like an intellectual one, but it is likely to be much larger than it now is, and have deeper roots in popular organizations and loyalties than it now does. But it looks as if an emerging and growing Revival Wilsonian movement will be the channel through which neoconservative insights will reach the American public. The rise in the number of Evangelical Protestants, combined with their increasing levels of affluence, political participation, and education, suggest that for the next generation, at least, one may witness the rise and consolidation of an Evangelical establishment that will view America's world role in a different way than the waning and dying mainstream Protestant establishment that once set the Wilsonian agenda. Mead argues (2004, 97) that anyone who thinks that Revival Wilsonianism is a passing or temporary phenomenon in US Foreign Policy is probably misreading the situation.

Meanwhile, Revival Wilsonians face the increasing unwillingness of the American people to spend billions of dollars and send military forces to all the places and for all the causes Wilsonians support. After the Iraq experience, a skeptical Congress and public opinion have to be convinced (sometimes over and over) that this is necessary and possible.

The rise of Hamiltonian and Wilsonian factions influenced the American Revival ideas and helped set the stage for a new era in US Foreign Policy, but the key to political change in American society and, therefore, to the changing orientation of US Foreign Policy is the decline in support for Fordism by the popular American nationalists, namely the Jacksonians.

Stripped of most of the legacy of racism and divorced from the naive agrarian that made the old American populism so skeptical of markets, the mix of American exceptionalism, a government populism, and defiant individualism have together become a major political force in the US by the twenty-first century (Mead 2004, 97). Jacksonian America hates the Fordist society of classes and blocs. It does not trust large institutions or bureaucrats and it believes in keeping experts on a short leash. Doubts about the long-term solvency of Social Security and Medicare have undermined popular confidence in the economic viability of the Fordist model. Many Jacksonians have more confidence that big government will collect big taxes than that it will pay out big benefits. The confluence of traditional American individualism with the cultural contradictions of Fordism has created a powerful anti-Fordist dynamic in contemporary American politics.

A popular revolt against the Fordist elites of experts and officials is gathering steam. The enemy of Jacksonian America has been largely defined as an arrogant 'clerisy' of administrative and cultural elites. Millennial capitalism has much less need of this intermediary class, and one of the main themes in American politics, as well as in US Foreign Policy, is the class war now raging as the swollen petite bourgeoisie of Fordist society comes under attack from aggressive capitalists, seeking to eliminate its regulatory and intermediary power. Resentful workers also fight against the petite bourgeoisie with its airs of superior moral and intellectual standing. This resentment is a testimony both to deep class-based dislike of the professional and administrative elites (university professors, experts of all kinds, think-tank fellows, lawyers) that Fordism has entrenched and enriched, and to a declining belief in the efficacy of Fordist economic solutions (Lukacs 2004, 432).

Jacksonian revolt against elites is running in harmony with the structural needs of the economy (Mead 2004, 101). Disintermediation is the hallmark of the new American economy: reducing costs and raising productivity by eliminating middlemen and middle management. Information technology and the Internet are reducing the need for middlemen like stockbrokers, bank clerks, and travel agents. Markups for middlemen like real estate and mortgage brokers are coming under increasing pressure as consumers use the power of information technology to increase their choices. At the same time, technology helps corporations increase their productivity and thin the ranks of middle management.

In foreign policy, Ronald Reagan inaugurated an anti-establishment, American Revival foreign policy, but it was hastily abandoned as the first President Bush moved back toward what were still the mainstream, consensus positions in foreign policy. In the Clinton years, international economic policy moved away from Fordism, as the 'Washington consensus' sought to replace the old economic orthodoxies of the Fordist period with 'neoliberal' or post-Fordist ideas. In politics and security policy, however, the Clinton administration remained Fordist as it was reflected in the US Balkan policy and was illustrated in the US stance in the Security Council.

President George W. Bush made a much more determined and systematic attempt to place US Foreign Policy squarely on the basis of American Revival ideas. A mix of incredulity, outrage, shock, anger, and despair is running through the foreign policy establishment as many of its most cherished ideas and institutions are impatiently brushed aside by Jacksonians and Revival Wilsonians. At times it has seemed as if the whole world was united in hate and execration for the new direction in US Foreign Policy. As Mead (2004, 104) has put it: 'In the vision of the diplomatic establishment in the US and abroad, the Neanderthals have escaped from their cages and the abomination of desolation has been set up in the holy of holies'.

However, this is much too simple a view. An American society increasingly reshaping itself along millennial lines was likely to find increasing problems as it conducted foreign policy in a world in which millennial capitalism is deeply unpopular. To this one may add the discomfort and fear that the increase in American economic and military strength has brought to many states in the world, including great powers like France, Russia and China. All these problems have been exacerbated by the shocks that roiled the international society as the US responded to the attacks of 11 September.

But what do all these mean for the present and future of US Foreign Policy? What might the implications of US Foreign Policy be for international society and its institutions?

US Foreign Policy and International Society

There are two reasons for which it is very difficult to predict with great accuracy the implications of the US Foreign Policy for international society. First, due to the nature of the American political system, the President is constrained by the Congress and Senate. Depending on the issue in question, the US President may find that the Congress and Senate are unwilling to support his/her policies, even if the majority in, at least, one of the two Houses is of the same political affiliation as the President. It becomes even more difficult if the President comes from a different political party than the majority in one or both of the two Houses. Second, US Foreign Policy may – to a considerable extent – be determined by the way in which international actors decide to deal with American power. If it is challenged, the US will be very actively involved abroad to secure its place in world affairs through the exercise of hegemonic policies. This does not, by any means, imply that the US – even without new challenges – will not continue pursuing hegemonic policies since it has already been challenged. Despite this difficulty, the rest of this section will proceed to an analysis of the impact one should expect the US Foreign Policy to have on the primary institutions of international society.

Sovereignty

Given the willingness of the old and Revival Wilsonians to export the American values of democracy and human rights, one should expect that US Foreign Policy will have significant implications for the institution of sovereignty. There are many places in the world where domestic groups would welcome US interference in the internal politics of their political communities to create what is seen by these groups as a more 'just' political order. Because of the influence of Revival Jacksonianism, one should also expect that any direct or indirect challenges to US security will attract US involvement abroad. For example, depending on how they will present their case, Iran or North Korea may eventually be targets of such intervention. In any case, active US involvement abroad will challenge the doctrine of non-intervention.

However, one should not expect that the US will act continuously against international law. This is for three reasons. First, no country in the world – no matter how powerful it is – can afford isolating itself by totally disregarding international law and ignoring international organizations. Second, in many instances and depending on the case, US diplomacy may be successful in gathering wide international support for its interventionist policies thereby legitimizing them. Third, international law is very wide in scope and covers a wide range of international activities. Although in some areas US activities may be questionable in terms of international law or clearly against it, in many other cases the US will play an active role in protecting and enforcing international rules while contributing to the creation of new rules in other areas of common international concern. In the short- and medium-term, one should not expect the US to sign and ratify international environmental conventions or accept the jurisdiction of the World Criminal Court, but meanwhile the US will act as the guardian of international law. What one should certainly expect is that the US will not bind itself to any rules that would affect its economic performance and/or restrict its efforts to secure itself by acting away from home.

Territoriality

Due to its own experience at home and consequently its sensitivity with ethnic and cultural differences, one may expect the US – under the influence of the Revival Wilsonians – to play an active role in promoting international political and territorial arrangements to effectively deal with ethnic conflicts. Domestic political pacts of Dayton's kind or recognition of new states following civil wars and long divisional arrangements, like in Cyprus, should not take anyone by surprise. This could have significant implications for territoriality as an institution of international society.

Diplomacy

Diplomacy is the field where Wilsonianism confronts Jacksonianism. While for the Wilsonians, diplomacy is an important foreign policy instrument, the Jacksonians see the exercise of power as providing the more effective way to settle an issue.

Reflecting a Jacksonian attitude, the George W. Bush Administration has been judged – and rightly so – to be quite 'undiplomatic' in the conduct of US' foreign affairs. Being 'undiplomatic', however, may imply two different things: first, that one may not be willing to really engage in a diplomatic dialogue; and second, the diplomatic agent may lack the so-called 'diplomatic tact' in his/her interaction with his/her colleagues. Many scholars tend to associate diplomacy with agreement. This means that US Foreign Policy is judged to be 'diplomatic' as long as there is a wide international consensus for action and as 'undiplomatic' if there is not. But diplomacy is not defined by agreement but by the willingness of states first, to pursue a settlement through the means of dialogue; and second, to exhaust those means in an effort to arrive to a solution even if such a solution is not eventually found.

After the unfortunate diplomatic events leading to the war in Iraq, the US has temporarily abandoned its Jacksonian tactics and has shown its willingness to make diplomacy the main tool for dealing with important international issues like the nuclearization of North Korea and Iran. In many other areas of international affairs, especially in the field of international economic relations, the US is constantly engaged and will continue being engaged in diplomatic interaction with the other members of international society. The basic tactics of US Foreign Policy, however, will not change. The US will therefore pursue multilateral, Wilsonian type policies whenever possible but will build Jacksonian 'coalitions of the willing' if and whenever necessary. Bilateral diplomacy is essential in building such coalitions.

It is very difficult to see the US being strictly unilateral in the sense of 'going it' entirely alone on an important issue. The reason is that all states wish to avoid being or appearing to be isolated, and they always seek for allies to legitimize their actions. The US is not an exception even if it is the greatest world power. Economic and military power is one thing, the power of acceptance and sharing of ideas in international relations is another.

One should refrain from using the concept of 'unilateralism' when coalitions of states are involved no matter how small they might be. The reason is that 'unilateralism' as a term has been used within the framework of the United Nations to signify the lack of support by major powers for US Foreign Policy. By doing so, with reference to an institution like the UN which is based on the notion of equality of member states, one relegates the importance of other states in world politics.

Great Power Management

Great power management has always been essential in dealing with the question of international order in an anarchical society. The post-Cold War or post-September 11 international system is not an exception. Formal alliances, like NATO, and informal ones, reflected in 'coalitions of willing', will continue playing an important role in the US foreign and security policy. Apart from stabilizing political regimes in countries that have experienced civil wars, like Afghanistan, Bosnia and Yugoslavia (Kosovo); contributing to international humanitarian missions, like in Darfur; and performing counter-terrorist missions, NATO will be crucial in dealing with any re-assertiveness on the part of the Russian Federation. The transatlantic alliance may also be proved essential in balancing the rising power of China and/or a possible coalition between Russia and China.

In the post-September 11 world, deterrence has once again become central to US security. If the Wilsonian instruments of diplomacy and international law fail to provide effective response to the questions of terrorism and weapons of mass destruction proliferation, then the Jacksonian US will use preemptive strikes, military intervention, and war, and will employ new weapon technologies as means of deterrence. This may, on the one hand, have negative implications for the institution of sovereignty but, on the other hand, it will add to the importance of great power management as a primary institution of international society.

Finally, challenges to US power by international actors, like the European Union, China and Russia, will lead to hegemonic policies on the part of the United States. The reason is that states do not really act to balance the power of other states but actually to create imbalances of power in their favor. This is simply because such imbalances provide them with greater security. However, a balance of power may be the eventual result of such a process. One should not expect the US to give up its power supremacy; especially while being under the influence of Revival Jacksonianism. The more its power is challenged the more hegemonic policies the US will pursue. The hegemonic state needs to project enough power to stabilize the system in order to make it safer for itself thereby maintaining its central position within it.

Equality of People

There are two reasons for which US Foreign Policy will have significant implications for the 'equality of people' as a primary institution of international society. First, historically the Wilsonian US has been very active in exporting the values of democracy and human rights. One should not expect the US to change direction on this issue. With the exception of countries where important strategic interests are involved, like Pakistan and China, whenever there will be a country where democracy is lacking and human rights are not respected, the US will play, at least, a vocal role if not a more active, interventionist one. Second, due to its sensitivity with ethnic and cultural differences, US will be prone to involve in humanitarian interventions abroad. The length and degree of such interventionist engagements, however, will be constrained by the country's existing worldwide military stretch and the possible human and financial (less important) cost involved.

On the other hand, the human rights record at home will continue be negative as long as terrorism remains a primary security threat. Under the influence of Revival Jacksonianism, citizens' surveillance, citizens' arrests and the treatment of imprisoned 'terrorists' will continue be a challenge to the international human rights regime. In Jacksonian US, order and security take priority over individual rights. This, however, provides the fertile ground for an intra-American dispute between Jacksonians and Wilsonians, which for the time being is won by the former.

Market

Revival Hamiltonianism will put a greater pressure on US Foreign Policy to achieve greater international trade and financial liberalization, while Wilsonianism will induce the US Administration to work with the other members of international society within the confines of global and regional organizations. Thus one should expect an extensive US international engagement through the means of international organizations, such as the WTO, the World Bank, IMF, and the Group of Eight (G-8). On the other hand, Revival Jacksonianism will put some constraints on trade liberalization since it will make necessary the protection of certain American economic sectors from foreign competition. Moreover, the confidence of Revival Jacksonianism will push the US to maintain its hegemonic position within the international economic system.

Nationalism

As it has been stated before, historically the Wilsonian US has been very active in exporting the values of democracy and one should not expect the country to alter its orientation on this issue. There are many places in the world where domestic groups would welcome US interference to assist the establishment of a democratic order. In the process of establishing a democratic order, the US views the organization and undertaking of national, regional, and local elections as a reflection of the exercise of popular sovereignty, which, in turn, legitimizes the new regime. However, strategic interests will determine whether there is an unconditional support for democracy abroad or a more realistic case by case policy will be adopted. Moreover, because of its own experience at home, and if all other means fail, the US will actively promote the principle of self-determination for repressed political communities. To this end, the US will support particular political and territorial arrangements.

On the other hand, challenges to US security, migration, and increasing anti-Americanism in world politics have created a strong nationalist movement in the US which is represented by the Jacksonians. But efforts of the Jacksonian America to strike back have resulted in increasing levels of nationalism in many parts of the world and especially in the Middle East. This trend is likely to continue.

Environmental Stewardship

In principle, the US will not turn its back to diplomatic efforts and negotiations regarding global environmental issues. Nevertheless, one should not expect the US to become part to any treaty that would affect its economic performance or to a convention that many other states and major powers are not willing to be parts. It appears that from all primary institutions of international society, environmental stewardship will be the one that the US Foreign Policy will affect by its relative absence rather than presence.

Conclusion

The purpose of this chapter was to examine the implications of US Foreign Policy for international order. In doing so, it sought to address certain weaknesses in the existing literature on US Foreign Policy and in particular the tendency to view it as a static phenomenon related to a particular administration. Instead, it considered US Foreign Policy as an evolving and dynamic process that is influenced and determined by developments in American society. It has challenged the idea that the orientation of US Foreign Policy is absolutely tied to a particular administration and has argued that it is necessary to examine the societal roots of US Foreign Policy in order to comprehend its complexity and future orientation. This means that change of administration will not necessarily lead to change in the direction of US Foreign Policy. In other words, changes in the American society may induce the new US administration to follow the same foreign policy as its predecessor although the new President may manage it in a different manner.

After discussing the 'paradox of American power' and the post-Cold War US Foreign Policy and its dilemmas, the chapter examined the four competing American visions regarding the goals and means of US Foreign Policy: the Hamiltonian, the Wilsonian, the Jeffersonian and the Jacksonian. After doing so, it examined how recent changes in the American society have led to the revival of and changes in these traditions and analyzed what this means for contemporary US Foreign Policy. In its final section, the chapter discussed the implications of US Foreign Policy for international order by pointing out how it will affect each of the primary institutions of international society as they are identified in Buzan's work.

Stemming from this analysis is the belief that although all primary institutions of international society will be affected by US Foreign Policy, great power management is the institution that one should expect the US impact to be the greatest. But due to the interdependence among international society's primary institutions, this impact will also be considerable on the institutions of sovereignty, diplomacy, nationalism and equality of people.

References

Art, Robert (2003), *A Grant Strategy for America* (Ithaca: Cornell University Press).

Brands, H.W. (2005), *Andrew Jackson* (New York: Anchor Books).

Brooks, Stephen and Wohlforth, William C. (2002), 'American Primacy in Perspective', *Foreign Affairs*, 81: 4.

Brown, Seyom (2003), *The Illusion of Control* (Washington DC: Brookings Institution Press).

Brzezinski, Zbigniew (2004), *The Choice: Global Domination or Global Leadership* (New York: Basic Books).

Bull, Hedley (2002), *The Anarchical Society*, 3rd edition (New York: Columbia University Press).

Buzan, Barry (2004), *From International to World Society?* (Cambridge: Cambridge University Press).

Callinikos, Alex (2003), *The New Mandarins of American Power* (Oxford: Polity).

Chernow, Ron (2004), *Alexander Hamilton* (London: Penguin).

Copeland, Dale (2003), 'A Realist Critique of the English School', *Review of International Studies*, 29, 427–41.

Ellis, Joseph J. (2001), *American Sphinx: The Character of Thomas Jefferson* (New York: Vintage).

Fry, Craig and O'Hagan, Jacinta (2000), *Contending Images of World Politics* (London: Macmillan).

Fukuyama, Francis (1992), *The End of History and the Last Man* (New York: Free Press).

Gaddis, John Lewis (2003), 'An American Foreign Policy Dilemma', in Rosemary Foot, John Lewis Gaddis and Andrew Hurrell (eds), *Order and Justice in International Relations* (Oxford: Oxford University Press).

Gaddis, John Lewis (1990), *Russia, the Soviet Union and the United States: An Interpretive History* (New York: McGraw Hill).

Haas, Richard N. (2005), *The Opportunity: America's Moment to Alter History's Course* (New York: Public Affairs).

Haas, Richard N. (2002), 'Defining US Foreign Policy in the Post-Cold War World', <www.state.gov/s/p/rem/9632.htm>.

Hirsh, Michael (2003), *At War with Ourselves: Why America Is Squandering Its Chance to Build a Better World* (Oxford: Oxford University Press).

Hofstadter, Richard (ed.) (1982), *Great Issues in American History From Reconstruction to the Present Day, 1864–1991* (New York: Vintage Books).

Huntington, Samuel (2004), *Who are We? The Challenges of the American National Identity* (New York: Simon & Schuster).

Huntington, Samuel (1998), *The Clash of Civilizations and the Remaking of World order* (New York: Simon & Schuster).

Ikenberry, John G. (2001), *After Victory: Institutions, Strategic Restraint, and the Rebuilding of Order after Major Wars* (Princeton: Princeton University Press).

Jervis, Robert (2006), *American Foreign Policy in a New Era* (London: Routledge).

Kagan, Robert (1998), 'The Benevolent Empire', *Foreign Policy*, 111, Summer 1998, 24–35.

Keohane, Robert (1989), *International Institutions and State Power: Essays in International Relations Theory* (Boulder, CO: Westview Press).

Kissinger, Henry (2001), *Does America Need a Foreign Policy?* (New York: Praeger).

Krauthammer, Charles (1990), 'The Unipolar Moment', *Foreign Affairs* 70: 1.

Kristol, William and Kagan, Robert (1996), 'Toward a Neo-Reaganite Foreign Policy', *Foreign Affairs* 75: 4.

Layne, Christopher (1993), 'The Unipolar Illusion', *International Security* 17: 4.

Levin, Gordon N. (1968), *Woodrow Wilson and World Politics* (Oxford: Oxford University Press).

Little, Richard (2003), 'The English School vs. American Realism: A Meeting of Minds or Divided by a Common Language', *Review of International Studies* 29, 443–60.

Little, Richard (2000), 'The English School's Contribution to the Study of International Relations', *European Journal of International Relations* 6, 395–422.

Lukacs, John (2004), *A New Republic* (New Haven: Yale University Press).

Lukacs, John (1984), *Outgrowing Democracy* (New Haven: Yale University Press).

Mead, Walter Russell (2004), *Power, Terror, Peace, and War* (New York: Alfred A. Knopf).

Mead, Walter Russell (2002), *Special Providence* (New York: Alfred A. Knopf).

Mearsheimer, John (2001), *The Tragedy of Great Power Politics* (New York: Simon & Schuster).

Mitchell, Broadus (1999), *Alexander Hamilton: A Concise Bibliography* (New York: Barnes and Noble Books).

Nye, Joseph S. (2001), *The Paradox of American Power* (Oxford: Oxford University Press).

Nye, Joseph S. (1990a), 'Soft Power', *Foreign Policy* 80, Fall 1990.

Nye, Joseph S. (1990b), *Bound to Lead* (New York: Basic Books).

Press-Barnathan, Galia (2003), 'The War against Iraq and International Order: From Bull to Bush', *International Studies Review* 6: 2, 195–212.

Randall, Willard Sterne (1993), *Thomas Jefferson: A Life* (New York: Harper Perennial).

Remini, Robert V. (1988), *The Life of Andrew Jackson* (New York: Harper Perennial).

Reus-Smit, Christian (2004), *American Power and World Order* (Cambridge: Polity).

Rice, Condoleezza (2000), 'Promoting the National Interest', *Foreign Affairs* 79: 1, 45–62.

Robertson, Pat (1991), *The New World Order* (Dallas, TX: Word Publishing).

Russett, Bruce (1993), *Grasping the Democratic Peace* (Princeton, NJ: Princeton University Press).

Sofer, Sasson (2002), 'Recovering the Classical Approach', *International Studies Review* 4: 3, 141–152.

Stephanson, Anders (1995), *Manifest Destiny: American Expansionism and the Empire of Right* (New York: Hill & Wang).

Stivachtis, Yannis (2006a), 'Power, Strength and American Hegemony: Hannah Arendt and Power of Association', under consideration.

Stivachtis, Yannis (2006b), 'Power, Strength and American Security', paper presented at the American Political Science Association (APSA) Annual Convention, Philadelphia, August 30 – September 2, 2006 and at the International Consortium for Social Theory (ICST) Annual Conference, Roanoke, May 26–28, 2006.

The National Security Strategy of the United States, September 2002, <www.whitehouse.gov/nsc/nss1.html>.

Walt, Stephen M. (2005), *Taming American Power* (New York: W.W. Norton & Company).

Waltz, Kenneth (1993) 'The New World Order', *Millennium: Journal of International Studies* 22: 2, 187–95.

Chapter 3

Triangulating Power: Russia, Europe and the United States Security Policies and Interests Projection in a Globalizing World

Maria Raquel Freire

At the dawn of the twenty-first century, the international order is growing plural and interdependent in political, economic, military and security terms with fundamental consequences in the (re)alignment of powers. The United States (US), the European Union (EU) and Russia are major actors in this challenging 'uni-multipolar world' (Huntington 1999, 35), sharing fears and concerns and competing regarding the most appropriate way of addressing these. In the face of the many threats to global security and in a world marked by growing interdependence in the context of profound changes, such as the demise of communism and the rise of Islamic radicalism, the proliferation of weapons of mass destruction (WMD), illegal trafficking and corruptive regimes, what might be the impact of transatlantic dis(unity) and Russia's inputs in the process?

A multiplicity of elements, both of an endogenous and exogenous nature, shapes the transatlantic relationship and its links to Moscow. While the complex interdependent and globalized international system does not allow for isolated conduct of political issues and economic affairs, internal approaches also condition options and courses of action. Moreover, to this duality must be added the fact that in Europe[1] there is a combination of the national and intergovernmental dimensions, with decision-making taking place at different levels, further complicating the setting where the Russia, EU, United States relations take place.

This chapter investigates the Russian place in the post-Cold War international order and whether and how it affects and is affected by the dynamics of the transatlantic relationship, focusing on power projection and security policies as its main structuring vectors. This analysis is framed in an encompassing understanding of security, building on the concept of security community and following a normative model of socialization of security policies for the study of the Russia, EU, US relationship. Triangulating power, the competitive versus cooperative approach among them, means a continuous redrawing of the triangle linking Brussels, Moscow and Washington, for sure not equilateral, and in many instances distorted. Power

---

1 The term Europe is used here as a synonym to European Union.

projection, as a consequence of security policy options, is the reflex of the complexity where this triangulation of approaches and bargaining takes place, having impact over the transatlantic relationship and the Russian positioning in the global order.

The issue of security is transversal regarding international actors, of a governmental and non-governmental nature, and the decision-making centers from the highest level of the state to its regional dimensions. It takes place in a bilateral or multilateral context, as a way of responding to a multiplicity of relations, pressure factors and leverage power to direct, or at least, condition change. The feelings of insecurity associated with the terrorist acts in the United States in September 2001 followed by attacks in Europe (such as in Madrid and London), as well as in Russia, attest to the pertinence of this encompassing understanding of security, as well as the need for encompassing responses to these global threats.

This maturation in the conceptualization of security has had reflex in the way Russia, the EU and the US relate to each other. The post-Cold War order offers new rules for the international game, requiring adjustments to the new conditions. In this new setting, the US has assumed the lead; the EU, despite difficulties, has increasingly gained relevance and international capacity to act in external affairs; and Russia seeks to reaffirm its power, downgraded after the disintegration of the Soviet Union to that of a regional power. The US assertiveness of military superiority and unilateral and aggressive posture, particularly after 11 September, has contrasted with the European multilateral and more diplomatic approach, which has found Russian support, at least on paper, as evinced in official documents.

In this context, the building of a security community, as first defined by Karl Deutsch in the 1950s, should have as main ingredients values compatibility, mutual needs acknowledgement and reliable and transparent policy goals – all of these underlined by the 'no war' principle. Applying the concept to this triangle is a challenging exercise. In fact, in theory and wording it seems suited-to-fit. The transatlantic community and Russia share as values, stability and democracy-building; acknowledge the need for cooperation in the fight against terrorism, organized crime and other global threats; and have explicitly defined in their official documents the principle of 'no war', along with the clarification of goals in their security policy formulations. However, from words to action the distance is wide, and interpretation and implementation of words have raised doubts about these apparently compatible principles.

The EU as a security community shares a set of values and norms built on a soft and multilateral approach to security issues, from which benefit-driven outputs are both an end and a self-sustaining factor, both for the Union and for the promotion of security in its vicinity. 'If we consider security as a matter of dialogue, exchange, trust building and civilian action more than military superiority, then the EU has a role to play' (Charillon 2005, 522). These soft security areas, where the EU has increasingly been gaining relevance, are fundamental as a basis for the Union's involvement at the global level, and for its influence as a 'normative model' (Youngs 2002, 103). By a process of gradual socialization of security approaches, meaning a set of norms and values allowing an approximation to EU policies and ways of dealing, it aims at endorsing an enlarged security community in its still much uncertain vicinity, where Russia is its largest neighbor. However, this has not been a linear process, with Russia resisting from socializing a security conceptualization that it wants to be its own. This has been evinced in its reticence regarding the 2004 Wider Europe proposal and in its practices at home, independent and uncomfortable in the face of what it describes as external interferences.

In parallel and simultaneously in contrast to this soft approach, the US would also like to see an enlarged security community including Russia, allowing reliance and stability, but built over its own principles and following its own rules. Thus, while the goals of building a more secure and stable world are shared, the means to achieve them are different. The result is a patchy order, where the values-gap and differences in understanding render difficult the achievement of a common denominator for effective cooperation.

The Soviet imperial logic is still much present in Russian foreign policy: a logic of affirmation and regaining of influence. In this process, the contours of the Western-Russia agenda become tremulous. The values gap, the underlying norm-setting differentiation, and the distinct understanding about (un)democratic practices render a common understanding about security and stability difficult. Dialogue seems in many instances an almost deaf talk, with Russian accusations of interference in its internal affairs and Western uneasiness about Russian practices at home and in the near abroad. Thus, cooperation, competition and uncooperative practices underlie this unbalanced relationship, which nevertheless presents differentiated traces when addressing Moscow's relations with the US or its dealings with the EU.

By analysing the Russian political options in the post-Cold War setting, further catalysed by the 11 September events, including its reaction in the face of an American 'go-it-alone' policy, and of the weak European response, balanced by the search for further international projection, this chapter understands the Russian course as ambivalent. This ambivalence is filled up with pragmatism, a realist look at means and capabilities, and a touch of pride recovering the imperialist feelings that persist in Russian politics. Objectives are balanced by means, the national interest is modeled and readjusted according to opportunities and constraints, and regional power projection is conditioned by the need for collaboration with other major players. This bargaining takes place in such a way that the Kremlin aims at pursuing Russian foreign policy goals, particularly in the geostrategic areas defined in Russian terms as of major relevance, while assuring new ingredients of competition will not be added to this already complex game, particularly in its vicinity. This is a balance difficult to attain, as further analysed.

The Political-Security Dimension of Russian Foreign Policy

Russian foreign policy has been shifting according to several factors, of an endogenous and exogenous nature, though the main post-Cold War structuring principles and goals have remained over time. What has been changing and conferring a sense of undulation to Russian policy making has been the conjugation of means and opportunities in the definition and pursuit of interests. The Commonwealth of Independent States (CIS) has remained a key area of intervention and influence, and relations with the EU, the US and the Asian powers (in particular India and China) have fluctuated according to opportunities for cooperation, clashes of competing interests, and pragmatic considerations of power projection and security reassurance. These adjustments have been clear throughout the Yeltsin years, balancing from rapprochement to the West, to a more Asian look, and keeping an eye over the former Soviet area. With Vladimir Putin, the concept of a multi-vectorial policy in political-security issues has conferred on Russian foreign policy a sense of continuity and instilled some stability by including the CIS as a priority area, as well as the Western and Asian dimensions. However, by enlarging the package, Putin also got added leeway, playing with these different dimensions to its best interest and in the broader game of projecting power in a growing interdependent international order.

The Yeltsin Years

At first showing a wish of approximation and integration into Western structures, usually termed as the romantic period (1992 and early 1993), Moscow defined itself as a natural ally of Europe. It did this by joining Partnership for Peace in the context of the North Atlantic Treaty Organization (NATO), as a formal signal of the new collaborative posture of the Alliance. Formerly NATO's number one military enemy, Russia initiated talks with the Council of Europe and fostered cooperation with the EU, leading to the signing of the Partnership and Cooperation Agreement (PCA) in June 1994 between it and the Union. Generically, the PCA envisages cooperation in different areas with the goal of integrating Russia in the wider area of cooperation in Europe, the strengthening of trade and economic ties, the promotion of security and international peace, and the development of a democratic society in a spirit of partnership and cooperation.[2] This was followed by the drafting of the EU strategy towards Russia in December 1995 which reflected the Union's concern over the need for a stable Russia in its proximity, with rapprochement built on economic assistance. Regarding its new neighbors, Moscow kept an introspective attitude, focusing on its internal problems.

However, the Western aid proved insufficient and the conditionality principles associated with it generated anti-Western feelings. These were explored by the nationalists and communists who pressured Boris Yeltsin and the Minister for Foreign Affairs, Andrei Kozyrev, for a change in policies. Severe criticism about Western interference in Russian affairs, including claims of mistreatment of Russian citizens abroad, particularly in neighboring republics, sustained the demands for further interventionism by the central authorities in Moscow.

In a new phase of its internal and external policy, Russia sought for reaffirmation as an influent power in its traditional area of influence, maintaining economic influence, political pressure and a considerable presence in military terms in some of these republics. This period (1993–1995), which might be labeled as the reaffirmation phase, translated the Russian nationalist aspirations at affirmation as a great power. Moscow aimed at becoming the 'guarantor of stability' in the area, maintaining a

---

2   www.europe.eu.int/comm/external_relations/ceeca/pca/pca_russia.pdf.   Signed   in June 1994, the PCA only entered in force in December 1997 due to the cooling of relations between Europe and Russia over the Chechen war.

tough stance at home, as evinced in the Chechen war, and intending to be recognized as the legitimate protector of its neighboring republics. In this way, the former Soviet space was defined as an area of strategic national interest, and the influence of third countries was not welcomed.

The Eastern enlargement of both NATO and the EU, understood in Moscow as a direct threat to its interests, highlighted differences. In a speech at the United Nations in 1995, Yeltsin appealed to a more ample framing of European security, if possible through the strengthening of the Organization for Security and Cooperation in Europe (OSCE), more than to an expansion of alliances which could conduct to a new confrontation (see Freire 2003). The new Duma, elected by year's end, with a stronger communist presence, meant less popular support for pro-Western politics in comparison to the first years of post-communist administration.

In early 1996, Andrei Kozyrev stepped down from office and was replaced by Yevgeni Primakov in the Foreign Affairs Ministry. Primakov conferred a new direction on the Kremlin's policies, demonstrated by the search for parity with the US, the cooling of the rapprochement to Europe, further involvement in the former Soviet space, and an enhanced Asian-look. Less pro-Western, Moscow launched a pragmatic policy, searching for more effective answers to the problems it faced, through the implementation of social and economic reforms at home, a change in its politics of intervention in the CIS from direct meddling to the search for consensus, and an international agenda focused on the CIS and Asian countries, in particular China and India.

The Russian relationship with Europe and the US was further aggravated by the armed intervention of NATO in former Yugoslavia, where the historical ties of Russia with the Serbians could not be ignored. Sanctions were, for that reason, not welcomed in the Russian Duma. Even among more moderate opinions, there was anxiety about NATO's overstretching beyond its natural borders, independently of what Russia or others could think. Despite Yeltsin describing the attack in the spring of 1999 as an 'act of aggression', Russian involvement helped in ending the conflict and easing tensions, though not without highlighting traces of disagreement underlining the relationship with the West.

On 4 June 1999, the EU Common Strategy on Russia was launched in Cologne, setting the basis for a 'strategic partnership', as a way of responding to the mounting tensions, with the Chechen issue and former Yugoslavia on top of discord. It represents the most consistent effort at coordination of European policies and programs towards Russia, defining objectives as well as drawing immediate priorities for action. The political message is clear: a stable Russia governed by democratic principles at the EU borders. However, the strategy will only have practical relevance if 'Russia think Europe and if Europe think Russia' (Nyberg 1999), meaning mutual and sincere commitment to the development of this relationship. This strategy is different from the 1995 document in that it clearly states soft security threats, and that EU-Russia cooperation promotes not only regional but also global security (Haukkala 2003, 13). However, this identification of common threats does not mean a common understanding about the ways of dealing with them.

Moscow responded in October the same year with the adoption of a document about the Medium Term Strategy for Development of Relations with the European

Union.[3] The document aims at assuring national interests and expands the image of Russia in Europe as a partner of confidence in the building of a system of collective security, while mobilizing the potential and experience of the EU in the promotion of the Russian market economy and democratization. In addition, it envisages strategic cooperation in the prevention and search for solutions to local conflicts, with emphasis on international law and peaceful means. In this way, it envisages a unified Europe, without dividing lines, and the balanced and integrated strengthening of the positions of the Russian Federation and Europe regarding political issues and international security. According to the document, the proposed objectives go into line with the European strategy towards Russia.

However, if at first sight the two documents seem to be in alignment, looking at them more carefully reveals after all some misalignment. The 'EU focuses on values and Russia's need to change profoundly, while the Russian document stresses national interests and sovereignty. The CSR [Common Strategy on Russia] is vague, while the Russian strategy is quite specific' (Lynch 2003, 59), revealing the pragmatic and realist tone Russian foreign policy has been assuming. This distant way of formulating guiding principles remains very present in the EU-Russia relationship, showing both the distance in the underlying conceptualizations about values and norms and the difficulties in understanding the 'other'. The complex EU structure and multi-level decision-making dynamics render it an opaque partner, while the Russian way of formulating policies and its precarious commitment to many international principles shows its obscure side. Difficulties in understanding that persist in time.

Putin's Pragmatic and Realist Approach to Foreign Policy

On 31 December 1999, Yeltsin resigned from the presidency. His interim successor, Vladimir Putin, was elected as the new president of the Russian Federation in March 2000, suggesting both expressions of support about his realist look at Russian politics and criticism about his tough stance at home and abroad. The three main foreign policy documents adopted by Putin at the beginning of his first mandate point to a multilateral approach in foreign policy. Those documents referred to the potential destabilizing role of a 'unipolar structure of the world with the economic and power domination of the United States', the CIS as an area of strategic importance and the Eastern dimension (the Asia-Pacific region) as a relevant region in Moscow's external policy (National Security Concept 2000; Russian Military Doctrine 2000; Foreign Policy Concept 2000).

Generally, Putin seeks to maintain a privileged relationship with the West. This follows a clear reasoning: 'not trying to play off the US and Europe against one another, or to give preference to one or the other ..., but rather to seek everywhere for opportunities to become part of the West' (Hunter 2003, 40). The events of 11 September 2001 and the global fight against terrorism constituted such an opportunity. Putin offered its support to the global fight against terror and the Western critical voices regarding disrespect and the violation of human rights in Russia,

---

3   www.eur.ru/eng/neweur/user_eng.php?func=apage&id=53.

and particularly in the Chechen Republic, were almost silenced. Putin recognized Russia's weaknesses and sought the revitalization of the state, with 11 September revealing itself as an accelerator of this tendency (Lynch 2003, 9). The concrete realization that Russia could not do much in the face of inevitable developments, such as EU and NATO enlargement, made Russia change its discourse since direct confrontation in wording by poisoning its relationship with the West could lead to isolation and consequently add to the country's fragility. In fact, this process could be used to Russia's advantage, since integrating countries at Russian borders into NATO and the EU might lead to further involvement of Moscow in these processes. This was realized by these organizations as convenient and benefit-driven: a policy of cooperative inclusion allowing both the alienation of exclusion fears in Moscow and not requiring formal integration of Russia in these structures.

For Russia, the primary threat to its own security comes from within – the menace of civil unrest and violence within its borders, such as in the most cited case of Chechnya (Freire 2005). This is followed by developments in its near abroad, defined as an area of vital interest. In this political orientation, it seems clear the recognition by the authorities in Moscow that the Russian geostrategic power is under threat. This feeling of vulnerability, with concrete justification in the wider involvement of other actors in its neighboring area, helps to explain the Russian collaborative approach. According to the Russian model, one way of preserving international security is through the clarification of the level of Western engagement in the former Soviet space, a delicate matter for Russia and regarding which Moscow likes to keep an attentive look. This new posture means a multilateral attitude towards its multiple security problems, but it also seems to be a way of counterbalancing Washington's unilateral hegemonic policy. If this is a strategy to oppose Washington's moves, then it might neither be consistent nor effective.

'The essence of Russian policy under Putin, therefore, has little to do with Kozyrev's pursuit of pro-Westernism in the early 1990s, where Russia was to merge into the Western 'family of civilized countries'. Current policy has a much sharper edge. Russian differences with the West have not disappeared. Simply, Putin has decided that they are best resolved with Russia comfortably inside the tent rather than with one foot jammed in the doorway. 'Russia's changes in foreign policy since 11 September, therefore, are based on calculations of priority and interest, where risk is distinguished from threat and real needs are separate from false ambitions' (Lynch 2003, 29–30). Thus, normative considerations are being surpassed by *realpolitik* principles.

Russia, Europe and the US: Security Policies and Power Projection in a Globalizing World

The contours of Russian security policies and options demonstrate the careful dealing Putin attaches to the relationship with the West, as well as with its Asian neighbors, playing both with transatlantic divergence and building on cooperation among them, of which the war on terrorism has been a clear example. In fact, the global fight against terrorism has conferred on Russia added power, allowing less restraint at home and in its near abroad.

> [T]he very weakness of the concept of a 'war against global terror' becomes its greatest strength; the inherent ambiguities and ambivalence embodied by this 'war' provide Russia with an ideological pretext for foreign policy change through strategic realignment, while the disparities and fractures within the Euro-Atlantic security community allow the opportunity for President Putin – the most consistent Westernizer since Catherine the Great – to pick and choose which of the core values and interests of a divided transatlantic community Russia shares (Herd and Akerman 2002, 370).

In addition, Russia plays off Western fears over a solid Russian-Chinese rapprochement, which despite growing contacts does not seem to have a far-reaching effect given the regional dynamics of competition, particularly regarding energetic sources and power projection (see Lo 2004; Katz 2006). Nevertheless, this is also part of the complex triangulation of power between Russia, Europe and the US, with which Putin plays to the most, though not always getting all he wants, as further analysed regarding both Moscow's relationship with the EU and Washington.

Russia and the EU: Two Unequal Partners, Ever Strategic Partners?

The EU and Russia are two unequal partners, different actors with different agendas, not always easy to reconcile. The EU is a regional organization with 25 Member States built over democratic principles and a multi-level decision-making system where individual interests do not necessarily coincide with the collective, particularly on foreign policy issues. On the other hand, the Russian Federation is a wide country with a unified policy and well-defined political, strategic and economic interests, based on a strong hand at home and tough stance towards foreign issues considered vital to Russian interests, pursued in many instances outside the traditional contours of democratic practices. From these disparities in cohesion and from the means to achieve political objectives, there have been resulting difficulties in the building of a strategic partnership between the sides.

There are internal divisions within Russia among the Euro-Atlanticists, the Eurasianists, and those who put Russia first. The Euro-Atlanticists favor closer ties to the US and Europe, the Eurasianists look to the Eastern scenario for strategic alliances with China and India in their horizons, and the Russia-first seeks an affirmation of Russian power on the basis of the country's imperial legacy, political strength and influence, and economic resources such as energetic assets. Russia's scenario at home reveals, in this very much simplistic analysis, the divergences in discourse. President Putin's power and powerful saying in foreign policy has nevertheless managed to transform these divergences in a unified foreign policy, allowing some coherence in both wording and action.

Within the EU, the scenario is not one of unified and coordinated policies. The multi-level decision-making system, where bargaining is necessary for attaining common positions, demonstrates how difficult it is to conciliate objectives of 25 national governments with different foreign policy visions. Moscow plays with these differences to get support, attention and a winning strategy for its foreign policy goals. For example, the Moscow-Paris-Berlin axis in the Iraqi affair (2003), against the assertive posture of the US, allowed the Kremlin a say in the transatlantic bargain. While cooperating with Washington, particularly after 11 September on terrorism related issues, Moscow does not preclude from criticizing the unilateralist stance of Washington's policy as countervailing international interests, and Russian interests in particular. In addition, Russia played with differences within the Union, with the old debate between the Europeanists and the Atlanticists resurfacing in the case of Iraq. However, the drivers behind this bilateral relationship are not clear: is it based on conventional power logic and rivalry or on genuine civilian power built over normative considerations?

The fast changing tone in dialogue, from good neighbourliness to mutual accusations and signs of distrust, show how the marking differences between these two major actors cannot simply be rubbed out. The mixing in cooperative and competitive approaches confers on this relation an interesting dimension: both acknowledge the relevance of the other, the strategic benefits arising from mutual understanding, and the possible gains from collaboration not only for the two but for regional and global stability. But, they also acknowledge deep differences in understandings and approaches. As formulated by Alexander Motyl, 'the gap between these states and the rest of Europe is *identitaire* and systemic, not because their identities are accepted as being non-European and, therefore different, but precisely because they are "European-*plus*" – plus Slavic, plus Russian, plus *unique*' (Lynch 2003a, 35). In this context, the framing guidelines for the EU-Russia relationship are not tight or defined to suit.

After the Union's enlargement to 25 Member States, the PCA was extended to the new members, in such a way that the privileged relationship Moscow had with the Union was also extended to the new members. It should be noted that many of these states were till then preferential trade partners of Russia, a status that to some extent is in this way maintained. The EU is a main trade and economic partner for Russia, carrying also strategic weight, as evinced in the Energy Dialogue established at the EU-Russia Summit in October 2000, though the results have so far been modest. In addition, the EU has sought a more active Russian involvement in security actions of the Union, such as for example the integration of Russian forces in EU missions (Bosnia-Herzegovina).

For Moscow, this involvement is important, clearly demonstrating its understanding that a European security and defense policy, which does not interfere in its vital issues and to some extent counterbalances and minimizes the presence of NATO, is welcomed in Russia. However, the way it has been conducted has generated discomfort in Russia.

[T]he EU makes decisions on the conduct of peacekeeping operations, while relegating Russia to observer status. I can say frankly that our cooperation on such a basis will flounder, going nowhere. We participate in the EU Police Mission in Bosnia-Herzegovina, but this is the first and only case of such participation. We have already declined the EU invitation to take part in several other peacekeeping and policing operations. I believe that our response to subsequent proposals will be the same unless we agree on an acceptable format for crisis management operations that takes into account the interests of all participants' (Chizlov 2005, 137).

This is a clear evidence of the differences in understanding resulting from distinct conceptualizations about security and normative considerations. But, in the midst of these differences, there has been room for collaborative policies.

There has been progress in the Kaliningrad issue,[4] a bilateral protocol was concluded regarding EU support to Russian integration into the World Trade Organization (WTO), and dialogue and cooperation on political and security matters has been strengthened after the November 2003 Joint Declaration signed in Rome between the EU and Russia. On its part, Russia ratified the Kyoto Protocol, allowing its entry into force in February 2005. In March of the same year, the first round of contacts on human rights, minorities and fundamental rights took place in Luxembourg, opening the ground for debating delicate issues. On 10 May 2005, an agreement on four common spaces was signed, having as a goal a Europe without dividing lines, built around four areas of cooperation, including a common economic space; a common space of liberty, security and justice; a common space of cooperation in the field of external security; and a common space of research, education and culture. These words still need to be translated into concrete actions. Despite the sides not directly relating the issues, it seems certain that concessions are becoming clearer in a relationship built over fragile foundations, in the sense of the disparity of values and principles that sustain them. 'A rapprochement with Europe would mean a "new game" according to different, civilized rules. Russian political establishment usually calls it "concessions" and "restrictions of sovereignty"' (Kuznetsova 2005, 69–70). The differences in discourse evince once more the difficulties in talking the same political language.

However, dissension runs through a wide range of aspects including democratic issues and human rights, of which Chechnya and criticism regarding the way Russia handled the Beslan hostage crisis are examples. Border control, migration policies, visa regimes, corruption, veterinary certificates, aviation royalties, or the settlement of border questions with Estonia and Latvia, add to disagreement. The ways in which Russia reacts to the strengthening of the Union regarding its military capacity reveal an ambiguous posture of support if this means a counterbalance to NATO and the US, but also of distrust for a powerful neighbor that might become more an adversary than a partner. 'Russian policy is pro-Russian and not pro-Western; the strategy of alignment is a means to an end. The most important end is that of domestic revitalization' (Lynch 2003, 94). Thus, a clear tension between the expansion of the normative agenda of the EU and Russian power politics considerations exists.

Russia and the US: Ups-and-downs in an Asymmetrical Relationship

The Bush administration policies focusing on geopolitical military considerations (Calleo 2001, 376), translate the Hobbesian belief in the need for superior force to survive in a conflicting world. These differences were exacerbated with the Iraqi crisis where multilateral institutions, such as the United Nations and NATO, were excluded. This demonstrates how these institutions are appreciated mainly to the

---

4   *Joint Statement on Transit between the Kaliningrad Region and the Rest of the Russian Federation*, Brussels, 11 November 2002.

extent that they support and legitimize American foreign policy. While Washington justifies its option on the high-tech military campaign where the use of Special Forces, paramilitary intelligence assets and precision-guided munitions made the eventual contribution of the Alliance members minor, the fact is that it preferred to avoid the complications of another 'war by committee' (Neuhold 2003, 464; Bereuter and Lis 2004, 157). As a consequence, 'while the EU was split, NATO was sidelined' (Hoffmann 2003, 1034). For Russia, this meant an opportunity to oppose Washington's presumption, and joy for the weakening of NATO, despite the Russian enhanced engagement in the organization's activities. These political moves led to an understanding that NATO's role in Washington's policy has been reduced, with the Atlantic Alliance moving from a central asset to the diminished role of providing candidates to ad hoc coalitions (Kanet 2005, 3).

Russia is very critical about NATO's enlargement policies and the deployment of military forces close to its borders, showing a persistent fear over Western institutions. The Alliance is equated with the US, serving its interests and being regarded as a vehicle for accelerating the unipolar trend driven by the US and thus widening the existing power gap (Splidsboel-Hansen 2002, 445). Nevertheless, Putin followed a soft approach to the enlargement of NATO, which elicited inflamed reactions at home. General Anatolii Kvashnin, chief of the general staff, has defined the NATO-Russia Basic Act as 'an informational cover' under which Cold War thinking persisted (Kvashnin cited in O'Loughlin *et al.* 2004, 13). Agreement over the creation of the NATO-Russia Council at its new format as 'NATO at 20' (now at 27), meaning an equal status to Russia in decision-making regarding European security ('NATO-Russia Relations' 2002), diminished the voices of discontent, though it did not silence them. From time to time the traditional image of the 'enemy', a remnant of the Cold War, is recovered along with the argument that the geostrategic context changed at Russia's expense. This image is extended to political-military issues from arms control treaties to the war on terrorism (Freire, 2007).

This reasoning leaves space for suspicion and a sense of transparency lacking in the US-Russia relationship. Moreover, misguided perceptions regarding discourse often render obscure motives and give ground to disagreement. According to Mikhail Margelov, Russian Chairman of the Foreign Affairs Committee of the Federation Council:

> American propaganda machine fits any new problems related to the conflict of interests into the context of the US concern with the future of democracy in Russia and associates it with the current issues such as strengthening the 'vertical of power' in Russia. This makes it harder to continue bilateral cooperation and develops into another type of the fluctuating system of relationship priorities (Margelov 2006, 25).

Following the same lines of the EU, Moscow and Washington collaborate in the fight against terror and organized crime, the proliferation of WMD, fostering of democratic political systems, the protection of individual rights, and the consolidation of economic benefits. These goals have been stated in the Moscow Declaration on the New Strategic Relationship signed in May 2002, and reaffirmed in meetings and statements in both capitals. Moscow shut down some Cold War military facilities, amply supported the US campaign in Afghanistan, and gave its consent on the stationing of American military forces in Central Asia, showing a cooperative stance (Blagov 2004). In response, it received recognition as a market economy, full membership in the G8 group, and support for its accession to the WTO, which has nevertheless been revealing problems, as evinced at the G8 meeting in St. Petersburg, in 2006.

These areas of cooperation have found resistance in topics over which disagreement prevails. Russia has criticized the US for meddling in its internal affairs, particularly regarding governing practices, human rights and the war against terror, with the latter translated into 'attempts to classify terrorist acts as "ours" and "theirs", as "moderate" and "radical"' ('Putin Accuses West' 2004). In addition, certain American actions reinforced the suspicions of some Russians that the US is seeking to parlay the war against terror into a war for control of oil, gas, and pipeline routes (Foglesong and Hahn 2002, 11), thus directly linking political and economic issues in a delicate way (Freire, 2007). Moreover, the US withdrawal from the Anti-Ballistic Missile (ABM) Treaty in 2001, despite the signature of a new treaty in May 2002 concerning the reduction of long-range nuclear weapons – the Strategic Offensive [Arms] Reduction Treaty (known as SORT), and the development of the national missile defense shield, raised suspicion in Russia. In reaction, Moscow announced the adoption of a pre-emptive military doctrine following the footsteps of Washington, as well as the development of a new nuclear missile system as an assurance of Russia's security.

The Sino-Russian relationship is also under close scrutiny in Washington. While the US understands the difficulties in empowering a strategic partnership between Russia and China (two competing powers in the region), it sees with caution rapprochement between the two giants. They share the multipolar and terrorism-fighting discourse, have taken the same path regarding Iraq in 2003, and hold important commercial ties, particularly in military and energetic terms. 'China's defence policy is aimed ever more pointedly at the defence capability of the US. It is also destabilizing an already volatile region. There can be no systemic security without Asian security and there will be no Asian security without a strong role for the west therein' (Lindley-French 2006, 55). Cooperation within the Shangai Cooperation Organization and the Joint Declaration on the International Order in the 21st Century, of July 2005, add to fears. Washington's reactions and criticisms might propel further approximation between the two states (Vnukov 2006, 133; Titarenko 2005, 5; Pant 2004, 313–5), though not meaning full engagement.

The war in Iraq (March 2003) clearly marked the lowest point in Russian-US, post-Cold War relations. By the end of May 2003, the gathering in St. Petersburg for the celebrations of the city's 300 years made clear the underlying differences between Moscow and Washington.

> Putin had re-established links with his neighbors near and far, and put Russia's relationships on a more sober, realistic footing. But there was also a new assertiveness, as he demonstrated that he might not be a pariah but neither was he a lackey of the west. It was a relationship of realpolitik, a balance of forces and economic interests far more than it was a true meeting of minds or values (Jack 2004, 296).

The rules of the game became clearer, with pragmatism and a realist look leading the Kremlin's policy-formulation. Russia pursued its own course, disagreeing with the US when necessary, but maintained a diplomatic and certainly contained approach (Freire, 2007). Washington should base its policies towards Russia on 'mutual interests, not the expectations of mutual values' (Trenin 2005), since it is increasingly clear that the underpinning values are different, as are the interpretations about democracy.

Despite dissension and in the midst of accusations, both sides acknowledge mutual gains from cooperation. The war on terrorism, non-proliferation, and Russia's integration into the international economy are three main themes which might bring mutual rewards. Changes in the format and style of communications between the US and Russia are necessary, in order to minimize the perception of Russia as a second-rate country, which Moscow cannot accept. In addition, counter-terrorism cooperation might be pursued through intelligence-sharing, the development of joint threat assessments, and the implementation of confidence-building measures through, for example, active work with Russia and other states on border security and anti-trafficking. These issues touch sensitive matters for Russia, particularly regarding its and others' involvement in the near abroad.

Conclusion: (Un)balances and (Mis)matches in the Triangulation of Power

In a global and interdependent world, the way in which Russia, the EU and the US interrelate is a demonstration of the complex international order, where the internal and external dimensions in the formulation of security policy and in the projection of power are interconnected. Traditional conceptualizations about war, power, security, diplomacy and international law have increasingly been under challenge. Despite fundamental concepts to bring order to the international disorder, these have been manipulated, interpreted and implemented according to differentiated understandings and approaches. As analysed before, the desire to expand the security community principle to an enlarged transatlantic relationship involving Russia, the EU and the US, built over a normative model of socialization of security policies, remains unfinished. Following Deutsch, values compatibility, mutual needs acknowledgement, and reliable and transparent policy goals should form a solid basis for guaranteeing the 'no war' principle. By respecting international law principles, and following diplomatic procedures, dialogue would be fostered and misunderstandings avoided. In this line of reasoning, great power management would be conducted under predefined lines of consensus, allowing a sense of prediction in the international order.

However, reality is not coincident with ideal-types, as evinced in the continuous alignment and realignment of power. The transatlantic relationship should, therefore, be developed in a balanced perspective built over a complementary logic. Europe should be capable of affirming itself in the world community not in a reactive, but proactive manner, and with an innovative posture be able to combine the differing perspectives, approaches and means of its 27 Member States. The US should adopt a less assertive stance and look at Europe as a valuable partner in the promotion of general stability and security. This should be pursued in a context of enhanced dialogue and institutionalized procedures underlying the working relationships within a security community for managing traditional diplomatic rivalries at the states' level, by offering a kind of supra-national-and-Atlantic framework where erroneous perceptions and conflicting leadership roles could be diluted. This should be grounded on the solid principles underlining the transatlantic relationship, sown decades ago and which have proven their invaluable strength, particularly democratic rule, liberal economy and avoiding mismanagement of dissension. These same old principles should forge the relationship with Russia, based on normative driven and consensual-built principles.

Many issues of discord shadow the transatlantic relation, further expanded by the inclusion of Russia, but many other shared concerns throw light over this puzzle of differentiated interests. Hegemonic assertiveness or isolationist inaction might be source of resentment, and differences in perception and understanding might endanger opportunities for dialogue and cooperation. But partnership, instead of competition, should be the dominant approach in order that global security might be enhanced. Europe needs the US, but the US also needs Europe. Just like Russia needs Europe and the US, and both of them need Russia. 'Americans cannot satisfy themselves by saying 'my way or no way'. They must transform their considerable power into consensus' (Bolkestein 2003, 243), while the Europeans must demonstrate a more solid approach to security issues and be able to affirm the advantages of a normative model of democratization and stability-building. The Russians should offer more flexibility in their positions, while not meaning an abandonment of vital interests or a simple bow before Europe or the US.

The relationship with Russia has been marked by ups-and-downs, according to developments in the international scene. However, in general terms, its evolution has been showing signs of progress, demonstrating the recognition that partnership and cooperation are necessary despite the remaining divergences in an increasingly volatile and unstable scenario. Transnational phenomena such as terrorism, organized crime, illicit activities and trafficking in drugs, arms and human beings, are shared problems. In addition, more pragmatic aspects, such as sharing a common border of over 1,500 kilometers, more than 50 per cent of trade exchanges being made with the EU, of Russia being the highest provider of hydrocarbonates (a fundamental source of energetic resources) and presenting high potential as a market, despite its still fragile economy, are fundamental aspects that demonstrate the positive sum game that might result from dialogue, and from its much needed translation into effective forms of collaboration.

In this relationship the conduct of dialogue and the rendering operational of initiatives must be sufficiently clear to dismiss Russian fears about EU enlargement, which have risen with the diminution of Moscow's power in the world stage. Neither of the sides sees its interests as best served by excluding the other, but they also realize the need to deepen cooperation. President Putin has mentioned the need for improving the quality of this cooperation, however, always following a realist perspective in the sense that when in some way Russian vital interests might be under threat, Moscow does not cooperate. So, a cooperation underlined by interest, compromise and rational calculus of opportunities and benefits exists.

This same reasoning applies to a large extent to the US-Russia relationship, regarding opportunities for cooperation, areas of competition, and a realist and pragmatic understanding of the global order, underlined by asymmetrical bargaining where the US power surpasses Russian capabilities. However, Moscow still has an enlarged leverage power in most of the former Soviet space, and retains a saying in international affairs, even if diminished and in instances almost unheard. A demonstration, nevertheless, that Washington finds a cooperative and amicable relationship with its Russian counterpart as beneficial for stability in the country and in the region and for the pursuit of American goals at the world scale.

The diminishing of NATO's role with the US unilateral moves after 11 September, has contributed to a downgrading of the organization's relevance in Russian politics, and to improvement in bilateral contacts between Washington and Moscow. In fact, Washington has been showing a less critical approach than the EU regarding internal politics in Russia. The EU has maintained a more active and less reserved attitude, openly criticizing the ambiguity and dualism inherent to the opposition between 'strategy' and 'democracy' in Russia, an attitude which has been suggesting problems to this relationship (Lynch 2003, 57).

The EU has been following a policy of influence over Russian internal developments through the definition of concessions and bargains in the face of shared interests and objectives. A policy of 'giving, but', which intends through the introduction of conditionality elements to pressure Russia in delicate matters, in particular regarding human rights and democratization. The US formulation is different in terms, though sharing the EU objectives of stability building in a country of mass proportions and vast resources. The accommodation of mutual interests has suggested a 'yes, but'[5] policy in the Russia-US relationship, with Washington conceding on the democratization sphere by allowing Russia's own democratization course, in exchange for concessions in the pursuit of its global role. But these exchanges have been reciprocal, with mutual accusations and the exchange of compliments marking the ambiguities inherent to the contours of foreign policy options and approaches.

The pragmatism and realism in Russian policy making clashes, in many instances, with the soft power and normative idealism proclaimed in the EU house, and with the hard unilateral approach followed by the White House. Despite differences, Moscow, Brussels and Washington recognize the relevance of a 'strategic partnership'. The means to empower it have, however, revealed difficulties. 'Europe's major institutions seek cooperative arrangements with Russia but do not include Russia in their agendas of enlargement. Western states and organizations appear to want Russia to reform economically and to enter the global economy, yet they impose restrictions on Russian trade' (MacFarlane 2001, 286). This ambivalence demonstrates that not only has Russia been having difficulty in adjusting to Western standards, but also that the West has been having problems in integrating Russia.

---

5   I borrow this expression from Stanley Sloan, *NATO, the EU and the Atlantic Community: The Transatlantic Bargain Reconsidered* (Lanham: Rowman and Littlefield), 2003.

Differences in approaches and perceptions have been clear, similarities in discourse have been underlined by disagreement over the interpretation of words, and mismatches in policies and actions have thus been frequent. But, Russia combines in its identity a European and a non-European trace, expressed in its multi-vector foreign policy, which should be explored by Europe and the US in its rapprochement and further integration of the Russian state into the Western club. However, this should not be pursued as an imposition or no-way option. 'The West sets the standards, and Russia has to adapt if it wishes to be accepted as an equal partner. As a consequence, Russia is declared responsible for its inclusion in or exclusion from 'the West' depending on whether it emulates or rejects 'Western' norms and procedures. These, in turn, are increasingly declared non-negotiable. This procedure is likely to result in one-sided adaptation rather than in mutual social learning' (Möller 2003, 316). In addition, its results will be limited.

Declarations of intention or claims of responsibility do not suffice in the building of a broader security community. Common action, the sharing of strategies and mutual gains must be clear: there is a basis, even if not solid, for such enlarged understanding. This is based upon common endeavors to fight terrorism in its various dimensions, the fostering of economic cooperation and further political dialogue on democratization. A rapprochement should be sought through inclusion, not in the sense of formal integration, but more of non-exclusion from existing processes and organizational dynamics.

In this regard, *The Economist* noted that '[s]ixty years ago a wise American diplomat, George Kennan, proposed that the right policy of the West towards an expansionary Soviet Union under Joseph Stalin should be 'containment'. Russia today is clearly no such threat. But it still matters, and the West should care about where it is going. The best policy now is no longer containment but 'wary engagement' ('Living with a Strong Russia' 2006), a wise advice.

References

Bereuter, D. and Lis, J. (2004), 'Broadening the Transatlantic Relationship', *The Washington Quarterly* 27: 1, 147–62.

Blagov, S. (2004), 'Putin Aims for Higher Russian Profile', Power and Interest News Report (PINR), www.pinr.com.

Bolkestein, F. (2003), 'Commentary: Europe, America and the Middle East', *European Review* 11: 3, 239–44.

Calleo, D. (2001), *Rethinking Europe's Future* (Princeton: Princeton University Press).

Charillon, F. (2005), 'The EU as a Security Regime', *European Foreign Affairs Review* 10: 4, 517–33.

Chizlov, V. (2005), 'Russia-EU Cooperation: The Foreign Policy Dimension', *International Affairs, A Russian Journal of World Politics, Diplomacy and International Relations* 51: 5, 134–8.

Deutsch, K. *et al.* (1957), *Political Community and the North Atlantic Area: International Organizations in the Light of Historical Experiences* (Princeton: Princeton University Press).

Fawn, R. (ed.) (2003), *Realignments in Russian Foreign Policy* (London: Frank Cass).

Foglesong, D. and Hahn, G. (2002), 'Ten Myths about Russia: Understanding and Dealing with Russia's Complexity and Ambiguity', *Problems of Post-Communism* 6, 5–16.

Freire, M.R. (2007), 'Russian and Other CIS Responses to the War on Terrorism', in Kolodziej, E. and Kanet, R. (eds), *Consensual or Coercive Hegemon: Either or Neither? American Power and Global Order* (University of Georgia Press).

Freire, M.R. (2005), 'Matching Words with Actions: Russia, Chechnya and the OSCE – A Relationship Embedded in Ambiguity', *UNISCI Discussion Papers*, 9, 159–71.

Freire, M.R. (2003), *Conflict and Security in the Former Soviet Union: The Role of the OSCE* (Aldershot: Ashgate Publishing).

Herd, G. and Akerman, E. (2002), 'Russian Strategic Realignment and the Post-Cold War Era?', *Security Dialogue* 33: 3, 357–72.

Hoffmann, S. (2003), 'US-European relations: Past and Future', *International Affairs* 79: 5, 1029–36.

Hunter, R. (2003), 'NATO-Russia Relations after 11 September', *Journal of Southeast European and Black Sea Studies* 3: 3, 28–54.

Huntington, S. (1999), 'The Lonely Superpower: US Military and Cultural Hegemony Resented by Other Powers', *Foreign Affairs* 78: 2, 35–49.

International Institute for Strategic Studies (IISS) (2003), *Strategic Survey 2002/2003: An Evaluation and Forecast of World Affairs* (London: Oxford University Press).

Jack, A. (2004), *Inside Putin's Russia* (London: Granta Books).

Johansson-Nogués, E. (2004), 'The Fifteen and the Accession States in the UN General Assembly: What Future for European Foreign Policy in the Coming Together of the "Old" and "New" Europe?', *European Foreign Affairs Review* 9, 67–92.

Kanet, R. (2005), 'Introduction: The New Security Environment' in Kanet, R. (ed.), *The New Security Environment: The Impact on Russia, Central and Eastern Europe* (Aldershot: Ashgate Publishing).

Katz, M. (2006), 'Primakov Redux? Putin's Pursuit of "Multipolarism" in Asia', *Demokratizatsiya* 14: 1, 144–52.

Kolodziej, E. and Kanet, R. (eds) (forthcoming), *Consensual or Coervive Hegemon: Either or Neither? American Power and Global Order* (University of Georgia Press).

Kuznetsova, E. (2005), 'Will the Roadmaps lead Russia to Europe?', *International Affairs, A Russian Journal of World Politics, Diplomacy and International Relations* 51: 4, 67–71.

Kvashnin cited in O'Loughlin, J.; Gearóid, Ó and Kolossov, V. (2004), 'A "Risky Westward Turn?": Putin's 9/11 Script and Ordinary Russians', *Europe-Asia Studies* 56: 1, 3–34.

Lindley-French, J. (2006), '*Big* World, *Big* Future, *Big* NATO', *NATO Review*, www.nato.int.

'Living with a Strong Russia', *The Economist*, 15 July 2006.

Lo, B. (2004), 'The Long Sunset of Strategic Partnership: Russia's Evolving China Policy', *International Affairs*, 80: 2, 295–309.

Lynch, D. (2003), 'Russia Faces Europe', *Chaillot Papers 60* (Paris: Institute for Security Studies).

Lynch, D. (2003a), 'The New Eastern Dimension of the Enlarged EU', in Lynch, D. (ed.), 'Partners and Neighbours: A CFSP for a Wider Europe', *Chaillot Papers 64* (Paris: Institute for Security Studies).

MacFarlane, S.N. (2001), 'NATO in Russia's Relations with the West', *Security Dialogue* 32: 3, 281–96.

Margelov, M. (2006), 'Russia and the US: Priorities Real and Artificial', *International Affairs, A Russian Journal of World Politics, Diplomacy and International Relations* 52: 1, 23–30.

Möller, F. (2003), 'Capitalizing on Difference: A Security Community or/as a Western Project', *Security Dialogue* 34: 3, 315–28.

Neuhold, H. (2003), 'Transatlantic Turbulences: Rift or Ripples?', *European Foreign Affairs Review* 8: 4, 457–68.

Nyberg, R. (1999), 'EU Common Strategy on Russia', Moscow, 15 July.

Pant, H. (2004), 'The Moscow-Beijing-Delhi 'Strategic Triangle': An Idea whose Time May Never Come', *Security Dialogue* 35: 3, 311–28.

'Putin Accuses West of Double Standards on Terrorists', *Radio Free Europe/Radio Liberty (RFE/RL)*, 18 September 2004.

Splidsboel-Hansen, F. (2002), 'Explaining Russian Endorsement of the CFSP and the ESDP', *Security Dialogue* 33: 4, 443–56.

Stanley S. (2003), *NATO, the EU and the Atlantic Community: The Transatlantic Bargain Reconsidered* (Lanham: Rowman and Littlefield).

'The European Union Summit: Try, Try, Try Again', *The Economist*, 12 June 2004.

Titarenko, M. (2005), 'The Importance of Collaboration between Russia, China and India against the Backdrop of Current Global and Regional Challenges', *Far Eastern Affairs* 33: 4, 3–15.

Trenin, D. (2005), 'A Russia beyond Putin's Russia', *The Taipei Times*, 11 April.

Vnukov, K. (2006), 'Russians, Chinese – Brothers Forever?', *International Affairs, A Russian Journal of World Politics, Diplomacy and International Relations* 52: 2, 129–34.

Youngs, R. (2002), 'The ESDP: What Impact on the EU's Approach to Security Challenges?', *European Security* 11: 2, 101–24.

Chapter 4

China's Foreign Policy Dynamics and International Order

Xi Chen

The end of the Cold War transformed the landscape of international politics. Although everyone might agree that major changes have taken place in the international order, no consensus has been reached as to which direction the new international order is heading towards. Two distinct views regarding the current shape of the international order dominated the discussion. On the one hand, there are people who believe that a unipolar world headed by the US is the unquestionable reality of today's international society. According to this group of people, the collapse of the former Soviet Union and the Communist states in Eastern Europe signaled the 'end of the history' (Fukuyama 1989), which ushered in liberal-democratic values and ideas worldwide; on the other hand, there are people who believe that a multi-polar world in which the US, European Union, Russia, China and Japan are all key players has taken shape in the post-Cold War era due to globalization and increased interaction and communication.

The second point of view is more relevant for several reasons. Given the incomparable influences of the US in economic, military and cultural realms, its super power position in the years to come is an indisputable fact. However, globalization also brought about new developments that restricted the US but empowered countries and international organizations such as the European Union, Russia, China, Brazil, India and Japan. The interconnectedness of the world resulting from globalization increases the cooperation between and among countries and at the same time makes countries more dependent on each other for their own economic, cultural and military security. Therefore, it would be impossible for any individual country to solve its problems independently no matter how many comparative advantages it has. Countries like Japan, China, and Russia are not on equal footing with the US yet, however, they are in no way negligible forces in shaping international order in today's world. The ever expanding interactions in the international community enable each country to get involved in a mutually constitutive and changing process, in which countries become more like each other. The common interests and grounds resulting from the interactions provide countries with both bargaining power and space for maneuvering in the face of international crises, which renders power politics and a unipolar world impossible.

As the developing country with the most remarkable economic growth since the end of the Cold War, China is rising quickly as a great power economically, politically and militarily, which in turn has injected vigor and energy in its diplomacy.

However, what are the dynamics of Chinese diplomacy in the past decades? How will the Chinese government approach international affairs as a rising power? Will the rise of China pose a serious threat to the current international system or will it help to maintain stability and order in the international society? This chapter is designed to answer those questions by tracing and analyzing the development of both the Chinese conception of national security and the country's foreign policy.

Development of the Chinese Concept of National Security

Chinese foreign policy is largely shaped by the country's perception of national security, which centers on national survival and development (Scobell and Wortzel 2005). The concept of security has been constantly redefined as changes take place in international order. The international security has become increasingly complex due to the extensive interactions and interdependence among different countries in the post-Cold War era. As a result, the security concept has been enriched both in its width and depth. On the one hand, it has transcended the restrictions of national boundaries and become a more encompassing and global concept, according to which countries both contribute to and rely on the international security environment to achieve their ends. On the other hand, the concept of security has been expanded to include security concerns in areas such as economy, culture and society (Krishna-Hensel 2006). Military security remains a major security concern of most countries; however, its importance has given way gradually to combined economic, social and cultural security concerns. China is no exception in this regard. Although available studies have approached the evolution of the security concept in China from different perspectives, scholars nonetheless agree that it has experienced the following several stages since 1949 (Qin 2003 and Meng 2006).

The first stage lasted from 1949 to 1969. The establishment of the People's Republic of China (PRC) marked the beginning of this stage, while the Russian invasion into the Zhenbaodao and the election of Richard Nixon as the US president signified the end. During this 20 year time span, both military and political security was given top priority while economic security was largely marginalized, if not ignored. Given the fact that the PRC's legitimate status was not unanimously recognized worldwide in the beginning years of its history, the paramount task for the Chinese government was to vigorously seek worldwide recognition of its legal status. The US refusal to support this effort in the United Nations (UN) and its military involvement in the Korean War made it the biggest barrier and enemy for Chinese political security at the time. Therefore, confrontation with the US was the dominant characteristic of the Chinese security strategy during this stage. Mao's comparison of the US to a 'Paper Tiger' was a reflection of the conflictual relations between the two sides.

The second stage extended from 1969 to 1982. During this period of time, the emphasis on political security gradually gave way to military security. The declined attention to political security was a consequence of some unexpected developments in Chinese foreign relations. First of all, the Sino-US relations largely improved in 1970. The Pingpang diplomacy initiated communication between the US and China in 1971. Nixon's state visit to China in 1972 signified the thawing of the relations between the two countries. Moreover, the international environment surrounding China became fairly agreeable in the wake of the restoration of China's seat in the UN. All these breakthroughs in China's diplomacy increased the country's sense of political security and also allowed it to shift its attention to other security areas, military security in this case. While China was enjoying elevated status worldwide, its relations with the former Soviet Union started to deteriorate in late 1950s. As a result, 'diplomatic encirclement, counter-encirclement maneuvers, arms race and border violence obsessed both sides at the time' (Ditter 2004, 212). Despite the similar ideological position of the two neighbouring countries, the Soviet Union had become the major threat to China's military security by the 1980s.

The third stage spanned from 1982 to 1996. China's security concept was transformed completely during this period of time. Due to the rationality held by the second generation of leadership, China's major security concerns started to shift to the economic sphere. Because of the policy of economic reform and opening up to the outside world, the attention given to the political and military security constantly declined during this stage. Regional and international cooperation flourished out of economic concerns. The relations between China and the Soviet Union began to improve in the 1980s as a result of economic interdependence and interaction. Increased economic cooperation between the two sides has even increased after the collapse of the Soviet Union. The top level official exchanges between China and Russia in the 1990s further reinforced the partnership (*huoban guanxi*) between the two sides. Although the 1989 student movement put China's policy of reform and opening up to a severe test, the government cautiously maneuvered itself out of the harsh international environments and further consolidated its economic reform policy after a transitory slowdown. The pragmatic approached allowed China to triumph over the sanctions and isolation and enabled the country to survive the crisis (Qian 2005, 127).

Starting in 1996, China entered the fourth stage. The introduction of the Shanghai Five signified the start of this new stage. Instead of focusing solely on political and military security, formerly marginalized security factors such as environmental security, information and cooperation were also included in the strategic security thinking of the countries involved. This new security concept was emphasized formally by China during the regional conference of the Association of Southeast Asian Nations in 1997. The new security conceptualization was further publicized by the China-Russia joint declaration on the multi-polarization trend and the building of a new international order signed in 1997. Following China's elaboration of its new security rationale during the UN disarmament conference in 1999, Jiang Zeming explained the new security concept in a comprehensive way during the CPC's 80 years anniversary in 2001. According to him, the international society should cultivate a security concept based on mutual trust, mutual benefit, equality, and cooperation; countries should endeavor to maintain long-term stability, security of a peaceful international environment; and countries should strengthen economic and technological cooperation and communication with an aim to gradually change the current unjust international economic order and realize the mutual coexistence and win-win goal of economic globalization. By rejecting the zero-sum game rule and rendering the Cold War mentality of competition and antagonition outdated, the new security concept emphasized the role of economic and diplomatic interactions.

From countering US and Soviet power to practicing and promoting multi-lateralism, the Chinese government has adjusted both its foreign policy and perception of national security according to its ever changing international environment. These adjustments, in turn, have shaped Chinese diplomatic practices.

The Evolution of Chinese Foreign Policy

Leaning to One Side Policy

Chinese foreign policy centered on the principles of independence and self-determination in the early years of the PRC. Upon the establishment of the PRC, socialist China was eager to win recognition of its legal status. Given the division between the Soviet Union and the US, Mao's China took a clear-cut stand and adopted a 'leaning to one side' stance in making its foreign policy (Camilleri 1980). In other words, enemies and friends had been explicitly defined as two camps. For the socialist bloc headed by Soviet Union, China considered its relations with those countries as the priority of its foreign relations. For the western bloc led by the US, however, China made no efforts to hide its objection against hegemony and power politics. In terms of the relations with the countries that were devoted to the national independence movements, Mao Zedong put forward his famous 'middle group theory', which suggested that China should support those countries' just cause with an aim to overthrow the imperialism and hegemony in the international community.

The leaning to one side stance and the enemy-friend dichotomy well explained the rationality that guided Chinese foreign policy in 1950s. Due to the fact that China was heavily dependent on the Soviet Union for protection and support in 1950s, the two countries signed a thirty year treaty of peace, friendship and mutual assistance. Mao Zedong's first state visit paid to the Soviet Union actually signified the climax of the international Communist movement.

The leaning to one side policy was moderated in the mid 1950s due to the changes in China's relations with the Soviet Union and the rise of independent movements in the third world. With the rapid decolonization in the mid 1950s, China, under the premier Zhou Enlai, shifted the priority of its policy to support newly liberated former colonies in the third world. Most notably, Zhou announced conciliatory policies towards third world states in Asia, Africa and Latin America at the Bangung Conference in Indonesia in April, 1955, and put forward the famous Five Principles of Peaceful Coexistance. These policies even included a very modest foreign aid program and a stated willingness to start discussion with the United States. China continued to refer to the 'Bangung Spirit' in later years as the basis for its claim to leadership of the third world. Though never translated clearly into concrete institutions or actual leadership, China did receive international sympathy and increased formal recognition due to its efforts during this period.

In the late 1950s, under the guiding principle of 'opposing the imperialism, revisionism and reactionaries' (Wang 2000), China shifted its foreign policy even further away from the Soviet Union, culminating in the official Sino-Soviet split of 1960. After the Soviets denounced Mao's Great Leap Forward and pulled out their advisers, the stage was set to extend main policies of self-reliance to the area of foreign policy. Behind the self-reliance principles lay the deep distrust and skepticism against both the revisionist Soviet and an imperial United States.

Self-Reliance

The new policy included support for national liberation movements in the third world, including support for the attempted coup d'etat by the Communists in Indonesia and support for opposition parties and movements in Africa and Latin America. China also fought a war with India in 1962 over a border dispute and although China won militarily, its involvement in the war aroused concerns among other nations. When China began testing its own independently developed nuclear weapons in 1964, it aroused fears and led to declined support in the third world.

China was extremely isolated during the early years of the Cultural Revolution with its foreign policy collapsed and most of its ambassadors recalled. The Soviet Union was denounced at this time as a revisionist and social imperialist country that was led by capitalist roaders.

The soviet invasion of Czechoslovakia in August, 1968, escalated the conflicts. Tension with the Soviets increased to the point that Beijing initiated a series of border clashes in March 1969 (Dittmer 2004).

Rapprochement with the US

When the Soviet Union was seen as the main enemy in the late 1960s, Mao and other CPC leaders began to favor re-engagement with the rest of the world, including the return of most ambassadors to their posts. Mao put forward his famous 'three world theory' as the guiding principle for China to practice diplomacy in the early 1970s. According to Mao, the world was composed of three parts: the superpowers, the developing countries and the countries in between. China has claimed to be part of the third world since then (Camilleri 1980). After dividing the world into three parts, China adjusted its policy towards each group of countries. As a result, China initiated a new policy of rapprochement with the US in the early 1970s, beginning with the 'pingpang diplomacy' of April, 1971, when an American table tennis team was allowed to visit China. In response, the US acquiesced to the PRC taking over the Chinese seat in the UN and acquiring a permanent seat in the Security Council in October 1971. Nixon's 1972 visit signified a big step forward of the bilateral relations of the two countries. As a result of this visit, the Shanghai communiqué was issued jointly, according to which, the two countries declared 'all Chinese on either side of the Taiwan strait maintain that there is but one China and that Taiwan is part of China (LaFleur 2003).

The full normalization of relations with the US occurred at the start of Deng Xiaoping's reform era. Deng initiated reform for both China's domestic and foreign policies. Different from Mao's confrontational stance against the West, Deng adopted a rather mild and open approach in developing relations with the US and Europe. Although China adopted a confrontational stance towards the Soviet Union in the 1960s and 1970s, its relations with the Soviet Union have somewhat improved in the 1980s due to the increased Chinese frustration with the continued US arms sales to Taiwan and the US restrictions on imports of Chinese textiles. Consequently, China was able to develop a more balanced policy between the US and the Soviet Union. The strategic emphasis on peace and development gave rise to the policy of nonalignment and active participation in the international economy.

Multilateral and Regional Cooperation

Instead of being a bipolar world, the tendency towards globalization and a multipolar world became all the more evident after the crumbling of the former Soviet Union. Globalization not only strengthened the connection of the world but also increased the speed and density of this connection.

By exerting a multi-layer and multi-level impact on international politics, globalization blurred the dividing line between domestic and international issues, which increased the necessity of countries to cooperate with each other in solving certain shared problems. This has inevitably allowed international organizations to play a more active and important role: the scales of the international organizations kept expanding, its membership increased, and its influences reinforced. The increasingly important role of the United Nations in the political sphere but also in economic and security areas bespoke the potentials of the international organizations to pose serious challenges against the old international norms based on sovereign states. Various regional cooperative organizations also emerged in the post-Cold War era, which not only facilitated regional dialogue, but also led to increased regional cooperation and communication.

In the economic field, most countries, despite the different political systems adopted, have chosen market economy as their economic model, which facilitated and expanded international trade at unprecedented speed. Accompanying the rise of international economic interaction, various international, local and cross-regional economic organizations also started to emerge. As the biggest world trade mechanism, the World Trade Organization (WTO) was established formally in 1995. At the same time, the European Union (EU) also successfully expanded its common interests from the economic field to both political and security areas. In addition, regional organizations in North America, Asia, Latin America and Africa were also established one after another.

As to the security area, although the end of the Cold War eliminated the possibility of massive military confrontations between two super powers, various traditional security problems were yet to be solved and quickly emerging non-traditional security problems such as terrorism began posing serious threats to international peace. Facing such a situation, there have been increased multilateral and regional dialogues and conferences on international security, which rarely happened during the Cold War era. To respond to this changing situation, almost all countries made adjustments to their foreign policies. China was no exception.

The post-Cold War international environment for China was far from optimistic. The period following the 1989 Beijing Student Movement is the political winter for the Deng administration. However, none of the distracting factors have shaken the determination of the Chinese government to further open up its economy and integrate into the international society. The CPC has reiterated that opening up to the outside world is a long term national policy in both the 14th and 15th National Party Congress. The political decision to gradually adapt to the international system enabled China to extensively integrate into the international community. By the end of the Cold War, China was a member of only 37 inter-governmental international organizations and 677 non-governmental international organizations. By 1997, however, these figures increased to 52 and 1163 respectively. This active involvement in international organizations gives rise to multilateralism in Chinese foreign policy. Starting from the 1990s, multilateralism has become a buzz word in Chinese official rhetoric. The Chinese government not only talked about the importance of multilateral cooperation on different occasions but also made concrete efforts to make this part of Chinese diplomatic practices. China was involved in the ASEAN Regional Forum (ARF) from its beginning. It is also an active member of other multilateral dialogue mechanisms such as the Conference of Interaction and Confidence Building Measures in Asia (CICA), the Council on Security Cooperation in Asia and Pacific Region (CSCAP), and the Northeast Asia Cooperation Dialogue (NEACD). Different from the 1980s, China actively involved itself in most of the major multilateral and bilateral arms control and nonproliferation accords. Its commitment to the Treaty on the Nonproliferation of Nuclear Weapons, the Chemical Weapons Convention, the Biological Weapons Convention and the Comprehensive Nuclear Test Ban Treaty as well as its involvement in the Missile Technology Control Regime, the Zannger Committee and the Australian Group are all evidence of changes in Chinese foreign policy (Gompert, Godement, Medeiros and Mulvenon, 2005, 31).

Besides multilateralism, another recent development in Chinese foreign policy is the stress on regionalism. With the rise of East Asia and Asia-pacific regions, regional cooperation has become intensified in recent years. Although it was not until 2004 that China's government formally expressed its support for regional cooperation, it started to participate in regional cooperation in security areas as early as the mid 1990s. The decade-long experience has allowed China to develop a rather comprehensive policy for regional cooperation. China's involvement in regional cooperation has proved to be both rewarding and fruitful. It not only strengthened the regional cooperation in various areas including economy and security but also effectively counterbalanced US efforts to agitate hostilities against China among its Asian neighbors. Chinese top officials have paid frequent state visits to its neighbouring countries in recent yeas and they have also addressed numerous decades old territory disputes with countries such as Laos, Russia, Vietnam, Kazakhstan, Kyrgyzstan and Tajikstan (Gompert, Godement, Medeiros and Mulvenon 2005, 30). All these pragmatic efforts improved the image of China and established China as a responsible and benevolent power, which, in turn, effectively diffused the tension and uncertainties that arise out of China's rise among its Asian neighbors.

While making constructive contributions to multilateral and regional cooperation, China also experienced the redefinition of its national identity, and reconstruction of the strategic culture and the rethinking of security interests, which led to the improvement of the national image on the stage of international politics. While further developing its economic and military power, the Chinese government also become aware of the importance of strengthening the country's soft power. Beijing has made serious efforts to bolster its international image in recent years. The exploitation of the Internet, regular press briefings, and frequent publications of "white papers" by the foreign ministry increased the transparency of China's foreign policy-making process to a great extent (Lu 2005). Various public diplomacy efforts such as scholar and student exchanges and cultural festivals also contributed to the improvement of the country's image.

The process of China's adoption of multilateral diplomacy and its integration into international system is a rather rational process which reflected the changes in Chinese understanding of the international security and its perception of its role in international politics. China's open stance towards international cooperation created an image of a rising Asian power. How would China impact the international order? In what way will China change the landscape of international politics? The following section will address these questions.

The Impact of Chinese Foreign Policy on International Order

Upon the rising of China in the 1990s, there have emerged various arguments regarding China's future role in the international order. On the one hand, there is the hostile China threat rhetoric, arguing that 'China's emergence as a regional hegemon in northeast Asia will be the most dangerous scenario the US might face in the early twenty-first century' (Liu 2004, 353). This is the most frequently cited comment among the US politicians prior to 9/11. On the other hand, however, there are more benevolent and open attitudes towards China's future role on the world stage, confirming that 'China has begun to take a less confrontational, more sophisticated, more confident, and, at times, more constructive approach toward regional and global affairs. In contrast to a decade ago, the world's most populous country now largely works within the international system' (Liu 2004, 387). For those who believe China's rise as a potential super power will overthrow the current international order, they made their arguments based on China's radical efforts to replace the international order during Mao's era. Given that fact that China has had strong opinions of building a new international order in which both developed and developing countries will have equal say and no single country like the US will monopolize the system as in Mao's era; it is believed that China has always had the ambition to challenge and change the current international order despite various changes taken place within the country during the past decades. For those who have adopted a more benevolent and embracing stance for China's rising, they argued that China's recent efforts in joining international organizations and active participation in international cooperation demonstrated the determination of the government to be part of the current international order. Instead of being a revolutionist of the current international system, China is actually increasingly acting as a system maintainer or reformer.

Given the defiant past of Mao's China to challenge the international system, China's voluntary and active participation in multilateral dialogues and activities in the 1990s was interpreted as a tactic to dissolve the existing system led by the United States. This 'China threat' argument was nothing but a sheer misunderstanding of both China's current intention and capability. Undoubtedly Mao's China once acted as a revolutionist of the international system. It tried hard to break the US monopoly then. However, history has redefined China's national interests and goals over time.

If one still remembers that the weapon that proved to be extremely instrumental in Mao's revolutionary success in China was the communist or socialist ideology, it will not be difficult to understand the position taken by the Chinese government on issues such as international law and order in the beginning years of its history. It was the ideological differences that gave China its independence and distinct identity. Therefore, it is logical for the Chinese government to stick to the same socialist ideology at least rhetorically to further consolidate its independence in the international arena by proposing a new international order which is different from the one that has been imposed by the imperial West. For Mao's new regime, it urgently needed a kind of consistence in its government rhetoric in justifying the legitimacy of the new China. Besides, the very fact that China's revolutionary success has inspired national independence movements in its neighbouring developing countries also provided the opportunity for the Chinese government to take lead in proposing a new international order. It is, therefore, rational to believe that there would be a certain kind of continuation in Chinese policies throughout its history. However, the enormous domestic and international changes in post Mao's China has shifted the ground of Chinese foreign policy, which in turn makes the policy orientations during Mao's era less relevant. In other words, the China threat arguments have lost much ground in today's China.

After the failure of the Great Leap Forward and the disaster of the Great Proletariat Cultural Revolution, the Chinese government and the CPC have reexamined both the domestic and international environments and adjusted the national policies accordingly. As a result of the political calculation, the government decided to give priority to economic development, which they believed could be best achieved by opening up to the outside world and pursuing multilateral diplomacy.

China does have multiple goals in practicing multilateral diplomacy. The primary goal for the Chinese government has been to create a favorable environment for domestic economic development. China takes multilateral diplomacy as an instrument to strengthen its domestic stability and speed up its economic development as the main channel for its integration into the international community, and as the guarantee of both party legitimacy and the larger healthier environment for China's domestic politics. As Chinese foreign minister Tang Jiaxuan put it, China's diplomatic work 'should unswervingly be subordinated to and serve the strategic goal for the establishment of a well-off society in an all-round manner' (Buzan and Foot 2004, 43). Lampton's explanation of China's four goals in practicing multilateral diplomacy also reinforces the position of the Chinese government (Lampton 2001). Although there have always been worries about the potentials for the US to impose its values and standards by way of multilateral organizations, the confidence that active participation in multilateral cooperation can give China increased leverage capability in international affairs against superpowers like the US overshadowed the uncertainties felt on China's part. The result of a recent evaluation of the challenges faced by China during the next decades conducted by professors from Peking University is rather revealing about the Chinese stand. The absence of foreign elements from the top eight challenges China might face during the next decades confirms the fact that the current paramount task and top priority for the Chinese government remains domestic sustainable development. Therefore, the rise of China is the consequence of rapid and stable domestic development rather than the result of a grand political and strategic ambition (Li, 2006, 155).

The policy of reform and opening up to the outside world allowed China to benefit enormously from global capital and foreign markets and also increased the interdependence between China and the rest of the world, which in turn strengthened the determination and confidence of the Chinese government to further integrate into the international system. Membership in various international organizations imposed various restrictions on what China can and can not do. However, it also offers China increasing bargaining and leveraging power in determining the future landscape of both its own country and the whole world. Although China's expansion in its cooperation with the rest of world was remarkable during Deng's era, it was not without limitations. On the one hand, quality participation in various multilateral mechanisms was yet to be developed. Its frequent abstention in critical votes in the UN Security Council was an example of the lack of initiative on China's part. On the other hand, the decision making in Chinese foreign policy was rather centralized. The rigid use of the socialist rhetoric greatly hampered the effective communication between Beijing top officials and their counterparts in the US, Asia and Europe. As observed by the western scholars, 'Beijing did a poor job of articulating and communicating its world views' (Gompert, Godement, Medeiros and Mulvenon 2005, 28). This situation is being changed gradually under both the Jiang and Hu administrations. By adopting a more flexible diplomacy, expanding its bilateral relations, engaging in multilateral organizations, participating in various conflict resolution mechanisms, and emphasizing soft power building, China has remarkably improved the quality of its interactions with the international community under the Hu administration. Its votes in support of both the UNSC Resolution for weapons inspections in Iraq and cooperation on tracking down financing for terrorists reveals its growing confidence in its role in international institutions.

China's rise in recent years aroused great concerns among both the US and its Asian neighbors. This can be attributed to China's past ideological position as well as its past role as a revolutionist of the international order. In order to ease the stress, China has obviously chosen to conform to current international norms. Its reaction to the Asian financial crisis, participation in UN peace-keeping activities in recent years and active involvement in both the North Korean crisis and global anti-terrorism campaign are examples in this regard. With the improvement in relations with East Asian countries, the fear of the 'China threat' among Asian countries has largely decreased, which in turn has facilitated further economic cooperation between the two sides. Due to the timely communication between China and the US, the two sides have been able to seek common ground and cooperate in multiple fields. Although the US has never really given up its intention and efforts to constrain the power of China in Asia, the proactive stance of the Chinese government to improve its relations with its neighbours and form regional alliances has greatly mitigated the US efforts (Li, 2006, 150). Its strategic relations and recent joint military exercises with Russia, initiatives to improve relations with India and expanded interactions and communication with its neighbours are all signs of China's efforts to actively explore its maneuvering space and break the US chains in Asia.

The China threat argument is developed from a misunderstanding of China's motives in participating in international affairs. It is also partially a result of the exaggeration of Chinese economic and military power. Scholars who believe that China poses a threat to the international order and the current balance of power, nonetheless believe that China is a potential superpower. Richard Bernstein and Ross Munno predicted with confidence in 1997 that 'within a few years, China will be the largest economy in the world' (Liu 2004, 353). The country's past glory, vast territory, huge population and unprecedented economic development definitely make it a perfect candidate for another super power after the US and the former Soviet Union. However, a close look at the country's economic and military capabilities would reveal that China is far from being a super power although the potential remains great.

The over two decades' economic reform bears impressive fruits in China; however, the results are not achieved without costs. Various social and economic tensions created by the imbalanced economic development are greatly impeding the further development of the country's economy. The fourth generation of leadership is facing formidable challenges ranging from maintaining high rates of economic growth, protecting domestic industries from external competitions, and maintaining social stability to dealing with various environmental problems. The need to ease those domestic tensions overshadows its international ambition and military expansion. Besides, the military modernization in recent years is very little more than a routine process to upgrade the outdated weaponries.

Conclusion

Both the policy orientation of Chinese government and the country's capability made it impossible for China to pose a threat to the current international order. In contrast, China actually demonstrated its determination to maintain and improve the existing systems by not adopting a confrontational approach towards the US power projection in Asia, taking initiative to improve its relations with Asian countries though all-round diplomacy, getting involved in multilateral dialogue mechanisms in solving international security crisis, and playing constructive roles in promoting international laws. Actually it was believed that China has begun to play a role in shaping the evolution of the rule and function in regional and multilateral organizations (Gompert, Godement, Medeiros and Mulvenon, 2005, 26).

However, the country's future options are not free from restraints. A number of uncertainties ranging from the country's ability to further develop its economy and enhance its overall national power to the way it manages the cross-strait relations with Taiwan, the US and its Asian neighbors will greatly limit the future course of Beijing's foreign policy. Despite the fact that China has become an active member of a great number of multilateral dialogue mechanisms, consensus between China and other members of the organizations is yet to be reached on the specific way multilateral dialogue is supposed to be conducted. By putting the

Chinese foreign policy initiatives in perspective, it is not difficult to realize that Chinese foreign policy has been constantly redefined throughout the course of the country's development. However underneath the seemingly constant changes, there have been principles left untouched ever since the PRC was established in 1949, one of which is the adherence to national sovereignty, stability and territorial integrity. China's precautiousness with its national sovereignty, its indifference to the institutionalization of the multilateral dialogue mechanism, its insistence on policy flexibility, and its anxiety about possible US dominance of the multilateral mechanism all limit the outcome of China's seemingly active participation in multilateral cooperation. Furthermore, various potential threats and problems in the international society also make it too early to develop a very optimistic prediction of China's future foreign policy development and its potential impact on international politics.

In the international arena, the US still poses the most serious threat to China's future security. Through increased economic interaction, the two countries have become unprecedently dependent on each other today, the Taiwan issue remains the source of uncertainty for the bilateral relations. As mentioned above, China tends to refrain from adopting a confrontational attitude towards the US but that does not mean that China will react passively to the US efforts to encircle and constrain China. China is actually acting increasingly confident in the international arena. Its recent objection to the US motive to sanction Cambodia is an effort to restrain the US influence in Asia. Besides, the peaceful evolutionary efforts by the West continue to exert influence on Chinese society, which poses serious challenges to the CPC's legitimacy to rule in China. Furthermore, the rise of terrorism both within Chinese territory and along the border area poses immediate threat to China's national integrity and security. Moreover, although economics and social security have become major concerns for Chinese government, it is reluctant to marginalize its military security, given the potential to increase the bargaining power of the Chinese government in economic and political negotiations with the international community. Despite the fact that China has time and again explained that the modernization of the Chinese military is nothing but a routine practice, the US has never given up the idea that China is increasing its deterrence power in the Asia-Pacific region. It is therefore predictable that China will encounter continued resistance and confrontation in modernizing its military in the years to come. Furthermore, new challenges such as environmental problems, various epidemics and informational security issues are all testing the Chinese government's crisis management capabilities. If the Chinese government can successfully tackle these problems, it will have increased power to shape the future international order. Otherwise, its increased participation in multilateral and regional cooperation will be rendered less meaningful. Finally, the regional strategic competition for resources and sovereignty with neighbouring countries such as Japan puts restrictions on the effectiveness of the open regionalism pursued by China.

To sum up, China's rising economic and military power renders it more negotiating power in managing international affairs; its adherence to multilateralism and open regionalism also generates opportunities for China to play an increasingly significant role in international politics. However, various limits on China's participation in multilateral cooperation and the potential threats the country faces in both its regional and international environment add uncertainties to the country's capability in shaping the future course of international politics.

References

Buzan, B. (2004), *From International to World Society* (New York: Cambridge University Press).

Buzan, B. and Foot, R. (2004), *Does China Matter? A Reassessment* (New York: Routledge).

Bull, H. (2002), *The Anarchical Society: A Study of Order in World Politics* (New York: Columbia University Press).

Camilleri, Joseph. (1980), *Chinese Foreign Policy: The Maoist Era and Its Aftermath* (Oxford: M. Robertson).

Deng, Y. and Wang, F. (eds) (2005), *China Rising: Power and Motivation in Chinese Foreign Policy* (Lanham: Rowman & Littlefield Publishers).

Dittmer, Lowell (2004), 'The Sino-Russian Strategic Parternership', in *Chinese Foreign Relations*, Guoli Liu (ed.).

Foot, R., Gaddis, J. and Hurrell, A. (2003), *Order and Justice in International Relations* (New York: Oxford University Press).

Friedman, E. (ed.) (2006), *China's Rise, Taiwan's Dilemmas and International Peace* (New York: Routledge).

Fukuyama, Francis (1989), 'The End of History', *The National Interest*, Summer.

Goldstein, A. (2001), 'The Diplomatic Face of China's Grand Strategy: A Rising Power's Emerging Choice', *The China Quarterly* 168, December 2001, 835–64.

Gompert, D., Godement, F., Medeiros, E.S. and Mulvenon, J.C. (2005), *China on the Move: A Franco-American Analysis of Emerging Chinese Strategic Policies and Their Consequences for Transatlantic Relations* (Santa Monica, CA: RAND Corporation).

Hao, Y. and Su, L. (eds) (2005), *China's Foreign Policy Making: Societal Force and Chinese American Policy* (Aldershot: Ashgate Publishing).

Harrison, E. (2004), *The Post-Cold War International System: Strategies, Institutions, and Reflexivity* (New York: Routledge).

Heinzig, D. (2004), *The Soviet Union and Communist China, 1945–1950: The Arduous Road to the Alliance (*Armonk, New York: M.E. Sharpe).

Hill, C. (2003), *The Changing Politics of Foreign Policy* (Hampshire: Palgrave Macmillan).

Johnston, A. and Ross, R. (eds) (1999), *Engaging China: The Management of an Emerging Power* (London: Routledge).

Lampton, D. (2001), *The Making of Chinese Foreign and Security Policy in the Era of Reform, 1978–2000* (Stanford, California: Stanford University Press).

Li, Qingsi (2006), 'The International Conditions of China's Peaceful Rise', in Sijian Guo (ed.), *China's Peaceful Rise in the 21st Century* (Aldershot: Ashgate Publishing).

Liu, G. (ed.) (2004), *Chinese Foreign Policy in Transition* (New York: Aldine de Gruyter).

Lu, Xin-an (2005), Ministry of Foreign Affairs in the Age of the Internet, In Yufan Hao and Lin Su (eds), *China's Foreign Policy Making* (Aldershot: Ashgate Publishing).

Men Honghua (2006), '"Anquankuijin" yu guojiaanquan guannian de chuangxin' ('"Security Dilemma" and the Innovation of the National Security Concept') henankejidaxuexuebao, issue 6.

Qian, Qichen (2005), *Ten Episodes in China's Diplomacy* (Harper Collins).

Scobell, A. and Wortzel, L.M. (2005), *Chinese National Security: Decision-Making under Stress* (Carlisle Barracks, PA: Strategic Studies Institute).

Shambaugh, David and Seiichiro Takagi (2007), *China Watching: Perspectives from Europe, Japan and the United States* (New York: Routledge).

Shambaugh, D. (2004/2005), 'China Engages Asia: Reshaping the Regional Order', *International Security* 29: 3, Winter 2004/2005, 64–99.

Sutter, Robert G. (1978), *Chinese Foreign Policy after the Cultural Revolution, 1966–1978* (Boulder, CO: Westview Press).

Swaine, M. (1995), *China: Domestic Change and Foreign Policy* (Ithaca: RAND Corporation).

Swaine, M. and Tellis, A.J. (2000), *Interpreting China's Grand Strategy: Past, Present, and Future* (Ithaca: RAND Corporation).

Wang, H. (2000), 'Multilateralism in Chinese Foreign Policy: The Limits of Socialization', *Asian Survey* 40: 3 (May–Jun, 2000), 475–91.

Yahuda, M.B. (1989), 'The People's Republic of China at 40: Foreign Relations', *The China Quarterly* 119, Special Issue: The People's Republic of China after 40 Years (Sep., 1989), 519–538.

Yaqing Qin (1999), 'Zhongguo guojia anquan guannian de fazhan he yanbian' ('The Development and Evolution of China's National Security Concept'). Tianze shuangzhou taolunhui, issues 5.

Zheng, B. (2005), *China's Peaceful Rise: Speeches of Zheng Bijian, 1997–2005* (Washington, DC: Brookings Institution Press).

Zhao, S. (ed.) (2004), *Chinese Foreign Policy: Pragmatism and Strategic Behavior* (Armonk, N.Y.: M.E. Sharpe).

http://www.fmprc.gov.cn/chn/wjb/zzjg/gjs/gjzzyhy/1136/1138/t4548.htm.

http://www.fmprc.gov.cn/chn/wjb/zzjg/gjs/gjzzyhy/1136/1138/t4547.htm.

http://www.irchina.org/xueren/china/view.asp?id=547.

http://www.irchina.org/news/view.asp?id=1253.

PART II
The Transatlantic Dimension of International Order

Chapter 5

The Expanding EU Role in the Neighbourhood: Implications for the Transatlantic Relations and International Order

Emel G. Oktay

The eastern enlargement of the European Union (EU) was considered as a key success story of the Union's soft power approach dealing with the challenges of the end of the Cold War. In the aftermath of the big-bang enlargement in 2004, the EU faces the task of presenting itself as a foreign policy actor towards the new Neighbourhood (Lynch 2004). With the strengthened claim that it has developed a unique capacity to promote the internal transformation of states as a civilian force, the EU's new policy is presented as expanding the zone of prosperity, stability and security beyond its borders (Ferrero-Waldner 2006, 139).

The geographical expansion has brought new geopolitical perspectives and diverging geopolitical priorities and national interests into the enlarged EU. The same goes for wider disparities in threat perception. In addition, international security environment had changed considerably especially after 11 September 2001 and the United States-led war that was launched to eliminate the alleged weapons of mass destruction in Iraq. The 2003 Iraq war caused rifts in both transatlantic and intra-European security relations. Although, the EU is a powerful economic actor in the global context, it is only in its regional context that the EU has been gradually engaging the full range of capabilities – economic, political, diplomatic and military – for a comprehensive projection of European power (Dannreuther 2006, 184).

In the absence of new enlargement prospects, to validate its distinctive claim to be a transformative post-modern power (exerting influence through encouraging internal transformation of societies rather than through physical coercion), the EU had to formulate a new policy to prevent new 'dividing lines' in Europe by embracing countries on the margins of the newly expanded Europe.

The work had begun much before the last enlargement was completed. In 2002, following a joint initiative by the Commission and High Representative Javier Solana, the development of a 'proximity or Neighbourhood policy' moved onto the Agenda of the Council.[1] The Council recognized the need to take an initiative with respect to its new neighbours seeing this as an opportunity:

> The EU enlargement will provide a good opportunity to enhance relations between the European Union and the countries concerned with the objective of creating stability and narrowing the prosperity gap at the borders of the Union (Cremona 2004, 2).[2]

The Commission policy paper on the European Neighbourhood Policy (ENP), 'Wider Europe-Neighbourhood: A New Framework for Relations with our Eastern and Southern Neighbors' dated March 2003, therefore, focuses on the key ideas of stability, prosperity, the Union's borders and shared values. One of the main concerns was to build a series of relationships that would enhance the security of the Union in its own periphery.

This study aims to examine the European Neighbourhood Policy (ENP) and its implications for the transatlantic relations and international order in general. It analyses the complex set of circumstances that lie behind the creation of the Neighbourhood initiative, explains the strengths and weaknesses of that particular policy and tries to assess its implications on transatlantic relations and order in international society. In conclusion, the paper tries to evaluate whether the European Union could emerge, through the Neighbourhood strategy, as a new security actor in its Neighbourhood and whether its interests are complementary or in conflict with the US interests in specific regions such as Eastern Europe, the Caucasus, the Middle East and the Mediterranean.

The Security Dimension of ENP: Building a Secure Neighbourhood for Europe

The long thought security dimension of the EU's new standing was enunciated by Javier Solana in his paper on 'EU Security Strategy' for the Thessaloniki European Council in June 2003:

> It is in the European interest that countries on our borders are well-governed. Neighbours who are engaged in violent conflict, weak states where organized crime flourishes, dysfunctional societies or exploding population growth on its borders all pose problems for Europe. The reunification of Europe and the integration of acceding states will increase our security but they also bring Europe closer to troubled areas. Our task is to promote a ring of well-governed countries to the East of the European Union and on the borders of the Mediterranean with whom we can enjoy close and cooperative relations.

The Council in June 2004 firmly endorsed European Neighbourhood Strategy Paper just few days after enlarging the EU to 25 member states in May 2004. It was obvious that the objectives of the European Neighbourhood policy served the broader goals of the European Security Strategy, the first ever-common strategic

---

1   See Solana-Patten Letter dated September 2002 and Prodi's speech at the Commission on December 2002.

2   GAER Council Conclusions on the new neighbors initiative, 30 September 2002.

vision of the member states, which had already been adopted six months ago (12 December 2003) by the Council and vice versa.

Overall, the European Security Strategy (ESS) is considered as a general strategy for EU external action at the global and regional level. It provides an assessment of EU's perception of the security environment (global and regional), presents the challenges and threats it is facing and points out the possible mandates and resources (Toje 2005; Duke 2004).

The ESS specifies five key threats: terrorism, proliferation of weapons of mass destruction (WMDs), regional conflicts, state failure and organized crime (European Council 2003, 3–5). The most frightening scenario is considered as the one in which terrorist groups acquire weapons of mass destruction and they are willing to use them to cause massive casualties (European Council 2003, 4). The ESS also sees terrorism as a 'strategic threat' that is global in its scope and is linked to violent religious extremism. EU recognizes that Europe is not only a target of terrorism but 'a base' as well. Violent or frozen, regional conflicts (either far away such as Kashmir, the Great Lakes and the Korean Peninsula or much nearer as the Middle East conflict) can lead to 'extremism, terrorism and state failure' as well as providing 'opportunities for organized crime,' of which Europe is the 'prime target'. All the threats mentioned are intertwined in a complex web of reasons and what results is a dilemma, making it more difficult to deal with a single policy and requires a mixture of instruments.

Perhaps requiring urgency for the promotion of 'a ring of well governed countries' at the periphery of EU and closely related with the ENP are a set of challenges mentioned in the Strategy. Energy dependence, for example, is considered as a 'special concern for Europe'; taking a stronger and more active interest in the problems of the Southern Caucasus, continued engagement with Mediterranean partners and resolution of Arab/Israeli conflict are also acknowledged as strategic priorities (European Council 2003, 5 and 10).

The ESS underlines the need to build security in 'our neighbourhood' rendering geography is still important in 'an era of globalization' (European Council 2003, 7). With the purpose of preventing new dividing lines and conflicts spreading into Europe, the delicate neighbourhood is demarcated as extending from the Balkans to the Southern Caucasus and from the Middle East to the Mediterranean (all are included in the ENP except the Balkans in which the countries have the Stability and Association Agreements with the EU). In pursuing strategic objectives, the EU is advocated to be more active and deploy full spectrum of instruments for crisis management and conflict prevention at its disposal including robust intervention when necessary (European Council 2003, 11).

At the more global level, ESS offered an ambitious agenda by 'promoting international order based on effective multilateralism,' as well as 'the development of a stronger international society, well-functioning international institutions and a rule-based international order' (European Council 2003, 9–10). In addition to upholding and developing international law and strengthening the United Nations as the primarily responsible body for the maintenance of international peace and security, another objective is widening the membership of what are considered as key institutions of the international system such as the World Trade Organization

(WTO) and other international financial institutions. One of the core elements of the international system considered as indispensable is the transatlantic relationship and NATO as an important expression of it (European Council 2003, 9).

Because of its comprehensive approach to security, ESS has the potential to serve as a reference framework and driving force for policies in all fields of external action, from trade to development to the Common Foreign and Security Policy (CFSP) and European Security and Defence Policy (ESDP). Biscop explains the starting point of comprehensive security as the recognition of interdependence between all dimensions of the security-political, socio-economic, cultural, environmental, military, hence the need to formulate integrated policies on all of them (2004, 25). With regard to its Neighbourhood, the EU will itself assume a leading role in building security. The same approach is to be applied at both levels: dialogue, cooperation and partnership in all fields of external action, putting to value the whole range of instruments at the disposal of EU (Biscop 2004, 25–6).

Geography of the EU Neighbourhood

The failure to define the borders of Europe has been viewed as a critical weakness in its self-projection (Zielonka 1998). The Treaty of Rome leaves open the prospect of membership to all states that can be defined as 'European', which might exclude countries from North Africa and Middle East but potentially includes countries of South-Eastern Europe and the Newly Independent States (NIS).

As a practical policy, keeping open or leaving uncertain the future borders of the Union preserves the most powerful instrument available to the EU for promoting economic liberalization and democratization; that is the possibility to invite new countries to join in on the basis of conditionality. However, ENP definitely rules out the prospect of membership for neighbouring countries by removing the 'golden carrot' which can most effectively activate the necessary internal political and economic transformations among these states. In fact, the basic underlying purpose of this policy is to find an alternative to enlargement.

After the enlargement of the Union to 25 members in June 2004 and the subsequent inclusion of Romania and Bulgaria by January 2007, three broad categories of concentric circles of neighbouring countries surrounding the EU appeared to be emerging (Dannreuther 2004, 204–205). The first circle comprises the countries that have a short or medium term prospect for membership: Turkey (which started negotiations in October 2005), Croatia and Former Yugoslav Republic of Macedonia and potential candidates in the western Balkans as part of the Stabilization and Association Process launched by the EU in 1999 (Albania, Bosnia and Herzegovina, Serbia, Montenegro).[3] The second group of countries includes those that are neighbours of an enlarged Europe and considered as part of 'wider Europe' but have no immediate or medium-term prospect for membership (Communication from the Commission 2003a). These are the countries of the Western NIS, Belarus, Russia, Ukraine and Moldova, countries of the Southern Caucasus, Armenia, Azerbaijan

---

3   http://ec.europa.eu/comm/enlargement/croatia/index.htm.

and Georgia, and the countries of the southern Mediterranean, from Syria, Lebanon and Morocco, including Israel and Palestine.[4] The third category encompasses those countries that are not immediate neighbours of the enlarged Union including countries of Central Asia and the non-Mediterranean countries of the Middle East, such as Iraq, Iran and the Gulf States.

This study covers only the second group of countries – all those included in the European Neighbourhood Policy, except Russia. EU-Russia relations have been developing along a separate track upon Russia's will. From the very beginning, Russia made it clear that it preferred to develop a strategic partnership and to be recognized as equal, not restrained by what is offered to it by the EU alongside very diverse countries extending from Moldova to Morocco (Leigh 2005, 111–112). The self-exclusion of Russia from the ENP framework that is supposed to address difficult cross border issues leaves a large hole in the centre of the policy.

Still the countries in the second group are very diverse in terms of their geography, politics, economy and culture. Therefore, it could also be considered as one of the important weaknesses of ENP to treat them under a single, broad policy. Roughly, they could be divided as Eastern Europe (Ukraine, Belarus and Moldova), Southern Caucasus (Georgia, Armenia and Azerbaijan),[5] Northern Africa or Southern Mediterranean (Morocco, Algeria, Tunisia and Libya) and Middle East (Egypt, Israel, Palestine Authority, Jordan, Syria and Lebanon). To elaborate analyses from different geographical perspective, it is also possible to make various combinations out of these regional groupings. For example, the countries of Eastern Europe included in the ENP and Southern Caucasus could be considered as Black Sea countries comprising a geographical unit (Aydin 2004, 5). On the other hand, the Broader Middle East (in EU terminology) would include all the countries of the Middle East and Northern Africa constituting a bigger unit. However different the presentation of the geography is, the task that the EU is trying to handle with ENP, that is providing security, stability and prosperity to its periphery, seems insurmountable.

Methodology and Content of the ENP

Through Neighbourhood strategy, the Union's policy is to use the pre-accession processes including plans (Action Plans), targets, the principle of conditionality and regular monitoring in order to achieve a high level of integration, strengthened cooperation on border management and common management of cross-border and regional issues. Only as the partners fulfil their commitments to strengthen the rule of law, democracy and respect for human rights; promote market-oriented economic reforms; and cooperate on key foreign policy objectives such as counter-terrorism and non-proliferation of weapons of mass destruction will EU offer an ever-deeper relationship (Ferrero-Waldner 2006, 140).

The ENP departs from previous regional initiatives and focuses on developing bilateral relations between the EU and the individual countries, in an attempt to

---

4   http://ec.europa.eu/comm/world/enp/index_en.htm.

5   In June 2004, after lobbying by the Caucasian republics and a peaceful 'Rose Revolution' in Georgia, the Council extended ENP to Armenia, Azerbaijan and Georgia.

influence their internal and external policies (Smith 2005a, 762). Thus, there are essentially two scales of the balance. One contains commitments by partner countries, and one contains commitments by the EU. The contents of the two scales differ from country to country (differentiation), according to its particular needs and capacities and its existing relations with the EU. Action Plans are mutually agreed documents (joint ownership) and they serve as a reference for programming EU assistance and mutual commitments.[6] The EU will monitor implementation (by association or partnership councils issuing regular progress reports) and if, after an initial three-year period, sufficient progress has been made, it will replace the existing document with a more ambitious agreement (Leigh 2005, 108–109).

The ENP's claim is that it represents a new approach in the EU's relations with its neighbours and it goes beyond classical foreign policy to support reform and modernization. Main policy instruments are brought together in a more focused way, and it covers wider range of issues with greater intensity. EU offers to partner countries a measure of economic integration and closer political cooperation. The argument is that the incentives are as engaging as membership and the best under the circumstances. The benefits are economic and social development, deeper political cooperation and economic integration (a stake in EU's internal market), as well as inclusion into other key EU policies through participation in community programmes in fields such as education, training, youth, research, environment, culture, and so on.[7]

The Action Plans are one of the key instruments for the implementation of the ENP and, although the content of each individual Action Plan is said to be tailor made for the partner country, the structure of each of them is similar. Each contains chapters on political dialogue and reform, economic and social cooperation and development, trade-related issues, market and regulatory reform, cooperation in justice, liberty and security issues (Justice and Home Affairs), sectoral issues (for example transport, energy, information, society, environment, research and development) and human dimension (people to people contacts, civil society, education, public health).[8]

Funding of the ENP is provided by a new European Neighbourhood and Partnership Instrument (ENPI), which will replace existing funds (TACIS, MEDA and others such as the European Initiative for Democracy and Human Rights – EIDHR) and include a cross border cooperation component. Under the cross-border module, 'joint programmes' bringing together regions of Member States and partner countries sharing a common border will be co-financed by the European Regional Development Fund (ERDF). The Commission has proposed that funding for the next budget cycle, between 2007–2013, should be significantly increased to match the political priority given to ENP partners plus Russia (Commission 2003b).[9]

---

6   These are not new legal agreements; the Partnership and Cooperation Agreements (PCAs) and Euro-Med agreements will remain the key framework for bilateral relations.

7   http://ec.europa.eu/comm/world/enp/index_en.htm.

8   http://ec.europa.eu/comm/world/enp/index_en.htm.

9   In December 2004, it was announced that the Commission would seek a budget of 14.9 billion Euros for the ENPI for the period 2007–2013 which would represent a significant increase from the 8.5 billion Euros allocated to TACIS and MEDA from 2000–2006. On 17

In fact, with its neighbourhood policy the EU offers 'sharing everything but institutions' in a 'privileged form of partnership'. However, the most important question remains as whether the envisaged structures would work in the absence of membership as the 'golden carrot'.

Criticisms and Weaknesses of ENP

It is far from evident that the ENP, as currently constructed, will be able to act as an instrument of the EU's ambitions for promoting its 'transformational influence' and strengthening its claim as regional and international actor. Some of the challenges the ENP is going to face stem from inside. Examples of these are the weaknesses the ENP has as a policy, institutional problems within the EU concerning implementation and other more substantial external challenges posed mainly by the United States and Russia which have their own agendas in these regions (Dannreuther 2006, 185).

Although ENP presents a shift towards a more differentiated approach and reflects recognition of the great diversity of countries included in its policy framework, it is still counterproductive for those genuinely seeking to engage substantively within the EU. As Dannreuther puts it 'There is a problem of distinct vagueness, similar to that of the eventual 'prize' to be offered, of how the multiple targets are to be prioritized, the time-scale for completion, and the exact benefits gained by their fulfillment' (2006, 191). In fact, despite all statements of hard work put in them, it is difficult to see how the Action Plans provide a real incentive for reform for three reasons: sometimes it is not clear who (the EU or the neighbour) is carrying the action, even when it is clear that the neighbour should be taking the action; it is not clear how progress will be judged; and finally, no time span for meeting particular objectives is given, there are no clear benchmarks (Smith 2005a, 764–5).

ENP claims to have provided the EU with the new tools for fostering friendly neighbours. However, it is not clear whether these extra tools are sufficient to promote fundamental economic and political reform in the neighbours and tackle the perceived problems posed by their geographical proximity to the enlarged EU. The task the EU set for itself is formidable: overcoming the 'welfare divide' between the enlarged EU and its neighbours. On the political side this divide is even greater. The majority of the countries in the region are either authoritarian or have weakly institutionalized democracies. Closely related to that is the presence of long-standing ethno-nationalist, religious or communal conflicts especially in the former Soviet space (Aliboni 2005, 3–11).

In addition, the pre-eminence of political objectives (such as respect for human rights and democratic principles, cooperation in the fight against terrorism and non-proliferation of weapons of mass destruction) and the EU protecting mostly its own

---

May 2006, the European Parliament voted for the agreement on the Financial Framework 2007–2013. The EU has decided that a total of 49.463 million Euros will be spent on its external activities in that period. In total, for seven years, a budget of 10.587 million Euros was spared for ENPI. This amount is inclusive of the funds also to Russia. See, European Commission, Multiannual Financial Framework 2007–2013, Fiche no 94, 11 April 2006.

interests concerning migration (readmission agreements) and energy issues while trying to promote its internal and external security agenda give the neighbouring countries an unpleasant taste about the true nature of the ENP.[10]

On the incentive side, despite talks about cross border cooperation, EU Member States are hesitant to take steps about visa facilitation and the establishment of local border traffic regimes or to allow border area populations to maintain traditional contacts, which means blurring the outer borders (Batt 2003). In addition, the trade incentives offered to agricultural products especially of Mediterranean Neighbours is far from being satisfactory. The EU in this area continues to be protective of its internal market. Although, the Commission policy paper on the European Neighbourhood Policy (ENP), 'Wider Europe-Neighbourhood: A New Framework for Relations with our Eastern and Southern Neighbours' dated March 2003 included the four freedoms (including free movement of persons) to partner states, there is no mention of them in the final strategy document.

The EU is still lacking the instruments to deal either with the countries of concern (Belarus, Libya, to some extent Syria) or conflicts in the Neighbourhood (from Moldova to the Southern Caucasus, the Middle East to the Western Sahara). Conflict resolution in the neighbourhood is considered as something that ENP should contribute by 'facilitating pragmatic advances on the ground'; even between countries otherwise divided by conflict through the emphasis on bilateral aspects of relations and on differentiation, as well as sub-regional cooperation. However, it is not clearly put forward what kind of pragmatic advances were actually meant or more simply what 'pragmatic advances' mean. The only explanation provided is that the ENP Action Plans take into account of special circumstances and include certain actions directed at confidence building. The assumption is, through its reform agenda, the ENP would serve to support more specific actions carried out in the context of CFSP.[11] The issue stems mainly from the tensions in the 'grey areas' that fall in-between the Community and the Common Foreign and Security Policy (Duke 2006, 21–7).

As Bretherton and Vogler (2006, 176) put it: 'in new areas of policy, where practices and understandings have yet to be constructed, cross-pillar tensions continue to arise'. The formal responsibility for the ENP lies with the Commission; the policy links economic development with security concerns, cross-border crime, democratization and human rights. The link between the ENP and the EU's Special Representatives in conflict areas is formulated by the following:

> The ENP Country Reports and Action Plans are developed by the European Commission, working in close cooperation with the EU's High Representative for the Common Foreign and Security Policy (Javier Solana) on matters related to political cooperation and the CFSP and where there are EU Special Representatives (paragraph 5), as in the Southern Caucasus or Moldova (Transdnistria) or in the Middle East, the Commission also works closely with them on the development and implementation of the political aspects of the relevant ENP Action Plans.

---

10 The exception is the Israel's action plan reflecting a more equal partnership document.

11 http://ec.europa.eu/world/enp.

However, in practice, the case is totally different. In March 2005, for example, the appointment of a CFSP Special Representative to Moldova, primarily in the context of conflict over Transdnistria, was met with the Commission's insistence that the person appointed should not be involved in the implementation of Moldova's recently agreed ENP Action Plan. The issue was resolved through negotiation of a compromise mandate, which states that Special Representative will deal only with the 'relevant aspects' of the ENP (Bretherton and Vogler 2006, 176–7). Considering the possibility that coordination problems in each political issue had to be resolved by negotiations for every case with a different ENP country and for each Action Plan, the ENP would not be able to serve in specific actions carried out in the context of CFSP.

EU as a Foreign Policy Actor in Its Neighbourhood

There are two different approaches in the literature that dominate existing analyses of the EU's international role. One is essentially actor-based, the other more broadly structure based (White 2004, 16). The first, the 'EU-as-actor' approach, concentrates on the impact of Europe on world politics. Scholars have tried to identify what sort of an 'actor' Europe is that has enabled it to be such an influential global player. Implicitly or explicitly, the working model has been the state, but increasingly scholars have moved beyond a statist model to identify a distinctive non-state yet collective entity, with the EC and latterly the EU providing the 'actor' focus of the analysis (White 2004, 17). The structure based approach is also related to actorness in the sense that the behaviour of the actor is also shaped by the structure of the system it operates in. Bretherton and Vogler (2006, 24–35) have offered a different perspective, seeing the various external roles of the EU as constructed from the 'interaction of opportunity (the external context of ideas, events and expectations), presence (representing the structural power of the Union) and internal capability'.

This study adopts the interactive approach by Bretherton and Vogler to assess the extent to which the EU has emerged as a strategic actor in its Neighbourhood and the strengths and weaknesses of this engagement. Later on, the analysis will focus on whether the EU's expanding role in the countries and regions of its periphery has significant implications to the US and transatlantic relations and on international order in general.

Is it possible to define the EU as a strategic actor in its Neighbourhood? A positive answer to that question has significant implications for the identity and purpose of the European Union both internally, in terms of its self-identity and its geographical expression, and also externally, in terms of Europe's status and role in the international order.

During the Cold War, the European Community constituted an important part of the Cold War global order as America's partner in the Euro-Atlantic Alliance. Besides, it became a model of regional governance developing a considerable attraction for outsiders. This European way of managing regional interstate relations through supranational integration came to be associated with the term 'civilian power' (Duchêne 1972).

The context in which Europe operates internationally has been dramatically changed since the end of the Cold War. The removal of the Soviet threat, the end of the bipolar divide, a unified Germany, the expansion of the EU to the East and a new problematic relationship with the United States all powerfully suggest a transformed political, economic and security context. Besides this transformation in the external context, the internal context has also been radically changed by progress in the process of integration which led to a single European market, the establishment of the European Union, a single currency in most Member States and further expansion in membership (Carlsnaes *et al.* 2004, 13).

These transformed, interacting external and internal contexts in turn have generated expectations from within and outside of the European Union to play a more influental role in international relations. These expectations focused mainly on the space created by the post Cold War world for 'civilian power' Europe to play its strengths in its immediate Neighbourhood by deploying non-military instruments. From a broader political economy perspective, Europe conceived as a regional actor fits neatly into post-Cold War analyses of regionalization and globalization.

The EU's ability to contribute to the global order will be shaped by its skill in governing its own realm and its Neighbourhood effectively. How could ENP, under the present international structure, contribute to EU's governance of its Neighbourhood effectively and therefore enhance EU's strategic role?

As Baun (2005, 17) specifies 'ENP contributes to the EU's strategic role in three ways': 1) Externally, simply by expanding the EU's influence in the geographic Neighbourhood, by also providing more direct involvement in regional and local crises (also with negative consequences); 2) Internally, by enhancing the EU's self-identity, institutional and cognitive capacity as a strategic actor and 3) by enhancing the EU's normative power and influence.

Greater Involvement in the Neighbourhood

The first kind of implication comes from the political significance given to neighbouring countries by the EU and strong and deep ties the EU aims to establish with them. Its objective is to increase considerably the level of economic integration as well as to upgrade the level of intergovernmental cooperation with regard to soft security issues such as illegal trafficking of various kinds, organized crime, terrorism, environmental degradation, and so on. As mentioned above, the long term goal is to create a secure, stable and prosperous 'ring of friends' around the EU.

If the ENP as a toolbox is successful in coordinating and systematizing EU policies towards its near abroad, the EU's influence in achieving its objectives will be greater. In view of the considerable geopolitical importance of some of those regions (in fact, all territories surrounding the EU borders today are strategically important, especially Eastern Europe, the Mediterranean and South Caucasus considering EU's growing energy demand), an expansion of EU influence through the ENP would increase the Union's overall strategic standing and also have significant implications for the transatlantic relations. It is also important to keep in mind that this intense and high-level integration makes any domestic and international crisis affecting the neighbours especially relevant and significant for the EU. This is due to the fact that such crises, challenges and risks could either prevent achievement of the planned integration within the ENP or impinge more directly on EU security (Dannreuther 2006, 3). With or without the ENP, the EU has to deal with these crises and challenges in its Neighbourhood sooner or later.

EU as a Strategic Actor in the Neighbourhood

It has long been argued by many experts that the EU has lacked the necessary infrastructure to be a significant external actor at the regional and global level. The European Security Strategy addressing this issue underlines that although 'the EU has made progress towards a coherent foreign policy and effective crisis management' (European Council 2003, 11) and 'a more coherent Europe is within our grasp', 'it will take time to realize our potential' (European Council 2003, 12). However, if the EU is to make a contribution that matches its potential, it needs to be more active, more coherent and more capable in pursuing strategic objectives. Being more active means applying the full spectrum of instruments for crisis management and conflict prevention at its disposal, including political, diplomatic, military and civilian, trade and development activities. Indicating its absence, the ESS emphasizes the need to develop a strategic culture that fosters early, rapid and when necessary, robust intervention (European Council 2003, 11). Preventive engagement is seen as a method to avoid more serious problems in the future. However, acting together and greater coherence are needed especially in addressing regional conflicts.

One of the objectives of the EU is to use ENP Action Plans to help increase security at its periphery. It has been announced that the Action Plans with Armenia, Azerbaijan and Georgia will address issues related to Nagorno-Karabakh and Georgia's internal conflicts (Ferrero-Waldner 2006, 141). The EU's border assistance mission to Moldova and Ukraine is designed to contribute to resolving the Transdnistria conflict. Aliboni argues that the ENP framework will result in greater, and in a sense upgraded, involvement of the EU in regional crises (such as the Arab-Israeli or Western Sahara disputes and the Israeli-Palestinian Conflict), domestic crises (coups d'etat, as in 1992 Algeria), or conflicts linked to secessionist or irredentist developments, eventually related to the outer ring of neighbours (Transdnistria, Abkhazia and South Ossetia, Nagorno-Karabakh, Armenia-Azerbaijan) (2005, 5). Therefore, in order to succeed, the EU by necessity will have to reinforce its CFSP and ESDP. Even if ENP seems like a civilian attempt based on economic and modest political cooperation with neighbours through bilateral Action Plans, its success will also be dependent on the EU's progress in developing the institutional capacities to plan, coordinate and manage external security operations in its Neighbourhood.

As important as the development of institutional capacity is cognitive development that is the extent to which the ENP is linked to the EU's emerging self-identity and adoption of a role as a strategic actor (Baun 2005, 20). Part of this emerging identity is also expressed in the European Security Strategy, which declares that 'building security in our Neighbourhood' is one of the three strategic objectives of the EU (European Council 2003, 8). However, while the ENP may push the EU to enhance its institutional and cognitive capacity to be a strategic actor, Europe still does not have the political will and leadership to play such a role beyond its borders (Baun 2005, 21). Therefore, it is fair to argue that despite the ESS, the EU still lacks a common strategic doctrine and understanding to act as a strategic actor in its periphery.

The EU as a Normative Power in the Neighbourhood

Despite the criticisms concerning the EU's capability as strategic actor in its neighbourhood, Maull (2005, 777) argues that in the post-Cold war period, the EU has acted as a flexible and adaptive strategic actor towards East and Central Europe and proved its strategic vision. With the Cold War over, the most likely role for the EU is considered as a pole of cooperation and stability in an order that is characterized by a pronounced diffusion of legitimate power and authority and hence an absence of effective institutional checks and balances. In the present state of international relations, that is under the conditions of globalization, 'the dualism is between patterns of integration and differentiation around specific identities; in the realm of global governance, the dualism is between modern and post-modern forms of governance' (Maull 2005, 777). The EU could, at best, supply only part of that balance, and probably only on a regional rather than global scale. It also represents the best, most effective example of a post-modern actor. In that capacity, it is best seen as a force rather than as a power in international relations (Maull 2005, 778).

As mentioned above, in the evolution of global order since the Cold War, Europe's importance has increasingly shifted from its role as a junior partner to America to that of a 'civilian power', a phrase coined by François Duchéne to capture Europe's alternative way of organising (or 'domesticating' as he put it) interstate relations (Maull 2005, 778). The European Community has been remarkably successful with this alternative mode of interstate governance. Not only has it succeeded in abolishing war within Europe, it has also created a way of life marked by individual freedom, prosperity and civility for its people, and has even begun to project stability, liberal democracy and prosperity beyond its own realm. However, it should not be forgotten that the very success of European Integration owes a great deal to American support and military presence in the continent (Kagan 2003). This made Europe a force in international relations, and in the new, uncertain international environment of globalization (Maull 2005, 778). As a post-modern force – like the physical force of gravity – rather than as a modern power, the EU exercises influence and shapes its environment through 'what it is', rather than through 'what it does' (See also Moller 2005). The gravitational pull which the EU exercises in international relations is based on the weight of its markets, capital and technological resources, as well as on the attractiveness of the European way of life (Maull 2005, 778–779).

Therefore, another way in which ENP enhances the EU's strategic role is by increasing its normative power and influence. 'EU's main contribution to regional security is related to what the EU is and represents rather than what it does' (Moller 2005). Moller argues 'Wisely, the EU has sought peaceful relations with its expanding ring of neighbours, both in Eastern Europe, in Balkans and the Greater Middle East, mainly by 'speaking softly but carrying big carrots.' The only thing is missing before the EU can really become a significant security actor thus seems to be political will (Moller 2005, 6).

Thus the EU's main contribution to European Security turns out to be what the EU is, in other words, an attractive community of nations. Not only has this rendered war within the EU inconceivable, but it also provides the EU with leverage over neighbouring states that would like to join in the future. Here it appears that the main weakness of ENP as an attractive force enhancing EU's 'transformational role' in the Neighbourhood is that it does not offer membership prospect, even to those countries most willing such as Ukraine and Georgia.

Transatlantic Implications of the ENP

Eastern Europe and the Southern Caucasus

Eastern Europe, considered by both Europe and Russia as a true backyard, is a 'shared Neighbourhood'. As regards to the EU-Russian relations, the most urgent problem is that Russia tends to view the EU's engagement in its near abroad in geopolitical terms and as a zero-sum competition for regional influence (See Löwenhardt 2005). There is also a triangular relationship between US, Russia and the EU with a potential to have a major impact on both US and EU policies towards these countries (Emerson 2004). However, contrary to the United States, the EU was not given to much geopolitical thinking or acting. Against the reassertion of Russian dominance in the former Soviet space including the Southern Caucasus, there is a considerable scope for EU-US cooperation. They both support the emergence of independent, democratic and western-oriented regimes and encourage their increasing integration into European and Euro-Atlantic institutions.

The Caucasus was at the very end of the EU's overcrowded policy agenda and Armenia, Azerbaijan and Georgia were not included in the ENP until June 2004 despite the region's strategic significance for the EU in terms of energy supply,[12] transport links with Central Asia and the prevention of trafficking in drugs and human beings (Leigh 2005, 117–118). The EU decided to raise its profile in the region by the appointment of a special representative to support efforts to resolve the frozen conflicts in the South Ossetia, Abkhazia and Nagorno-Karabagh.[13] Due to the beginning of Turkey's accession negotiations in October 2005, the Southern Caucasus has become, potentially, a region bordering the EU. Although there is no serious disagreement over the policies towards the region at the moment, US insistence on playing an active, even dominant role in the region and its unilateral actions especially regarding control of the energy flows could lead to increased friction with the EU.

---

12 Energy and transport links gained particular significance with the entry into service of the Baku-Tbilisi-Ceyhan (BTC) oil pipeline in July 2006. It is going to be followed by a parallel gas pipeline.

13 Council Joint Action 2003/473/CFSP of June 25, 2003, regarding a contribution of the European Union to the conflict settlement process in Georgia/South Ossetia, June 26, 2003.

On the other side of the Black Sea, the EU membership of two littoral states, Romania and Bulgaria in 2007, might add to that friction since they are very much willing to provide bases for the likely future US military operations in the Persian Gulf or in the Middle East.

In addition, although Turkey and the US have long been regarded as 'strategic partners', recent developments, especially with regard to the US invasion of Iraq, have created serious mutual distrust. A few examples are the Turkish Parliament's refusal in March 2003 to allow US troops to launch a second front against Iraq from the Turkish territory; the later US reluctance to pay attention to Turkey's apprehensiveness about the division of Iraq along ethnic and religious lines and to take action against the Kurdistan Workers Party (PKK), an illegal entity on the State Department's Foreign Terrorist Organization (FTO) list which is still being sheltered in Northern Iraq. Under the present circumstances, the membership of Turkey in the EU and its consequences on the EU neighbouring countries already adjacent to Turkish borders (such as Iran) could also have adverse implications for the United States. In many strategic issues and areas, Turkey's position is closer to the European Union (especially on Iraq). On the other hand, there is also a shared disillusionment by both Turkey and Russia with the United States and European policies and attitudes, as well as increasing common ground on issues in the broader Black Sea region which could have adverse strategic implications for the US and EU interests in the region (Hill and Taspinar 2006). US eagerness for infiltrating the Black Sea under the pretext of fighting international terrorism caused concerns in the two major Black Sea powers. The fact that the other littoral states (Bulgaria, Romania and Georgia) have already been cooperating with the US along its interests sends some alarming signals that Turkish-US relations could encounter new difficulties in the future.

The Middle East and the Mediterranean

The US' dominant strategic and military presence in the Middle East eclipses the EU's efforts at the political and military level. Despite numerous recent suggestions that US-EU collaboration in the 'Greater Middle East' could be a means of reconstructing the transatlantic partnership (Everts 2003; Council on Foreign Relations 2004), there is real potential for conflict between the EU's Neighbourhood goals and US strategic objectives in the 'war on terrorism' (Baun 2005, 8). Although through the ENP, the EU could provide a more pragmatic and structured approach to the countries of the region on a bilateral level based on differentiation and selectivity, the geo-strategic interests of the EU dictates the need for a more comprehensive regional framework replacing the Barcelona Process. This, however, directly places the EU on a collision course with a dominant external actor in the region (the US) and with its close ally Israel. In addition, the policies adopted by the latter two countries in the region could undermine the objectives and proper functioning of the ENP such as Israel's refusal to negotiate with the Palestinians or a further Iraq-style demonstration of the US attempts for imposed regime-change (Dannreuther 2006, 200).

Overall, the ENP does not, nor is not expected to, offer credible tools to the European Union in dealing with security challenges in neighbourhood. The European Union is often oscillating between action and non-action, where it issues declarations on political developments in neighboring countries but the member states do not have the will to push for concerted action at the EU level. As indicated above, there are important problems of consistency and cross-pillar coherence when it comes to important political issues, and the ENP has no remedy for that.[14]

The Maintenance of Order in International Society

The European Security Strategy indicates an awareness by European leaders that Europe's history, geography and cultural ties give it links with every part of the world and assets to build on: neighbours in the Middle East, partners in Africa, Latin America and Asia. They also consider it imperative to develop strategic partnerships with Japan, China, Canada and India as well as with all those who share the same goals and values and are prepared to act in their support (European Council 2003, 13–14). Above all, however, the transatlantic relationship is considered as 'irreplaceable' and the EU's aim should be an effective and balanced partnership with the US (European Council 2003, 13). The general agreement is that the EU can only achieve this by building up real foreign policy capabilities and increasing its coherence.

On the other hand, 'promotion of international order based on effective multilateralism,' and 'the development of a stronger international society, well-functioning international institutions and a rule-based international order' are part of the global agenda offered by ESS (European Council 2003, 9–10). Upholding and developing international law and strengthening the United Nations as the primarily responsible body for the maintenance of international peace and security, widening the membership of what are considered as key institutions of the international system such as World Trade Organization (WTO) and other international financial institutions are perceived as goals to be achieved.

Besides international law, functions of other primary institutional mechanisms for the maintenance of order in international society as defined by Hedley Bull (2002) such as diplomacy, the balance of power, war and great power management are highly susceptible to the course and nature of the EU-US relations. As for diplomacy which reflects states' efforts to influence the behavior of other states through bargaining and the use of various non-military activities (Bull 2002, Chapter 7), the EU as a 'soft security actor' has an increasing but often frustrating role in the broader diplomacy of world order (Hill and Smith 2005, 359). The ENP is basically designed to promote the EU's influence on the neighbouring states as a normative power and, therefore, to increase its bargaining power through diplomacy. On the other hand, it is widely acknowledged that the policy makers in the US are more ready to use military power (also unilaterally) rather than diplomacy in addressing foreign policy problems. This also brings forth the balance of power issue: is it possible that the EU can be seen as an alternative power counterbalancing the US for diplomatic and even for security purposes in the maintenance of order in international society? The distinct possibility is that the EU and the US could be more complementary than competitive in using power and, therefore, they could act in concert when necessary

---

14 For issues of consistency and coherence in the EU, see Bretherton and Vogler, 'The European Union as a Global Actor', pp. 174–178.

by preserving the general balance of power. Since the war is viewed as a necessary means to preserve the balance of power (Bull 2002, ch. 8), the most important issue is to achieve multilateralism and/or consent of other powers before going to war. Referring to great power management, multilateralism automatically leads to the EU and the US working in alliance and pursuing policies which work for, rather than against, the international order.

The promotion of multilateralism and keeping transatlantic relations intact are the most important tasks the EU faces today. As Wallace (2003) indicates:

> Each side of the Atlantic blames the other for this breakdown in trust and multilateral cooperation. Both deserve to share the blame, though for different reasons. The problem in Washington is that the foreign policy debate has been captured, to a remarkable extent, by ideological conservatives who reject multilateral constraints on American supremacy, see military power as the decisive factor in international politics, and underplay the importance to the US of the network of multilateral rules that underpin the global economy. The problem in Europe is that no government is thinking about the continent's contribution to global order, or attempting to define shared European interests in promoting a stronger framework for that order. There is, therefore, no basis for a constructive transatlantic dialogue. Washington policy-makers see no reason to listen, and European governments have nothing to say.

What is to be done? The US and Europe drifting apart and taking their own paths would not contribute much to order and stability in today's world. Therefore, close cooperation between them is essential. As Wallace (2003) mentions, American unilateralism 'rests both on domestically driven foundations and on the disillusioned perception of many in Washington that there are no others prepared to share the burden of global order'. Thus, disproving that view mostly depends on a more participatory approach on the part of EU towards global institutions and international order. A greater degree of European involvement in shaping the global order would enable Europe to exert an influence commensurate with its size and more in line with its interests.

Conclusion

The European Neighbourhood Policy reflects a greater European willingness to be involved in the resolution of conflicts and the spread of prosperity beyond the immediate physical boundaries of Europe. It is also a useful tool for the EU to project its soft power to a vast area encompassing North Africa, Middle East, Southern Caucasus and the Black Sea region, which could be seen as the enlarged EU's natural sphere of influence. Finally, through the ENP, Europe has an additional means of balancing the so far unchallenged global dominance of the US, albeit on a limited geographical scale. For these reasons, the ENP is a welcome initiative that deserves support.

However, it is far from clear how successfully the EU will steer this policy. In this regard, the lack of clear incentives for the target countries to embrace the ENP is troubling. The prospect of EU membership is at best based on the concept of 'constructive ambiguity'. It is highly doubtful that this ambiguity can be maintained very long. The EU may have to announce the limits of its expansion sooner than it would have done otherwise. Yet, even without offering full membership, the EU can demonstrate its seriousness in embracing relevant countries by adopting a longer-term, strategic approach towards them. This entails greatly increased institutional engagements, adopting new modes of economic interaction and investments, facilitating human contacts while fighting transboundary threats and educating and convincing the European public opinion about the long-term benefits of such engagement. In the ENP, some of these elements are present. However, the main weaknesses stem from the ambiguities inherent in the Action Plans and a lack of clear benchmarks. As long as the EU is successful in achieving the above-mentioned goals, the EU Neighbourhood Policy could affect important US economic, political and strategic interests in Europe's periphery.

References

Aliboni, R. (2005), 'The Geopolitical Implications of the European Neighbourhood Strategy', *European Foreign Affairs Review* 10, 1–16.

Attina, F. and Rossi, R. (eds) (2004), *European Neighbourhood Policy: Political, Economic and Social Issues*, Jean Monnet Center 'Euro-Med', Department of Political Studies.

Aydin, M. (2004), 'Europe's Next Shore: The Black Sea Region After EU Enlargement', *Occasional Paper* 53 (Paris: European Union Institute for Security Studies), June.

Batt, J. (2003), 'The EU's New Borderlands', *CER Working Paper*, October.

Batt, J. *et al.* (eds) (2004), *Partners and Neighbours: A CFSP for a Wider Europe*, Chaillot Paper No. 64 (Paris: European Union Institute for Security Studies).

Baun, M. (2005), 'European Neighbourhood Policy and Transatlantic Relations', Paper prepared for the 46th Annual International Studies Association Convention, 1–5 March.

Biscop, S. (2004), 'The European Security Strategy and the Neighbourhood Policy: A New Starting Point for A Europe-Mediterranean Security Partnership', in Attina and Rossi (eds), 25–36.

Biscop, S. (2004), 'Effective Mutlilateralism: Bringing the European Way into Practice', in Biscop (ed.), 27–32.

Biscop, S. (ed.) (2004), *Audit of European Strategy*, IRRI-KIIB, Brussels, December.

Bretherton, C. and Vogler, J. (2006), *The European Union as a Global Actor* (London and New York: Routledge), 2nd edn.

Bretherton, C. and Vogler, J. (1999), *The European Union as a Global Actor* (London and New York: Routledge).

Brimmer, E. and Fröhlich, S. (eds) (2005), *The Strategic Implications of European Union Enlargement* (Washington DC: Center for Transatlantic Relations, Johns Hopkins University).

Bull, H. (2002), *The Anarchical Society*, 3rd edn (New York: Columbia University Press).

Carlsnaes W. *et al.* (eds) (2004), *Contemporary European Foreign Policy* (London: Sage Publishers).

Communication from the Commission of the European Communities to the European Parliament (2003a), 'Wider Europe Neighbourhood: A New Framework of Relations with our Eastern and Southern Neighbours', COM (2003) 104 Final, 11 March.

Commission of the European Communities (2003b), *Paving the Way for a New Neighbourhood Instrument*, COM (2003) 393 final, Brussels, 1 July.

Council on Foreign Relations (2004), 'Renewing the Atlantic Partnership', Report of an Independent Task Force by Henry A. Kissinger and Lawrence Summers, March.

Cremona, M. (2004), 'The European Neighbourhood Policy: Legal and Institutional Issues', *CDDRL Working Papers* No. 25, 2 November.

Dannreuther, R. (2006), 'Developing Alternative to Enlargement: The European Neighbourhood Policy', *European Foreign Affairs Review* 11: 183–201.

Dannreuther, R. (ed.) (2004), *European Union Foreign and Security Policy: Towards a Neighbourhood Strategy* (London: Routledge).

Duchene, F. (1972), 'Europe's Role in World Peace', in R. Mayne (ed.), 32–47.

Duke, S. (2006), 'Areas of Grey: Tensions in EU External Relations Competences', EIPASCOPE 1: 21–27.

Duke, S. (2004), 'The European Security Strategy in a Comparative Framework: Does it Make for Secure Alliances in a Better World?', *European Foreign Affairs Review* 9: 459–481.

Emerson, M. (2004), 'The EU-Russia-US Triangle', *CEPS Policy Brief*, 52, June.

European Council (2003), 'A secure Europe in a Better World: European Security Strategy', Brussels, 12 December.

Everts, S. (2003), 'Difficult but Necessary: A Transatlantic Strategy for the Greater Middle East', Paper prepared for the GMF Conference, June 25th, Washington, DC.

Ferrero-Waldner, B. (2006), 'The European Neighbourhood Policy: The EU's Newest Foreign Policy Instrument', *European Foreign Affairs Review* 11: 139–142.

Gingsberg, R. (2001), *The European Union in World Politics* (Boulder, CO: Bowman and Littlefield).

Hill, C. and Smith, M. (2005), *International Relations and the European Union* (Oxford and New York: Oxford University Press).

Hill, F. and Taspinar, Ö. (2006), 'Russia and Turkey in the Caucasus: Moving Together to Preserve the Status Quo?', IFRI, France, *Russie.Nei.Visions* No. 8, January.

Kagan, R. (2003), *Paradise and Power: America and Europe in the New World Order* (London: Atlantic Books).

Laszlo, J.K. (2005), 'The Strategic Implications of EU Enlargement on Central and Eastern Europe', in Brimmer and Fröhlich (eds), 73–97.

Leigh, M. (2005), 'The EU's Neighbourhood Policy', in Brimmer and Fröhlich (eds), pp. 103–125.

Löwenhardt, J. (2005), 'Stuck in the Middle: The Shared Neighbourhood of the

EU and Russia, 2000–2005', *Clingendael European Papers* No. 2, October, The Hague.

Lynch, D. (2004), 'The New Eastern Dimension of the Enlarged EU', in Judy Batt *et al.* (eds).

Manners, I. (2002), 'Normative Power Europe: A Contradiction in Terms?', *Journal of Common Market Studies* 40: 2, 118–34.

Maull, H.W. (2005), 'Europe and the New Balance of Global Order', *International Affairs* 81: 4, pp. 775–99.

Mayne, R. (1972), *Europe Tomorrow: Sixteen Europeans Look Ahead* (London: Fontana).

Moller, B. (2005), 'The EU as a Security Actor, Security by Doing and Security by Being', *DIIS Report* 12.

Sjursen, H. (2003), 'Understanding the Common Foreign and Security Policy: Analytical Building Blocs', *ARENA Working Paper* 9/03, Oslo.

Smith, K.E. (2005a), 'The Outsiders: the European Neighbourhood Policy', *International Affairs* 81: 4, pp. 757–73.

Smith, K.E. (2005b), 'Still Civilian Power EU?', *European Foreign Policy Unit Working Paper* 1, LSE, London.

Smith, M. and Steffenson R. (2005), 'The EU and the United States', in Hill, C. and Smith, M. (eds), 343–63.

Solana, J. (2003), 'A Secure Europe in a Better World', S0138/03.

The Economist (2006), 'A Weakening Magnet', 1 April, p. 32.

Toje, A. (2005), 'The 2003 European Security Strategy: A Critical Reappraisal', *European Foreign Affairs Review* 10: 117–33.

Wallace, W. (2003), 'Can the Transatlantic Rift be Healed?' *The Observer*, 27 April.

White B. (2004), 'Foreign Policy Analysis and the New Europe' in Carlsnaes W. *et al.* (eds), 11–31.

Wohlforth, W. C. (2004) 'The Transatlantic Dimension', in Dannreuther (ed.), 186–201.

Zielonka, J. (1998), *Explaining Euro-Paralysis: Why Europe is Unable to Act in International Politics* (Basingtoke, UK: Macmillan).

Chapter 6

The Shape of the ESDP and the Transatlantic Link: Consequences for International Order

Constantinos Koliopoulos

The present chapter purports to examine 1) the factors that impede the development of an autonomous defence capability within the European Union (EU); 2) the prospects of the aforementioned enterprise, especially in the light of the continuing EU enlargement process; 3) the implications of the likely evolution of the European Security and Defence Policy (ESDP) on transatlantic relations and international order. The main argument of this chapter is that the prospects for an autonomous European defence structure are rather meagre; the ESDP forces are critically dependent on NATO infrastructure and will continue to be so for the foreseeable future. This is due to a number of pathologies that can be traced on three different levels: political, institutional and military. This, in turn, suggests that the US will continue to be the military powerhouse of the West, and NATO will remain the principal military instrument defending Western interests and, when necessary and possible, shaping the international order accordingly.

The chapter starts with a brief overview of the institutional history of European security from the aftermath of the Second World War till the 1990s. After that, there follows the examination of the political context in which the ESDP takes place. The lack of a common European identity, coupled with the varying and often contradictory political aims of both the European states (great and small) and the US thwart the evolution of the EU into an entity with a common foreign and security policy. Meanwhile, the ongoing enlargement process of the EU, which will highlight the disparities among its members, will further weaken the relevant attempts; these factors constitute the chief source of pathologies of the ESDP. This political context has decisively affected the institutional shape of the ESDP, to which the chapter next turns; it examines the strictly intergovernmental character of the ESDP, its very close institutional linkage with NATO, the practical function of the ESDP institutions and the emergence of separate institutional arrangements of defence cooperation among a number of EU members. After that, the chapter analyses the military dimension of the ESDP, namely the nature of the tasks of the European military rapid response forces and their – questionable – capability of performing them without NATO assistance. In light of the preceding analysis, the chapter concludes with an appraisal of the prospects of the transatlantic partnership in the military sphere and its likely impact on international order.

Historical Overview

The first post-war multilateral initiative on European security was the Brussels Pact, signed in 1948 by Great Britain, France and the Benelux countries. Interestingly enough, the pact had an anti-German character, aiming to deter German revanchism. Of course, such a conception was clearly out of date, and the Brussels Pact was soon superseded by NATO, which was formed in 1949.

The creation of NATO signified the institutionalization of the US participation in European security. Eventually, this participation led to a certain cleavage in Europe between the so-called Atlanticists and Europeanists. In the context of European security, the Atlanticists favour an enhanced US presence in Europe and the primacy of NATO in the European security architecture, whereas the Europeanists would like to see a reduction of US influence and the creation of more autonomous European security structures. However, as has always been evident and will also be demonstrated below, the realities of power distribution at the two sides of the Atlantic tend to bolster the Atlanticist conception of European security and correspondingly undermine the Europeanist one.

In the early 1950s, the Americans supported European integration, believing that an integrated and economically strong Western Europe would serve as a bulwark against the Soviet Union. After the creation of the European Coal and Steel Community (ECSC) – the first part of the institutional complex that is now known as the EU – in 1951, the United States actively promoted the creation of a European Defence Community; a bold attempt to bring about military integration in Western Europe. However, apart from being a sensitive matter in its own right, the project was ideologically and emotionally charged; thus, in France, left- and right-wing opposition, coupled with apprehension as to the re-emergence of West Germany as a military power, led to the rejection of the relevant motion by the French parliament in August 1954 and to the collapse of the project.

Soon after that, the initial signatories of the Brussels Pact extended an invitation to West Germany and Italy to join in by signing a protocol to the Pact, leading to the creation of the Western European Union (WEU). Finally, in 1955, West Germany joined NATO.

With the Cold War raging, it was natural that NATO would assume primary responsibility for European security. True, France developed its own nuclear forces and in 1966 withdrew from the military sector of the Atlantic Alliance, but there were no illusions as to which country and which security organization would take the lead in repelling the Soviets if need arose. Consequently, the WEU fell in a long slumber that was to last until 1984.

In 1970, the members of the European Community established the European Political Cooperation (EPC) process, a rather loose mechanism for the coordination of their foreign policies. This was the first step, though a rather wary one, towards expanding European integration into the sphere of 'high politics' (foreign and security policy).

The 1980s witnessed an increase in the tempo of European integration, affecting security matters as well. In 1984 the WEU was reactivated, whereas the Single European Act of 1986 formally associated the EPC with the European Community.

The cataclysmic events of the late 1980s and the early 1990s changed the systemic landscape and forced the European Community (that would soon be finally renamed European Union) to modify its institutions accordingly.

The chapter is now entering in earnest the subject of the present analysis. In 1992, the Maastricht Treaty replaced the EPC with the Common Foreign and Security Policy (CFSP). Still, though the latter bears a far more impressive-sounding name, it has been pointed out that the qualitative distance between the EPC and the CFSP is actually small (Christodoulides 1993, 298–9). After a while, especially due to the conflict in former Yugoslavia, it became apparent that the CFSP lacked the necessary military muscle. The creation of this military dimension was decided upon at the Cologne European Council in June 1999 (see below): the ESDP was born.

The Political Context of the ESDP

The enterprise of the ESDP does not take place in a vacuum. On the contrary, it is inextricably linked with the evolution of the EU into a federal entity with a common foreign and security policy.

At first sight, it seems that the Member States of the EU have strong incentives to proceed with the integration in the political and military spheres. This is the case because the economic integration that is already being achieved with the Economic and Monetary Union (EMU) is very likely to remain, so to speak, hanging in the air without the parallel development of the political dimension of European integration (La Malfa 2002). This is also what theory would expect. According to the neofunctional theory of international organization (Haas 1958), the implementation of integration in fields of relatively limited importance progressively creates further needs that eventually lead to a spill-over of integration in fields of greater importance, finally leading to integration in the spheres of foreign and security policy.

Nevertheless, as it becomes evident from the following analysis, the evolution of the EU into an entity with common foreign and security policy is not likely to take place in the foreseeable future. Four important reasons impede such a development: the national/state distinctiveness; the strategic choices of the three greatest powers in Europe (France, Great Britain, and Germany); the continuing enlargement of the EU, in disregard of the qualitative criteria of integration[1] and the US opposition. As a result, the EU displays a conspicuous lack of strategic self-sufficiency (Ifestos 1999a, 309–29; 1999b, 253–99).

Beginning with the first of these reasons, it is a fact that the loyalties of the citizens of the EU Member States are still directed towards their native countries rather than the EU. Since they remain first and foremost French, Danish, Spanish, and so on rather than Europeans, they are unlikely to consent to the absorption of their states in a greater political organization. If anything, the accession of ten new Member States in the EU increases disparities, highlights distinctiveness and weakens the

---

1   I am indebted to Professor Theodoros Christodoulides for pointing out this impeding factor.

integration process. Thus, it was most unjustified that a number of voices within the EU castigated as 'treason' the strategic choice of a number of Member States to sidestep the institutional organs of the Union and side with the US during the recent Iraq War. Simply put, there is no 'Europe' that the 'Europeans' regard as their homeland, hence no one can rightfully accuse them of betraying it.

The main implication of the lack of a common European identity and the continuing prevalence of national identities within the EU – a situation that is likely to hold for the foreseeable future – is that the EU Member States continue to have distinct national interests and distinct foreign threat perceptions. As a result, the mutual solidarity of the EU partners in security matters ought by no means to be taken for granted. In fact, as was demonstrated by the Great Britain's siding with Canada during the Spanish-Canadian conflict of 1995, the reverse may well be the case. In the same vein, threat perceptions vary across Europe, ranging from very low (Denmark, Ireland) to very high (Greece), thus affecting the relative commitment of the Member States to an autonomous ESDP. In other words, the notions of 'security' and 'defence' have different meanings across Europe; each of the EU Member States gives a different answer to the fundamental question 'defence and security against whom and against what?'

The national/state distinctiveness is reflected on the grand strategies of the three most powerful European states, strategies that stave off rather than promote the prospect of political integration of the EU (Ifestos 1999b). Beginning with France, one cannot but be struck by the great consistency with which this country pursues the maintenance of great-power status. In order to increase its international weight, France successfully sought to acquire nuclear weapons, notwithstanding various foreign reactions. Furthermore, though France has indeed promoted European integration, it has sought to keep it within an intergovernmental context, endeavouring to balance German power and secure a leading role for itself in Europe.

In contrast to France's striving after an autonomous international role, Great Britain largely bases its own great-power status on its special relationship with the United States. In order to increase its international weight, Great Britain consciously sides with Washington. As a result, it seeks the continuation of the US presence in Europe and the subordination of the ESDP to the Atlantic Alliance. In the same vein, defending its national sovereignty, it attempts to prevent, or even undermine, the supranational evolution of European integration.[2] Finally, Great Britain has been a champion of the continuing EU enlargement, in the belief that the accession of new members will stave off the danger of supranational integration.

Germany is well aware of the worries its growing strength creates to the rest of the Europeans, whereas the Germans themselves are largely haunted by the memories of the past. All this has led to serious obstacles in the formulation of German foreign and security policy. Judging from the limited German participation in the Gulf War and the Kosovo War, plus Germany's refusal to participate in the Iraq War, these

---

2   Supranational cooperation, in contrast to intergovernmental, involves the devolution of sovereign rights of the states to an entity that can make, within its jurisdiction, decisions *immediately executable* within its Member States. I am indebted to Professor Theodoros Christodoulides for clarifying this point.

obstacles are still present.[3] Consequently, Germany is quite reluctant to appear as the champion of an ambitious agenda of enhanced political integration of the EU with a view to creating an entity with a common foreign and security policy.

The above demonstrates that the political integration of the EU and the institution of a common foreign and security policy are not in the agenda of any of the three great powers of Europe. This, in turn, sets decisive limitations to the nature and the role of the ESDP.

The situation is not any different as far as the small powers of Europe are concerned. This is most conspicuous in the case of almost all the new-fangled and aspiring members of the EU. These states, far from being concerned with turning the EU into an entity with a common foreign and security policy, are chiefly keen on extracting resources from the Union in order to promote their development. Thus, the continuing enlargement process serves to further weaken the federal character of European integration.

The reaction of the US to the ESDP is a logical corollary of Washington's strategy that aims to maintain the global leadership of the US by deterring the emergence of rival powers.[4] Thus, the United States tries to prevent a possible evolution of the EU into a political entity that will seek independence from the US in security issues. As a result, Washington systematically endeavours to keep the ESDP within the bounds of NATO (Peters 2004).

At first sight, it might seem astonishing to claim that the EU lacks strategic self-sufficiency. This astonishment is due to a rather widespread tendency to compute the power of EU by simply adding up the elements of national power of the EU Member States. In fact, computations of this kind may serve only as indicators of the *potential power* of the EU, if and when the integration process is completed in the sector under consideration. Till this happens, the fragmentation of the EU results in the whole being less than the sum of its parts. For instance, the fact that the total population of the EU-15 was roughly 300 million people did not automatically mean that the EU constituted 'a common market of 300 million people', since the problems emanating from the existence of different currencies imposed a host of practical limitations to the extent of the EU common market. Only with the advent of the euro has it become possible – though still not completely – to equate the potential extent of the EU common market with its actual one.

The same is the case in the defence sector: though the personnel of the armed forces of the EU-25 is definitely more numerous than that of the US (1,780,598 vs. 1,546,372) (IISS 2006), these numbers, if taken alone, will lead to completely wrong conclusions regarding the distribution of power at the two sides of the Atlantic. In fact, lacking a central political entity that would allocate resources and exercise command on a pan-European scale, an autonomous European security organization

---

3   For the difficulties Germany faces both in the formulation of defence policy and in assuming a great-power role, see Maull 2000; Sarotte 2001; Meiers 2005.

4   Among others, an official paper of the Pentagon that was leaked to the Press declares that the United States ought to discourage the other industrially developed countries from challenging the American leadership or from seeking a greater regional or global role (Pentagon 1992).

would be pitifully weak militarily. And since, as has been argued above, the creation of such an entity does not seem likely in the foreseeable future, the strategic weakness of the EU is bound to continue.

With the maximalist scenario of supranational integration of the EU being out of the question for the foreseeable future, one has to examine the less ambitious scenario of an autonomous ESDP with intergovernmental structures. Actually, it has been argued that the very intergovernmental nature of the ESDP has been one of the reasons for its supposed progress (Heisbourg 2000). Well, it may be equally argued that it is also one of the reasons why the progress of ESDP is not likely to go much further. Apart from the aforementioned problems of the US reaction and the European strategic weakness, which continue to be present in this case as well, such an enterprise will require an increase in the defence expenditure of the majority of the EU Member States. However, given the lack of an obvious threat towards their national security, like the one posed by the USSR in the past, it would be difficult to persuade the electorates to approve increased expenditures for armed forces designed to meet threats of comparatively far lesser magnitude. Actually, the European countries display a marked tendency to continually reduce both their defence expenditures and the numerical strength of their armed forces. Characteristically, since 2000 the armed forces personnel of the EU-25 has been reduced by roughly 310,000 (170,000 for the EU-15), a reduction of roughly 15% (10% for the EU-15) (IISS 2000; IISS 2006). Finally, the greatest problem of an intergovernmental ESDP will be its tremendous difficulty to reach political and strategic decisions. As the recent Iraq War demonstrated for the umpteenth time, the EU Member States more often than not hold divergent views in crucial matters of foreign and security policy. This divergence has very often made the EU incapable of concerted action and is likely to paralyse an intergovernmental ESDP, especially as the number of the EU Member States is already inconveniently large and is bound to rise further in the future.

Supposedly, after the uncontrolled US action in Iraq, the issue of the ESDP gathered new momentum (see below for the initiative of France-Germany-Belgium-Luxemburg). Regarding this matter, the following observations seem in order: It is true that both the strategic dependence on the United States and US hegemony in general, occasionally annoy certain European governments and often provoke negative feelings in the public opinions of several European states. Nevertheless, no European country (or number of countries) is willing or capable of undertaking the investment that is necessary in order to eliminate the strategic dependence on the United States, or to challenge US hegemony. This fact clearly sets the limits of the ESDP.

In view of the above, it is no accident that the idea of an autonomous ESDP has been for all intents and purposes buried, and the whole discussion taking place at the moment pertains to the more efficient activation of the European states within the context of NATO. Even projects such as the European military rapid response forces are largely based on the use of NATO assets, as will become clear below.

To summarize: the continuing political fragmentation within the EU constitutes the source of the political pathologies of the ESDP; in turn, these political pathologies create a number of institutional and military pathologies. The EU Member States have a hard time achieving anything more than a minimum agreement in issues of foreign and security policy, whereas the shadow of the transatlantic colossus looms decisively over the ESDP. This is the political context that sets the tone for the institutional aspect of the ESDP.

Institutional Pathologies of the ESDP[5]

As was mentioned in the previous section, the ESDP, in contrast to the other common policies of the EU, takes place within an intergovernmental context; an inescapable condition that creates a host of problems. The Member States are entitled to participate completely and on an equal footing in all the decisions and deliberations of both the Council and the groups and committees of the Council that deal with operations under EU leadership. The commitment of national assets of the Member States in these operations is to be based on their sovereign decision. Moreover, the revised treaty of the EU provides that the relevant decisions will be made unanimously by the Council. True, the Council may occasionally, in deviation from the above provision, take decisions with special majority when adopting common actions, common positions or making any other decision on the basis of a common strategy, as well as when adopting a decision pertaining to the implementation of a common action or a common position. Nevertheless, if a member of the Council declares that, due to important and expressly stated reasons of national policy, it intends to oppose a decision that is about to be taken with special majority, then no voting takes place. In this case, the Council may, with special majority, refer the issue to the European Council where the decision will have to be taken unanimously. In other words, the unanimity rule is maintained as regards decisions deemed to have important consequences for the national interests of the Member States.

The main institutional pathology of the ESDP is its very close institutional linkage with NATO. In turn, this leads to a number of specific institutional pathologies, pertaining both to the relation of the ESDP with third countries and to the very way the ESDP functions in practice.

The very close institutional linkage of the ESDP with NATO is shown, among others, by the following: At the Cologne European Council in June 1999, where the ESDP was born, the leaders of the EU agreed that the Union must have the capability of autonomous action based on reliable military forces, the means for taking a decision to use them and the necessary readiness to react to international crises, without prejudice to NATO actions.

This initiative did not constitute an attempt to create a European army. Instead, it was launched in order to support the Common Foreign and Security Policy (CFSP) of the EU and to enhance and widen the overall foreign role of the Union through the development of a common European policy on security, defence and crisis management in the context of the so-called 'Petersberg tasks' (humanitarian and rescue missions, peacekeeping missions and missions comprising the intervention

---

5   The institutional information contained in the present section comes chiefly from the official website of the EU (European Union).

of fighting forces in crisis management, including peace-enforcement missions). The aim was to endow the EU with an autonomous capability to make decisions and, when NATO as a whole would not intervene, to initiate and then conduct military operations in order to deal with international crises.

For the effective conduct of the operations undertaken, the EU will have to determine, depending on the circumstances, whether these operations will take place under its leadership and with the use of NATO assets and capabilities or under its leadership without the use of NATO assets and capabilities. For operations of the second type, the EU can use national or multinational European assets predetermined by the Member States.

The decisive role of the Atlantic Alliance within the ESDP is also clearly stated in the introduction of the Presidency Report on the Meeting of the European Council at Nice (December 2000), where it is said that the 'autonomous nature' of the ESDP does not include the creation of a European army, and that NATO will play the main role in European defence. To this end, it was stipulated that during each six-month presidency of the EU there will take place at least three meetings between the European Committee of Policy and Security and the North-Atlantic Council, and at least one ministerial meeting between the EU and NATO. It is interesting to note that, concerning the operations of the EU where defence planning is common with NATO, there was disagreement between the French President Jacques Chirac, who proposed that the operations of the EU should be planned and conducted autonomously, merely maintaining coordination with NATO, and the British Prime Minister Tony Blair, who emphasized that it would be wrong to create a capability of independent planning that would conflict with NATO.

On 16 December 2002, the EU and NATO agreed on a framework of permanent relations enabling the former to have access to NATO assets for the purpose of crisis management. The 'Declaration of the EU and NATO for the ESDP' provides a formal basis for cooperation between the two organizations at the fields of crisis management and conflict prevention. It lays out the political principles for this cooperation and provides the EU with assured access to the planning and logistical capabilities of NATO. The crisis management activities of both NATO and the EU are mutually enhanced, but the autonomy of each organization is protected.

Finally, at the Brussels European Council (12–13 December 2003) it was approved, with NATO consent of course, that the European operational headquarters, rather modestly enhanced, would be kept within the NATO headquarters in Mons, Belgium. Furthermore, it was stipulated that the prospective crisis management campaigns of the EU would be explicitly subject to a NATO 'right of first refusal' (Gherghisan 2003, quoted in Peters 2004).

Incidentally, at this point it may be useful to say a few words about the overused term 'European Defence Identity'. In the present writer's opinion, this term constitutes another example of grandiose rhetoric that actually does not translate into very much in practice. The term implies that, since Europe possesses 'its own defence identity', it may well follow its own course in defence matters, a course distinct and even contrary to that of the United States. However, this notion was nipped in the bud: since 1990, in a number of European Councils it has been repeatedly stated that the European Defence Identity will contribute to the development of allied solidarity within NATO. In other words, the vaunted European Defence Identity translates into nothing more than the European pillar of NATO.

The very close institutional linkage of the ESDP with NATO led to a series of problems concerning the role of Turkey in the ESDP. As regards the European Member States of NATO that are not members of the EU – Turkey, Iceland, Norway, Bulgaria, Romania – the Helsinki European Council (1999) recognized the need for suitable arrangements to enable such states – and other interested states as well – to contribute to military crisis management by the EU, with due respect to the autonomy of the EU as far as decision-making is concerned. For the implementation of this decision, it was agreed to initiate dialogue and briefings with the aforementioned countries. It was also agreed that whenever the Union would undertake a military operation with the use of NATO assets, the European Member States of NATO that are not members of the EU would participate in the operation if they wanted to. In cases of military operations without the use of NATO assets, the Council of the EU could decide to ask these states to participate.

Probably the thorniest aspect of the relation of the ESDP with states that do not belong to the EU, is the one concerning Turkey. Turkey, though it had expressed its willingness to contribute up to 5.000 military personnel in future crisis-management operations of the EU, vetoed plans according to which the NATO assets would be automatically available to the Union. In order to withdraw its veto, Turkey asked the EU to allow it complete participation in the decision-making process of any EU military action in its surrounding region, including the Balkans and the eastern Mediterranean. The EU held the position that, by allowing Turkey to participate in the institutional machinery of the ESDP, it would put in jeopardy the autonomy of the latter. The deadlock was resolved at the Copenhagen European Council (12–13 December 2002): that summit witnessed the conclusion of an agreement ('Berlin Plus') giving the EU access to NATO assets for its own military operations (see above), providing at the same time some safety valves to Turkey. Thus, it is expressly stated that 'under no circumstances ... will ESDP be used against an Ally'; it is also stipulated that Cyprus (and Malta) will not participate into any ESDP operation using NATO assets. In the final analysis, given the dependence of the ESDP on NATO infrastructure (see below), it was inevitable that, one way or another, Turkey would participate in the ESDP.

As far as the practical function of the ESDP institutions is concerned,[6] the very close institutional linkage of the ESDP with NATO is reflected in the belief of many EU Member States, and consequently of their military officers that find themselves assigned to ESDP positions, that the ESDP enterprise is merely a branch of NATO. In particular, while countries like France, Belgium and Greece endeavour to bring about a somewhat more autonomous ESDP, the majority of the EU Member States do not even consider the ESDP as independent from NATO. As a result, they are not particularly willing to develop specific ESDP resources; since the ESDP is regarded as part of NATO, such an attempt is viewed as at best superfluous and at worst detrimental.

---

6   The writer was given invaluable information on this issue by a Greek senior officer with great experience in the ESDP.

Another institutional pathology that seems to be in the making is the development of separate defence cooperation sub-groupings among a number of EU Member States. A typical example was the so-called 'Quadrilateral Defence Summit' that took place on 29 April 2003, between Belgium, France, Germany and Luxemburg. The point of this initiative was that the close cooperation occurring between Belgium, France and Germany during the crisis preceding the Iraq War could lead them to a permanent 'enhanced cooperation' in defence matters, where Luxemburg could also participate.

The joint declaration of that summit (Joint Declaration 2003) contains specific proposals for the European Constitution, proposals that demonstrate the common stance of these countries on the matter. They include the reformulation of the Petersberg tasks and the inclusion of a general provision of solidarity and common security that will assist every member-state in dealing with all kinds of threats and not just terrorism. The four countries also proposed that the European Constitution should adopt a 'European Union of Defence and Security' as the institutional framework for enhanced cooperation in defence and security, allowing deeper integration than the one envisaged in the preamble of the Constitution.

Apart from their proposals on the European Constitution, the four countries launched a number of initiatives, open to the other Member States as well. In particular, their proposals involved:

- The creation of a 'common rapid-reaction unit' based on the existing Franco-German brigade, in which the Belgian storm-troopers and the Luxemburg reconnaissance squad would be incorporated.
- The creation of a common planning and operations centre, for the support of both independent EU missions and missions conducted in cooperation with NATO.
- The establishment of a European strategic airlift command, with a common transport unit entitled with dispatching forces in conflict areas.
- The creation of a general staff for the conduct of common operations in theatres of war.
- The creation of a common European unit to deal with the threat of chemical, biological and nuclear attacks.
- The creation of a European disaster relief system, ready to deploy civilian and military forces within 24 hours.
- The creation of European military training centres.
- The creation of deployable European command posts.
- The creation of a European arms procurement agency for the coordination of arms procurement.

In the present writer's opinion, these proposals are way too ambitious; rather than constituting realistic policy options, they probably reflect the disillusionment of several European countries with US unilateralism. Still, the disruptive potential of these separate defence cooperation sub-groupings should not be underestimated. While their material capabilities are relatively insignificant, they do create perceptions of disunity, or even hostility, both within Europe and as regards the US-EU relations.

Nevertheless, in order to give a balanced picture of the institutional scenery of the ESDP, it is worth noting that during the first semester of 2004 the Irish Presidency of the EU made significant progress in further expanding the ESDP, mainly in the following aspects:

- Establishment of a European Defence Agency based on Brussels, responsible for the expansion of crisis-management-related defence capabilities of the Member States. To this end, this Agency will be active in four fields: boosting capabilities, weapons policy, support of the European defence market and industry and promotion of research and development.
- Approval of new targets for boosting capabilities, stressing the transition from quantitative to qualitative goals (Headline Goal 2010 – see next section).
- Creation of six to nine battlegroups for rapid reaction intervention, each consisting of 1,500 military personnel; these groups are to be deployed on the request of the UN, mainly for operations in Africa.[7]

Military Pathologies of the ESDP

The Helsinki European Council (December 1999), set the so-called Helsinki Headline Goal, according to which the EU, through voluntary cooperation, ought to be able until 2003 to deploy rapidly and then maintain forces capable of implementing the full range of the Petersberg tasks, in operations up to army corps (15 brigades or 50,000–60,000 military personnel). These forces would be militarily self-sufficient and would possess the necessary command, control and intelligence assets, logistical capabilities, other battle support services and also, depending on the situation, air and naval elements. The Member States would have to be able to deploy these forces at that level within 60 days; also, they would have to be able to provide smaller rapid reaction assets with far greater readiness, plus their deployment capability, maintaining this deployment for at least a year. To this end, there would also be required a further reserve of deployable forces (and support assets) in lesser readiness, to replace the initial forces.

In practice, the implementation of this goal encountered considerable difficulties. Finally, according to an official assessment promulgated in 19 May 2003, the European military rapid response forces were now capable of conducting operations across the full range of the Petersberg tasks, 'limited and constrained by recognized shortfalls' (European Union, 2003). As the writer was told by a Greek senior officer with great experience in the ESDP, these shortfalls 'are basically the same as the shortfalls of NATO if America is taken out'.[8] In other words, one encounters once again the European lack of strategic self-sufficiency that was mentioned in the section of the political pathologies of the ESDP.

The military analysis of the various types of missions that the European military rapid response forces will be called upon to undertake, demonstrates the decisive

---

7   The projected number of these battlegroups has been further increased to 13.

8   Similarly, it has been argued that 'The EU's dependence on NATO (as opposed to US) assets and capabilities is actually marginal' (Hagman 2002, 103).

dependence of those forces on NATO infrastructure – that is, on US military power – since it is incapable, on its own, to perform the most important of these missions. As has been mentioned above, these missions are confined to the so-called Petersberg tasks, namely humanitarian and rescue missions, peacekeeping missions and missions comprising the intervention of fighting forces in crisis management, including peace-enforcement missions. Regarding each one of these, the following observations can be made:[9]

Humanitarian Assistance Missions and Peacekeeping Missions

These are the missions most likely to be undertaken by the European military rapid response forces. These missions are not particularly dangerous, whereas the EU has already undertaken numerous such missions (for example Albania, Bosnia-Herzegovina, Mostar command, Democratic Republic of Congo). Consequently, the European military rapid response forces possess considerable experience in this respect, and can be said to be capable of performing these missions successfully.

Rescue Missions

These are special missions that, due to their high degree of danger and the many imponderables involved, require specially trained personnel, considerable means of support and high technology systems. They are among the difficult missions that the European military rapid response forces will be called upon to perform, especially when they have to take place on enemy territory. The outcome of such an operation, when undertaken by European military rapid response forces, will depend on the available means and intelligence; this is where one sees clearly the importance of NATO infrastructure. Nevertheless, military sources estimate that the European military rapid response forces are indeed capable of performing such missions (Drymousis 2001, 16).

Crisis-management and Peace Enforcement Missions

These are the most difficult missions that the European military rapid response forces will be conceivably called upon to perform. They are unpredictable and dangerous missions, whereas the political decision-making associated with them is fraught with considerable difficulties. The undertaking of such missions by the newly created mechanisms of the European military rapid response forces will be a difficult and time-consuming process, especially when there is a prospect of these forces being used in areas where the EU Member States themselves have conflicting national interests. In such cases, it is very hard to envisage the use of the military component of the ESDP. Furthermore, an operational and tactical examination of these missions is bound to reveal several peculiarities of the potential theatres of operations, and a host of associated shortfalls of the European military rapid response forces (Drymousis 2001, 15–17):

---

9   The following analysis draws from Drymousis 2001.

- The nature of the terrain will probably favour commando operations, namely the very type of operations likely to be employed by the adversaries of the European military rapid response forces.
- The theatre of operation may possibly contain a maritime element. This can prove quite hazardous; for instance, it may make it imperative to conduct operations in closed waters. Once again, the importance of NATO naval infrastructure is manifest.
- The adversaries of the European military rapid response forces are likely to have substantial concealment capabilities due to their expert knowledge of the area, resulting in incomplete flow of intelligence for the European military rapid response forces. In addition, the latter may find it difficult to deal with their adversaries without engagements, since these adversaries are familiar with the ground and its surroundings, and may be able to move rapidly and respond quickly to developments.
- It is estimated that the means currently available to the European military rapid response forces do not enable them to form an accurate intelligence picture of the situations likely to be encountered in such missions.
- The various national components of the European military rapid response forces have been equipped in accordance with national interests and force structures that vary from case to case. The participation of military forces in the missions under examination requires special equipment, high-level training and close cooperation between the various services of the armed forces. The current composition of the European military rapid response forces, initially at least, does not conform to the needs of such missions.

These missions create new procurement needs. However, coping with these needs runs into considerable political difficulties; as has already been mentioned, the current political situation is generally not conducive to an increase of defence expenditure in the EU Member States. Here, a note is in order. Countries like Great Britain, France and Germany undoubtedly possess, either in combination or even individually, the latent power to overcome the aforementioned military pathologies. Still, the problem is that the current political context does not justify the undertaking of such measures. Only the emergence of a relatively great military threat could provide the political leaderships of these countries the necessary incentives to boost their military capabilities to a point commensurate with the needs of an autonomous ESDP. However, should a threat of such magnitude emerge, it is almost certain that the United States will not stand by idly. If that threat emanates from a resurgent Russia, we will witness the renewal of the Cold War. If it emanates from an important regional actor in the Middle East or the Balkans, we are more likely to witness conflicts resembling the Gulf War or the Kosovo War, than conflicts where the European military rapid response forces will be fighting alone against a third state or states.

This is what one should have in mind when examining the ambitious Headline Goal 2010. The European Council of June 2004 agreed upon the basic lines of development of the EU military capabilities up to 2010, especially concerning the rapid reaction battlegroups. According to the conclusions of the Council, rapid reaction requires rapid decision-making and planning process, as well as rapid deployment of forces. As regards the decision-making process, the EU aim is to be able to begin an operation within five days from the approval of the Crisis Management Plan by the Council. Regarding the deployment of forces, the aim is to have these forces ready to begin the implementation of their mission within ten days from the relevant EU decision. A basic element of the Headline Goal 2010 is the capability of the EU to deploy, in response to crisis, forces that will either operate alone, or will form part of a wider operation that will include subsequent phases (European Union 2004).

The Headline Goal 2010 is indeed ambitious. It remains to be seen whether it will be actually implemented, thus eliminating the existing military pathologies of the ESDP. Still, the continuing existence of the crucial political pathologies of the ESDP does not warrant optimism on this matter. Even if the military pillar manages to register progress, the political impediment is bound to be decisive – as Clausewitz has famously pointed out, war has its own grammar but not its own logic (Clausewitz 1989, 605).

ESDP: An Appraisal

When examining, on the one hand, the complex and laborious endeavours for the creation of an ESDP endowed with military rapid response forces and, on the other, the nature of these forces and the missions they are expected to undertake, one cannot help being struck by the discrepancy between effort and result. Basically, the result of all these endeavours is the creation of a military force that will deal with tasks of secondary importance that the United States, chiefly for financial reasons, is unwilling to undertake.[10] The bulk of the prospective missions of the European military rapid response forces are likely to involve humanitarian assistance and peacekeeping missions, that is by definition non-fighting missions. Even the comparatively more difficult field of crisis management has at best to do with coercing small Balkan states. It is inconceivable that any European military rapid response forces will perform on their own such missions in the former Soviet territories, let alone outside Europe. The very most one may expect, and for the time being this is not a realistic scenario, is that the European military rapid response forces will constitute a somewhat increased European presence in a future war that the Americans are expected to win militarily in any case.

A possible objection to the above might be that it is still too early for such criticisms, and that the modest beginnings of the ESDP do not necessarily predetermine its future development. The telling retort to this remark is given by the analysis of the political context contained in the beginning of the present chapter: there are

---

10 According to the estimate of a Greek senior officer with great experience in the ESDP, the saving of US resources by avoiding unwanted missions may not be the only way in which the financial incentive is influencing the US stance towards the ESDP. Since the boosting of the ESDP – under US tutelage of course – will require several arms procurement programs, the United States may be hoping that at least part of these programs will be undertaken by US defence industries.

compelling political reasons making it unlikely that the ESDP will 'take off' in the foreseeable future.

The second conclusion is that the enterprise of the ESDP takes place within a strictly intergovernmental framework. The EU Member States are extremely reluctant to cede their national sovereignty at the sensitive spheres of security and defence; this, among others, is reflected on the retention of the unanimity rule in the decisions pertaining to the ESDP. As has been mentioned above, this leads to enormous difficulties in political and strategic decision-making.

The third conclusion has to do with the autonomy of the ESDP. The above examination of the institutional framework that regulates this enterprise demonstrates its close linkage with the Atlantic Alliance; the ESDP will be simply the European pillar of NATO. This is not due to some caprice on the part of the creators of that institutional framework; institutional texts do not have an independent logic. On the contrary, the close linkage of the ESDP with NATO reflects the inescapable reality of the US international pre-eminence and the European lack of strategic self-sufficiency. The ESDP is dependent on NATO infrastructure, and its missions will be those that NATO is not willing to undertake.

To summarize: the ESDP is dealing with comparatively minor matters, is marred by disagreements and varying national interests among the EU Member States, and is bound to remain dependent on NATO.

Conclusion: ESDP, NATO and International Order

If the preceding analysis is correct, then it should not be particularly difficult to reach a number of pertinent conclusions regarding the relative role to be played in international order by the ESDP and NATO respectively. By extension, this will lead to an understanding of the relative influence the EU and the US are likely to possess in the shaping and management of international affairs. To be sure, though the ESDP is by definition representative of the EU, it is not accurate to view NATO as simply an extension of the US; still, judging from the way NATO functions, this view is not too far from the truth.

This is not the place for a detailed presentation of the prospects of NATO; suffice it to say that, in contrast to the lumbering ESDP, the Atlantic Alliance is in excellent shape indeed. Having proved its worth during the first post-Cold War decade, a period fraught with uncertainty about its future, NATO is acquiring an ever-expanding role as a convenient vehicle for the promotion of US interests around the globe. Furthermore, it has been aptly called 'the arm of Western civilization' (Coker 2002, 70); for third countries, cooperation with NATO signifies, if not civilizational, at least political affinity with the West as a whole (see for instance the recent overtures of Argentina and especially Japan – which definitely is not part of the West in civilizational terms – for partnership with NATO).

With the ESDP basically being overshadowed by NATO, the EU is bound to possess but little military muscle for the foreseeable future. This, in turn, is bound to result in correspondingly little international influence for the EU. To be sure, the EU is very active internationally, outspending the United States in many areas such as aid to developing countries. The EU is indeed so prominent in the management of international order, albeit with non-military means, that it has even been claimed that the world is actually bipolar (Moravcsik 2003). However, it has been correctly pointed out that 'Europe has little reason to be unduly proud of its soft power role. Despite European economic power, despite policing peace settlements around the world and despite providing enormous amounts of aid, the EU actually acquires relatively little influence in return for its money' (Eilstrup Sangiovanni 2003–04, 200).[11] When all is said and done, those who do the fighting are the ones that actually get influence and respect in the international arena. Thus, though the EU has, when all expenses are taken into account, far outspent the US in Kosovo (Eilstrup Sangiovanni 2003–04, 199, 206), there should be no doubt that the US is bound to play a far greater role than the EU in determining the political future of the Kosovo region.

Nevertheless, though the United States will continue to be the military powerhouse of the West, and NATO will remain the principal military instrument defending Western interests and, when necessary and possible, shaping the international order accordingly, the ESDP can still have at least some useful functions to perform, albeit in a subordinate role. For better or for worse, the chief utility of the ESDP as far as the international order is concerned, is to provide a diversification of the West's response to a number of eventualities. In other words, if need arises, the Western countries – whenever their interests converge enough to warrant the use of this all-inclusive term – may have at their disposal a variety of responses, including military. This may conceivably ease US resource constraints. It may also provide third countries with options more acceptable politically – for instance, whenever there is strong local reaction to the presence of US troops in an area. To be sure, the hardest military work will always be done by the United States; every move of the European military rapid reaction forces will depend on previous US sanction; and the ESDP will basically constitute the European pillar of NATO.

This may seem an intelligent division of labour, auguring well for international stability. If the cases of Kosovo or Afghanistan are any indication, the following picture is likely to emerge: 1) the US will undertake the bulk of the military effort during future wars; 2) after the end of those wars the EU may end up outspending the US in reconstructing the pacified areas; 3) still, the EU will probably lag far behind the US in influencing the fate of those areas. This does not sound like a rational arrangement. However, it may well prove a viable one, given the EU bureaucratic inertia and unwillingness to expand its military capabilities, plus the fact that the broad interests of the EU countries and the US are likely to remain convergent for the foreseeable future.

In conclusion, it would be interesting to reflect on what the above analysis of the EU/ESDP – US/NATO relations would imply for the function of a number of instruments for the maintenance of international order. According to Hedley Bull, international order is being maintained through the balance of power, international law, diplomacy, war, and great-power management (Bull 1977, 101–229). If the

---

11 This observation leads Eilstrup Sangiovanni to argue that, instead of strengthening its ESDP, the EU would do better to boost its capacity for what it is arguably doing best, namely non-military crisis management and post-war reconstruction.

preceding analysis is correct, then the ESDP can have but a marginal impact on international order. True, as was pointed out above, it may provide the Western countries with additional policy options, thus affecting the function of diplomacy – defined by Bull as 'the conduct of relations between states and other entities with standing in world politics by official agents and by peaceful means' (Bull 1977, 162). It may conceivably affect the function of war as well, though this is much less likely. However, when we come to the institutions of the balance of power and great-power management, stark realities emerge once again. Bull, following Vattel, defines the balance of power as 'a state of affairs such that no power is in a position where it is preponderant and can lay down the law to others' (Bull 1977, 101). The above analysis should leave no doubt that, at least in security matters, no balance of power exists currently in the West, and the ESDP is not changing this. Finally, as far as great-power management is concerned, besides what has been said above, Bull himself makes it graphically clear that it is pointless to use this concept when examining the EU/ESDP – US/NATO relations: 'Western Europe, while it is not amalgamated in a single state, is not a power at all' (Bull 1977, 204).

References

Bull, H. (1977), *The Anarchical Society: A Study of Order in World Politics* (Houndmills and London: Macmillan).

Christodoulides, T. (1993), 'The Indecisive Step: The Common Foreign and Security Policy in the European Union', in T. Christodoulides and C. Stefanou (eds).

Christodoulides, T. and Stefanou, C. (eds) (1993), *The Maastricht Treaty: A Comprehensive View* (Athens: I. Sideris) [text in Greek].

Clausewitz, C. von (1989), *On War* (edited and translated by Michael Howard and Peter Paret) (Princeton: Princeton University Press).

Coker, C. (2002), 'Globalization and Insecurity in the Twenty-first Century: NATO and the Management of Risk', *Adelphi Paper 345* (London: International Institute for Strategic Studies).

Drymousis, I., Lieutenant Commander, Hellenic Navy (2001), *European Security*, mimeo (Athens: Hellenic Naval War College) [text in Greek].

Eilstrup Sangiovanni, M. (2003–04), 'Why a Common Security and Defence Policy is Bad for Europe', *Survival* 45: 3, 193–206.

European Union [website], <http://www.europa.eu>.

European Union (2003) [website] *Declaration on EU Military Capabilities,* 19 May, <http://ue.eu.int/uedocs/cmsUpload/Declaration%20on%20EU%20Military%20 Capabilities%20-%20May%202003.pdf>.

European Union (2004) [website], 2582nd Council meeting, External Relations (Excerpt from the Press Release) EUROPEAN SECURITY AND DEFENCE POLICY – Council Conclusions <http://ue.eu.int/uedocs/cmsUpload/Excerpt%2 0from%20the%20Press%20Release.pdf>.

Gherghisan, M. (2003), 'European Defence Agreement Reached', *EU Observer* [website], <http://euobs.com/?aid=13877&rk=1>.

Haas, E. (1958), *The Uniting of Europe: Political, Economic and Social Forces, 1950–1957* (Stanford: Stanford University Press).

Hagman, H.-C. (2002), 'European Crisis Management and Defence: The Search for Capabilities', *Adelphi Paper* 353 (London: The International Institute for Strategic Studies).

Heisbourg, F. (2000), 'Europe's Strategic Ambitions: The Limits of Ambiguity', *Survival* 42: 2, 5–15.

Ifestos, P. (1999a), *Theory of International and European Integration* (Athens: Poiotita) [text in Greek].

Ifestos, P. (1999b), *Diplomacy and Strategy of the European Great Powers, France, Germany, Great Britain* (Athens: Poiotita) [text in Greek].

IISS (2000), *The Military Balance, 2000/2001* (London: The International Institute for Strategic Studies).

IISS (2006), *The Military Balance, 2006* (London: The International Institute for Strategic Studies).

'Joint Declaration', *Meeting of the Heads of State and Government of Germany, France, Luxembourg and Belgium on European defence – Joint declaration* [website], (29 April 2003) <http://www.ambafrance-uk.org/article.php3?id_article=4858>.

La Malfa, G. (2002), 'The Orphaned Euro', *Survival* 44: 1, 81–92.

Maull, H.W. (2000), 'Germany and the Use of Force: Still a "Civilian Power"?', *Survival* 42: 2, 56–80.

Meiers, F.-J. (2005), 'Germany's Defence Choices', *Survival* 41: 1, 153–66.

Moravcsik, A. (2003), 'The World is Bipolar After All', *Newsweek International*, 5 May.

Pentagon (1992), 'Excerpts from Pentagon's Plan: "Prevent the Emergence of a New Rival"', *New York Times*, March 8.

Peters, I. (2004), 'ESDP as a Transatlantic Issue: Problems of Mutual Ambiguity', *International Studies Review*, 6: 3, 381–401.

Sarotte, M.E. (2001), 'German Military Reform and European Security', *Adelphi Paper* 340 (London: The International Institute for Strategic Studies).

Chapter 7

Transatlantic Convergence or Divergence? Threat Assessment, Surveillance Technologies and Fundamental Rights

Angela Liberatore[1]

Did 11 September 2001 (9/11) make the European Union (EU) and the US closer or farther apart? And what can be learnt with regard to the relations between security and democracy post 9/11? An analysis of some instances of transatlantic cooperation or tensions is offered below with the aim of clarifying these questions. Rather than attempting a full fledged comparison of EU and US policies, the analysis takes the EU context as 'pivot' and focuses on the influence of – and implications for – transatlantic relations. The cases considered are threat assessment, the introduction of biometric identification, the EU/US Agreement on Passenger Name Records (PNR) and extraordinary renditions. From a broader conceptual perspective, these cases are useful illustrations of the relations between security policies and democratic debate, oversight and rights.

I argue that there is a general convergence between the EU and the US with regard to broad features of threat assessment and the resort to surveillance as one of the means to tackle terrorism. At the same time, there is divergence with regard to the stance towards multilateralism, the use of force and the protection of certain fundamental rights. The degree of 'securitization' of policy agendas and political discourse and the degree and type of pluralism to be found in the US and the EU post 9/11 contribute to explain both instances of convergence and of divergence. From a normative standpoint, some unsettling issues need attention. These include the difference between exceptions granted by law and exceptions to law, the risk these pose for the legitimacy of democracies, and the impacts of the violation of fundamental rights with regard to both the internal social cohesion and the external credibility of countries intending to foster democracy. Finally, a more stable international order could be expected by an increased convergence between the EU and the US, but such order will only be legitimate if international law and protection of fundamental rights are taken seriously.

1   European Commission, Directorate General for Research, Brussels. *The opinions expressed are those of the author and do not necessarily represent the views of the European Commission.*

Some Elements of Context

Security has always been at the core of transatlantic relations. The end of the Cold War and the related redefinition of geopolitics led to a change in how security cooperation is conceived, rather than to its decrease in importance: 9/11 and the Iraq War being the most prominent and problematic cases in point. At the same time, transatlantic relations are also embedded in broader issues of international cooperation ranging from trade to environment protection. Co-operation takes place on the regulation of financial markets and other areas, while significant divergences emerge on matters such as the Kyoto Protocol or the steel market. All these cases have been analysed in depth by other authors, are reiterated at bilateral high level meetings between the US and the EU and are recalled here as important contextual elements to avoid the risk of looking at 9/11 and related developments as isolated or self-standing. For obvious reasons of space and focus they will not be examined below; however, it is useful to note that transatlantic cooperation is punctuated by different perspectives on multilateralism and the role of international law in as diverse areas as environment, trade and security.[2] It is also important to consider that both the EU and the US are focusing on democracy as part of their own identity as well as a value to be further diffused in the world. Again, divergences emerge on whether democracy can be facilitated or also imposed. This, as well as the link with respect of fundamental rights, raises important considerations with regard to both the working of democracy within the EU and the US and how people outside see them.

With regard to the broader relations between democracy and security, they raise specific challenges in the EU context. These relate, on the one hand, to the very nature of the EU decision making process and, on the other, to the specific areas of policy under consideration. EU decision making is multi-level and thus, it can be inferred, involves a higher plurality of actors than national systems. At the same time, EU decision making is often criticized as technocratic and elitist – which makes the previous inference to be considered *cum grano salis*.[3] With regard to the policy areas relevant for our cases, these include the field of internal (justice and home affairs) and external (common foreign and security policy) security which are both 'newer pillars' as compared to Community policies. Newer policy areas are generally weaker, but specific events and actors might change such structural weakness. The same applies to the democracy side of the coin. After the initial focus of the European *Economic* Community on market liberalization, the issues of 'democratizing the EU' became prominent in the political agenda in the late nineties and in the Constitutional debate. Citizenship rights in the EU emerged first as economic and social rights, and later a broader range of fundamental rights was acknowledged in a Charter (politically important but not legally binding) and was incorporated in the EU Constitutional Treaty – ratification of which was shaken by two negative referenda in 2005. The US governance system involves some similarities but also crucial differences as compared

---

2   On perspectives of multilateralism see Telò 2006.

3   On EU governance and democracy see, for example: Chryssochoou 1998; Kohler-Koch and Eising 1999; Laffan *et al.* 2000; Liberatore 2004; Schmitter 2000; Wallace and Wallace (eds) 2000.

to the EU. Its federal structure involves multi-level decision making, but obviously a full-fledged federation and a supranational regional organization are diverse: just to mention one aspect, the strong Presidentialism of the US is in sharp contrast with the rotating EU Presidency held by one of the Member States. Pluralism is a key feature of the US polity including its very large number of advocacy organizations, the adversarial approach to regulatory policy making and the role of the Courts. However, such pluralism is submitted to a strong dominant paradigm when security is at stake, a phenomenon especially visible during the Bush Administration and helped by the consolidated nature of defence and foreign policies – which are rather 'beginners' in the EU context.

In the following pages, the focus will be on patterns of convergence and divergence post 9/11, with focus on security cooperation; this is further restricted to surveillance technologies plus the case of renditions – the point in common being that the latter have to resort to covert surveillance to be implemented. First a brief examination of four cases is presented: threat assessment (supposedly as the basis for surveillance or other options being pursued), biometric identification, PNR and extraordinary renditions. Then, some analytical lessons are drawn on the implications of these developments with regard to patterns of convergence/divergence and the relations between democracy and security. Finally, some normative reflections are suggested.

Threat Assessment

Accounts of transatlantic solidarity or misunderstandings post 9/11 often start with assumptions about similar or different perceptions of threats. For some, the attacks of 9/11 brought a new wave of cooperation against international terrorism; for others, they contributed to reciprocal misunderstandings on the novelty or significance of the terrorism threat. The US-led war on Iraq induced a split within the EU: for some, the Franco-German opposition in the UN Security Council involved a broader transatlantic divide; for others, the participation of some EU countries in the war amounts to a strong transatlantic alliance to fight the threat posed by the regime of Saddam Hussein. But what is a 'threat', who defines and identifies threats, how is the assessment verified and how does it influence policy options?

Threat is a complex notion that 'resonates' with other notions such as risk, vulnerability, danger and fear. Similarly to the notion of risk, sophisticated assessment methods are put in place to identify and measure threats. At the same time, it is normally recognized that threats, as well as risks, are subjectively perceived and related to a number of factors, ranging from belief systems to past experience. Threats refer to some actual events or actors, but are also socially constructed projections of how such actors or events could develop in the future, or new ones emerge. Here constructivist approaches in International Relations meet (and borrow from) similar approaches in the fields of sociology and epistemology. When entering such subjective and socially constructed dimension, notions of vulnerability, danger and fear come into play. Vulnerability has also being devoted important methodological attention with the development of indicators and other measurement tools, and evokes feelings too: namely of being exposed to something negative and having little or no capacity to protect oneself. Notions of danger and fear make the negativity even stronger and the sense of agency in face of negativity even weaker. Literature on danger and fears ranges from anthropological to psychological and political studies; an important contribution of such literature (for example Furedi 2002) is the questioning of causality: do we have more fears because there are more risks, threats and dangers 'out there'; is fear induced and manipulated to justify otherwise unacceptable measures; or is it caused by other – intentional or unintentional – factors? This chapter will not attempt to give a general answer to such question, but suggest it is important for the understanding of threat assessment.

A clarification must precede the brief examination of threat assessment in the EU and the US. As key actors of threat assessment are intelligence services, only the 'iceberg' of the matter can be explored through open sources. This chapter is limited to such sources, also comforted by literature on intelligence (Dewerpe 1994) indicating that some of the key features of the process can be inferred without gathering access to classified information. At the same time, the role of intelligence is crucial on both analytical and practical grounds: it is at the core of reflections on the relations between secrecy and accountability, as well as between knowledge and power (Brodeur 2003), and it is central to ongoing efforts to improve the sharing of intelligence (Nomikos 2004).

A key point of reference is represented by the two overall strategic documents where key threats are identified: the National Security Strategy of the US – NSSUSA (The White House 2002) and the European Security Strategy – ESS (European Council 2003a). A simple schematization of identified threats is offered below.

NSSUSA 2002	ESS 2003
1) Global Terrorism and States sponsors of terrorism	1) International terrorism
2) Weapons of Mass Destruction (WMD)	2) Weapons of Mass Destruction (WMD)
3) Regional Conflicts	3) Regional Conflicts
	4) State failure
	5) Organized crime

Both strategic documents identify terrorism (with focus on its international/'global' dimension) as the key threat, as well as Weapons of Mass Destruction (WMD). They agree also on the focus on some countries, but the NSSUSA uses the term 'state sponsors of terrorism' – popularized with the more aggressive label of 'rogue' states and the even stronger 'axis of evil' discourse, while the ESS focuses on the process of state failure: a difference which is not only semantic as it may point to different courses of action. It is also worth noting that different emphasis is put in the two documents on the possible links between terrorism and WMD and between them and 'rogue' or 'failing' states. Regional conflicts are also mentioned in both documents and the ESS also adds organized crime. This, together with regional conflicts, was added to the initial document after the European Council of Thessaloniki of June

2003, reflecting different emphasis by Member States and adding to an initial selection that fully mirrored – while with the differences discussed above – the preceding NSSUSA. A key element to be considered is the way threats are 'packaged' in governmental and media discourses, and what is the relation with response options. In the US context, the links between terrorism and WMD – in conjunction with the figure of an unpredictable dictator as Saddam Hussein – were the object of 'threat inflation' to justify the war with Iraq (Kaufmann 2004), and fears induced by such threat inflation were instrumental to the wide acceptance of the notion of a preventive war (Barber 2003). In the EU context, the diversity of positions on the Iraq War indicated different appreciations of the nature of the threat and, even more, of the suitability and legitimacy of war to tackle it. Also following the terrorist attacks in Madrid and London the link with war as a response to terrorism was very weak or negative (for example the new Spanish government – elected soon after the Madrid attacks – withdrew the troops from Iraq) and the focus was more on the links between international and home-grown terrorist organizations than between terrorists and 'rogue states'.

With specific regard to the assessment of terrorism threats, the two EU-level key actors are the European Police Office (EUROPOL) and the EU Situation Center (SITCEN). EUROPOL is the EU criminal intelligence agency that is operational since 1999; it offers intelligence and training but has no executive powers. Its threat assessment's focus is on organized crime (EUROPOL 2006) but a counter-terrorism unit has also been established and provides assessments. Some versions of those assessments are presented to the European Parliament and brief elements are published where the terrorist threat is assessed with regard to foreign and domestic terrorist groups (EUROPOL 2005, 2006b). SITCEN, located in the Council Secretariat, reports to the Counter-terrorism Coordinator, Gijs DeVries, and the EU High Representative for the Common Foreign and Security Policy (CFSP) Javier Solana. SITCEN has been working in cooperation with external intelligence services of Member States since early 2002 and was endorsed cooperation with internal intelligence since 2004 (Solana 2004). As stated by De Vries (2005), 'the European Parliament can have dialogue with the Council of Ministers on the work of SITCEN. But the specific products that come out of this work will have to remain confidential'. Actually, not only the 'specific products' are – obviously – confidential/classified, but even the methodology used to pool, select and synthesize information and analysis coming from external and internal, military and policy intelligence in several Member States (theoretically 25, but not all of them included in SITCEN cooperation) is not subject of any publicly traceable document. The fact that not only the results but also the methods of threat assessment are not submitted to review by peers outside the closed intelligence community continue to raise issues as to their validity and credibility. In addition, it has been persuasively argued that accountability of intelligence should be seen as a guarantee of quality, on top of legitimacy, rather than a problem (Müller-Wille 2004). This is, of course, not specific to the EU institutions involved. In the US case, for example, it is not possible to grasp the specifics of CIA's assessment methods through the CIA's user-friendly website, its Guide to Country Profiles, or the journal *Studies in Intelligence* burst forth with the backing of senior CIA leaders; but at least some effort is made to let some non sensitive methodological discussion be available at the surface level.

The point above is important when discussing efforts in intelligence cooperation, both with regard to the problems in sharing data and methods between services, and with regard to the accountability of the cooperative networks that may come into place. The matter is very complex and cannot be explored further here. What can be however concluded from this quick overview is that key elements of threat assessment, as expressed in published documents, seem to converge across the Atlantic, as is the case for the common emphasis on the need for further intelligence cooperation. On the other hand, both public statements and practice demonstrate that such apparently converging threat assessment gives raise to different policy preferences and frames: the 'war on terror' is a US frame quite different from the European 'fight against terrorism' based on law enforcement means. Similarly the war on Iraq is a US-led operation where some EU countries joined on individual capacity – not as 'Europe' (and mostly against their internal public opinion). In short, either the assessment is less converging than it seems at the surface, or at least its interpretation in terms of response option (namely concerning resort to war) is partly diverging.

Biometric Identification

Biometric technology (from the Greek: *bios,* life and *metron*, measurement) identifies individuals automatically by using their biological or behavioural characteristics. Biometric identification – already available but not massively used – played a significant role after 9/11. In the EU context, distinct initiatives were launched with regard to EU citizens and to third country nationals; while distinct, such initiatives partly converged over time.

Biometrics' first appearance at the EU level was in 2000 with regard to non-EU citizens, more specifically with regard to the inclusion in the EURODAC database of fingerprints of asylum applicants. The idea was actually much older: ministers responsible for immigration had agreed on a Community-wide system for the comparison of fingerprints of asylum applicants back in 1991. At the European Council of December 2001 it was resolved to establish a common Visa Information System (VIS) to also include biometric identifiers to prevent 'visa shopping', improve the administration of the common visa policy, contribute to internal security and fight terrorism. The VIS project, as well as the revision of the Schengen Information System (SIS II) became prominent during enlargement and post 9/11. During 2004, the year marked by the attacks in Madrid on 11 March, intense debate took place over VIS and its implementation. Reservations were raised in the European Parliament and by data protection authorities (Article 29 Data Protection Working Party – established with the Directive on data protection of 1995) on the storage of biometric data in a database due to the risk of such data being used in a way that is disproportionate or incompatible with original purposes, and wondering about the necessity of having the same data stored in SIS II, VIS, and EURODAC (Data Protection WP 2004; European Parliament 2004a). In November 2004, a report by the Council expert committee on visa stated that the proposals on biometrics in visa and residence permits presented in September 2003 suffered of a 'collision problem', that is a possible interference between chips with biometric data inserted in passports by different countries. At the Brussels Council of February 2005 the Council 'having regard to the technical problems related to the storage of biometric identifiers in visa', invited the Commission to bring the activation of biometric identifiers in the development of VIS forward to 2006 (Council of the EU 2005).

Following 9/11, developments on biometrics in documents of EU citizens ran partly in parallel with those concerning third country nationals. Two main factors pushed the introduction of biometrics in travel documents of EU citizens: an external factor – the pressure from the US, and an internal one – the consistency argument made at the Council in Thessaloniki in 2003 that similar requirement should apply to all travel documents issued by EU Member States (European Council 2003b). The Council invited the Commission to submit a proposal for the introduction of biometrics in passports and the proposal was presented in February 2004 (European Commission 2004a). It aims at rendering the passport more secure, meeting the requirements of the US Visa Waiver programme, providing coherence with requirements for third country nationals entering the EU, bringing new and older EU Member States in line, and implementing international standards set by the International Civil Aviation Organization (ICAO). It explains that ICAO chose the facial image as primary interoperable identifier – leaving fingerprint or iris image as optional biometric identifiers. It is also stated that a European Register should be established but its impacts on fundamental rights – especially data protection – should be first considered.

The year 2004 was a very intense period with regard to the finalization of biometric identification policies; this was partly linked to the revamped emphasis on fighting terrorism following the attacks in Madrid. On 25 March, the European Council endorsed a Declaration on Combating Terrorism that mentioned biometrics (European Council 2004). In October 2004 the Interior Ministers of five EU countries – France, Germany, Italy, Spain, United Kingdom – met in an informal meeting and agreed on the need to include biometric identifiers, facial image and fingerprints, in passports. Such proposal was debated at the Council of Justice and Home Affairs Ministers of 25 October where additional countries supported it. On 28 October, the Report of MEP Carlos Coelho on the Commission's Proposal of February 2004 was endorsed by the Committee on Civil Liberties, Justice and Home Affairs – and later by the EP plenary (European Parliament 2004b). The report agreed with the Commission proposal of having one identifier – facial image – as compulsory and others as optional, stressed that biometric data in passports should be used only for verifying the authenticity of the document and the identity of the holder, and argued that no central database of EU passports and travel documents with biometric data should be established due to the risk of 'function creep' (use of data for other purposes than originally envisaged). On 4–5 November, the Hague Programme, adopted by the European Council, recalled the importance of adopting biometric identifiers; interestingly it includes the topic of 'biometrics and information system' under the heading of 'strengthening freedom' (European Council 2004b).

On 13 December 2004, the Council Regulation on standards for security features and biometrics in passports and travel documents issued by Member States was adopted (EC 2004c). It provides for the inclusion of facial image (to be implemented within 18 months) and fingerprints (to be implemented in 36 months) in interoperable formats, for the right of holders to verify and – when appropriate – ask for rectification of data, for limitation of biometrics for verifying the authenticity of the document and the identity of the holder, and for the establishment of additional technical features. Criticisms to these provisions on biometric identification have been raised by NGOs (for example Statewatch, Privacy International) and in some national debates (for instance, in connection with the introduction of the electronic identity card in the UK).

While the US administration was successful in pressurizing the EU concerning the introduction of biometrics, it was much less proactive in introducing biometrics domestically (Koslowski 2005); this partly changed by initiative of the State Department that planned to issue biometrically enhanced US passports in 2005 (Harty 2005). In this case, the EU even 'outperformed' the US, and on this ground the EU could raise the issue of visa reciprocity (Council of the EU 2006) to modify the current situation where American citizens can travel throughout the EU without visa, while the US imposes visa obligations on nationals of ten EU Member States.[4] This can only reinforce the conclusion that biometric identification is a case of strong convergence between the US and the EU.

Passenger Name Records

While the diffusion of biometrics was being pursued, the US also pressed the EU and other countries on the control and transfer of technologically less sophisticated data such as names, addresses and travel routes. Following 9/11, airlines were asked by the US authorities to transfer PNR to the US Bureau of Customs and Border Protection. In March 2004, the European Commission presented a draft decision (European Commission 2004b) on protection of personal data contained in the PNR in view of the transfer of EU passenger records to US authorities by air carriers. This was rejected by the European Parliament which decided on 21 April (European Parliament 2004c) to refer the related international agreement with the US to the Court of Justice of the European Communities. However, on ground of urgency, and since the EP request for an opinion of the Court did not have a binding suspension effect, on 28 May 2004 Günter Burghardt, EU Ambassador to the US, signed an agreement on behalf of the EU with Tom Ridge, US Department of Homeland Security Secretary, on the exchange of PNR. The agreement, signed in Washington, entered into force immediately and legalized the transfer of data of passengers on transatlantic flights to the US authorities, transfer that had been taking place for over one year as airlines were not allowed to land otherwise. Under the agreement, airlines provided information about

---

4   Czech Republic, Estonia, Latvia, Lithuania, Hungary, Poland, Slovakia, Malta, Cyprus and – only one among 'old' Member States – Greece.

passengers – including name, address, phone number and birth date – to US security officials. NGOs such as Statewatch provided critical monitoring of the PNR issue.[5]

The case presented by the EP before the European Court of Justice in July 2004 was decided upon in May 2006 (ECJ 2006) following a detailed opinion by the Advocate General published in November 2005 (ECJ 2005). In its judgement, the Court decided to annul both the Commission Decision on the adequate protection of personal data contained in the PNR and the Council Decision on the conclusion of the agreement with the US. The judgement argues that the legal basis for both Decisions was wrong: in the first case with reference to the Directive of 1995 on data protection in relation to the internal market, and in the second case concerning Article 95 of the Treaty establishing the European Community. Such legal provisions do not cover data protection and conclusion of international agreements in the field of security, and the transfer of PNR has been demanded and agreed indeed on ground of (state) security. While the judgement cancels the agreement on procedural grounds, it does not challenge it in substance. For instance, it argues that the interference in the private life of passengers is to be considered in accordance with the law and proportionate to the objective of combating terrorism. For reasons of legal certainty and in order to protect the persons concerned, the effect of the Decision was preserved until 30 September 2006.

Following the judgement, the European Parliament – in a letter of its President to the Presidents of the European Commission and the European Council of 9 June 2006 – recommends that the Commission should avoid precipitate decisions, the Parliament should be fully kept involved in the replacement of the annulled decisions, and that an agreement on a Framework Decision on data protection in the third pillar should be found. On 16 June, the European Commission adopted two initiatives to put a legally sound framework in place for the transfer of PNR. One initiative would terminate the existing agreement while the other would authorize opening talks with the US in view of a new agreement. With regard to the latter, the Commission recommends that the Council give authorization to open negotiations for a new agreement with the US on the basis of Article 38 of Title VI, Treaty on European Union, pillar on justice and home affairs; this is considered the correct legal environment to conclude an International Agreement for matters dealing with public security and criminal law matters (European Commission 2006).

As the latter events took place at the time of writing, only some speculations can be offered with regard to the follow-up. The Council and Commission are likely to stick to the letter of the ECJ judgement and seek to change only the legal basis for the new agreement. The Parliament is likely to continue to voice concern not only on procedural but also on substantive grounds. Some NGOs will probably question the effectiveness of PNR transfer. For the purpose of this contribution, it can be noted a full convergence on the PNR issue between the US authorities and the European Commission and Council, with the European Parliament and some NGOs

---

5 (Statewatch, Observatory on PNR: http://www.statewatch.org/pnrobservatory.htm).

challenging such convergence on grounds of accountability as well as compliance with fundamental rights – namely privacy.

Extraordinary Renditions

While some passengers have their data transferred and shared between several public authorities and private companies across the Atlantic, the track of other passengers disappears through 'extraordinary renditions'.

'Rendition' is a 'surrender' or 'handing over' of a person or property, especially from one jurisdiction to another. 'Extraordinary rendition' however is not defined in international law. Wikipedia defines extraordinary renditions as 'an American extrajudicial procedure which involves the sending of untried criminal suspects, generally suspected terrorists or alleged supporters of groups which the US government considers to be terrorist organizations, to countries other than the United States for imprisonment and interrogations'.[6] Wikipedia as well as the Council of Europe report of 2006 state that a rendition programme targeting Al-Qaeda was launched under the Clinton Administration; such programme escalated and changed in focus during the Bush Administration.

First queries about extraordinary renditions post 9/11 were raised by US NGOs and lawyers, and news about the possibility of secret CIA prisons and abductions in Europe were published in November 2005 by US media (ABC television channel, Washington Post) and NGOs (Human Rights Watch). Such reports – amplified by media and NGOs in Europe – prompted some institutional responses. The Council of Europe (that gathers all EU countries plus several others) asked its Committee on Legal Affairs and Human Rights to examine the matter. The European Parliament established a temporary committee on the alleged use of European countries by CIA for the transport and illegal detention of prisoners. Extraordinary renditions were also prominent in diplomatic exchanges during the visit of US Secretary of State Condoleezza Rice to Europe in December 2005; Rice responded to Europeans' appeals for information regarding renditions by making clear that the practice would continue and implied that European governments co-operated with CIA.[7] Some legal investigations also were launched, for example in February 2006 by the Deputy Public Prosecutor of Milan on the abduction of Egyptian national Abu Omar.[8]

The report of the EP Temporary Committee, drafted by MEP Giovanni Fava, was published in April 2006 (EP 2006). It condemns the practice of extraordinary renditions, deplores the fact that CIA has been responsible for illegal abductions, considers implausible that European governments were not aware, and regrets that rules governing the secret services seem inadequate in several EU Member States. It calls for setting up more effective controls on secret services, recalls the prohibition of torture and the fact that information extracted upon torture may

---

6   Wikipedia, the free encyclopedia, http://en.wikipedia.org/wiki/Extraordinary_rendition, checked 20 June 2006.

7   *Washington Post*, BBC-News, *Der Spiegel*, *Le Monde*, *La Repubblica*, 6 –8/12/2005.

8   Milan Court, Sezione Giudice per le indagini preliminary, ref. 10838/05 RGNR and 1966/05 RGGIP.

under no circumstances be considered as valid evidence, and urges Member States to strictly comply with the principle of non-refoulement of the Convention against Torture: according to such principle no party can expel or return a person to a state where there are substantial grounds for believing that he or she would be in danger of torture.

Similar points are made in the detailed report of the Council of Europe, drafted by Dick Marty, Chairman of the Committee of Legal Affairs and Human Rights, and published in June 2006 (Council of Europe 2006). The report starts considering that Mr. Marty had no investigative power and that it is paradoxical to expect bodies without investigative power – as the Council of Europe and the European Parliament – to adduce evidence in the legal sense. In this regard, it acknowledges the assistance of some authorities in the EU (for example the European Commission, Eurocontrol, the EU Satellite Centre), but it is stressed that the Council of Europe and the EP had to undertake their inquiries due to a lack of willingness on the part of national institutions that could have clarified the allegations. The report also responds to charges of the report being an 'anti-American exercise' by stressing that American journalists, NGOs and politicians were the first to denounce extraordinary renditions. Interestingly, a key US witness interviewed by the Council's team was Michael Scheuer, chief of the Bin-Laden Unit in the CIA's Counter-terrorism Center for four years. To explain the situation, the report offers the metaphor of the 'global spider's web', spun over seven years and with the US as chief web's architect with capacity to capture individual targets abroad and carry them to different parts of the world. Several individual cases are then discussed and the conclusion is drawn that some Member States can be held responsible for violations of the rights of specific person object of extraordinary renditions: Sweden, Bosnia-Herzegovina, UK, Italy, Former Yugoslav Republic of Macedonia, Germany and Turkey are mentioned. In addition some states are charged of collusion in secret detention and un-lawful transfers: Poland, Romania, Germany, Turkey, Spain, Cyprus, Ireland, UK, Portugal, Greece and Italy.

In short, collaboration and/or collusion between CIA and some European countries' authorities are pointed out by both the Council of Europe and the European Parliament; and much stronger words are used by NGOs such as Amnesty International that published a report entitled 'Partners in crime: Europe's role in US renditions' (Amnesty International 2006). While such situation can lead to the conclusion that also in this case there is a convergence between the EU and the US, I suggest that the situation is more ambiguous than in the case of biometrics (where the EU even outperforms the US in speed), or PNR (induced by the US but adhered to by key European institution such as the Council and the Commission). While extraordinary rendition is a covert programme which is part of the US official governmental policy, the cooperation or collusion with it is clearly a matter of strong embarrassment for European governments and attracts clear resistance by some representative institutions – as exemplified by the reports by the EP and the Council of Europe. One reason for this is that such practice completely collides with the notion of full compliance with international law. Such notion characterizes the stand of European countries and institutions in areas that range from support to the International Criminal Court, to the addition of a European Charter of Fundamental

Rights, to the related international convention to make respect of fundamental rights more binding (while not legally binding until incorporated in a revised European Constitution or Treaty). Also, the landscape of authorities, media, NGOs and public opinions within, as well as between European countries, is even more diverse than the diverse US landscape, and in no European country the paradigm of 'being at war' – used as a justification for such unlawful practice – is as strong as in the US during the Bush Administration.

What Lessons?

Paths of both convergence and divergence characterize transatlantic relations. Factors that shape such paths include the relative strength of the security frame, the degree of pluralism in the institutional settings, the centrality of rule of law and fundamental rights in the understanding of democracy, and the weight of closed intelligence versus broader knowledge sources in influencing public debate and policy choices.

Secure vs Securitarian Democracy

The wish to be and feel secure is socially broad-based and very rarely contested. However, diverse views emerge as to from whom or what an individual or a collectivity wishes to be secure. There is also the question of whether security is a precondition for, on equal footing as or only guaranteed by liberty. Another point, specific to measures taken on the ground of security, is whether they actually enhance security and whether their 'side effects' are proportional and justified. The ultimate question related to all the above is, who can have a say and decide on the matter?

With regard to the first point, it is worth noting that Article II-66 of EU Constitutional Treaty states 'Everyone has the right to liberty and security of person'. This means that they are both considered fundamental rights worth Constitutional guarantee. The historical and philosophical roots of the article take us to liberalism, where the person is meant to be free and secure from abuse of power by states. In depth philosophical inquiries have been devoted to these issues, including the different perspectives of 'classic' and 'modern' liberalism towards the role of state, and this chapter will not attempt to synthesize or add to them. The point relevant here is that the current political discourse on biometric identification, PNR and other surveillance processes – and even more in the case of renditions – tends to focus on the responsibility of governmental authorities to protect citizens from security threats coming from 'abroad' or 'other' entities such as terrorists (domestically or internationally organized). What that Constitutional article and philosophical tradition reminds us is that citizens may be or feel threatened not only by those non-state actors but also by the very governments who are pursuing security policies; therefore, safeguarding liberties, rights, rule of law can be seen as the basis for legitimate governmental action in the field of security in democratic societies. One could paraphrase Benjamin Franklin's statement 'They that can give up essential liberty to obtain a little temporary safety deserve neither liberty nor safety'[9] and consider that a democracy or community of democracies that would put security as its supreme goal – or 'securitarian democracy' – would seriously undermine its own functioning and normative basis. The debate on this is acute in the US, for example in connection with the cases of Guantanamo and Abu Graib – with media, politicians, NGOs and Courts addressing the issue of whether the US democracy is hampered by allowing torture and suspension of rights such as defence and fair trial – and is crucial for the EU also.

The EU is establishing itself as a 'security actor' going beyond its longstanding role of contributing to regional and global stability through economic cooperation. Biometrics can be seen as one of the areas where the EU is experimenting with 'soft' security measures (while possibly with hard implications) while starting to build military capacity, is following an endogenous path (a shown by the establishment of biometric requirements in EURODAC) while responding to external pressures (namely from the US following 9/11), is applying its established preference for global liberalization (for example by endorsing ICAO standards and the goal of global interoperability) and needs to face the accountability problems this involve (global surveillance being as a sensitive issue as terms of trade). In short, continuity and change are linked: the EU as a 'new' security actor may be no longer exclusively civilian but indicates a preference for civilian means – eventually initiated for other purposes – than military intervention in dealing with new security threats. The EU also continues to see itself as a guardian of a global, multilateral system – whether this means joining the US in pushing for ICAO standards on biometrics or facing them with regard to the role of the International Criminal Court or the UN Security Council. While the overarching commitment is clear, its implementation in the cases under examination indicates that different and not fully compatible priorities may be at stake.

Who decides what and how security threats must be tackled is a key aspect in the making and legitimacy of security policies in democratic polities. To take the first step, the identification of security threats can be problematic due to the secretiveness of major players in such identification – that is intelligence agencies. While secretiveness of intelligence is accepted and legally provided for in democratic settings, the boundaries of necessary secrecy and the ways of guaranteeing some forms of accountability are far from uncontroversial. Even assuming that threat identification is reliable – both in terms of quality insurance of the information gathered and related analysis, and of enough accountability being provided – the formulation of policy options is a second step that involves a broad range of actors as 'providers' and 'receivers' of different security measures. The key issues here are the procedures for inclusion or exclusion of those having a stake in the definition and selection of options, the relations between different institutions, and the related 'checks and balances'. This takes us to the discussed pluralism and its limits.

Limited Pluralism

The case discussion above led to an apparently counter-intuitive finding: a topic such as biometrics – which might appear *prima facie* as a good candidate for purely

---

9   In his Historical Review of Pennsylvania of 1759.

technocratic decision making, dominated by technical experts and fenced from democratic debate – is instead debated by parliaments, advocacy organizations and the media. The authoritative experts in the field are not only those with technical knowledge, but also those with knowledge of legal and social aspects. Also extraordinary renditions – in principle a secret programme intended to be carried out, by definition, without democratic scrutiny and debate – has been object of inquiry and discussion from NGOs, Parliaments, governments and media. In other words, a certain degree of pluralism can be observed that leads to some disclosure of unlawful practices as well as politicization of technologies like biometrics both in terms of their contribution to security needs and their implications for fundamental rights.

A qualification of the term 'certain degree of pluralism' is necessary. Indeed such pluralism is mainly confined to a diverse but relatively narrow elite – with some articles in the media reporting on biometrics, PNR or renditions, some statements by industry (due to the significant economic stakes involved in bursting the biometric market or in making sure that the PNR issue does not hamper the air transport sector), and some official and non-governmental attempts to steer public debate. Threat assessment is rarely a matter of debate; for instance, the European Security Strategy was only discussed at experts' workshops and in a few Parliaments of EU Member States, and media tend to report and eventually amplify threat assessments. They question it if there are experts providing counter-assessments as was the case concerning the WMD in Iraq before the war: their existence was claimed by the US, they were not found by the IAEA inspectors, and the suspicious death of British scientist David Kelly spurred debate on its relation with that issue. Another qualification regards the notion of pluralism and debate in the EU context: research on the development of a European public sphere alerts us that not all issues are likely to be 'Europeanized' and that while trans-national networks and events can foster debate by people across Europe on issues seen as European, it would be illusory (due to media structures, political cultures, and so on) to think of a European public sphere as disconnected from national arena for debate (for example Koopmans and Erbe 2004). With regard to biometrics and PNR, the issues are distinctly 'European' (in terms of EU-level decisions, and of joint European response to US initiatives) – with some 'variations on a theme' at national level. The national level comes out even more strongly in the case of extraordinary renditions, with the European framework as the key reference point.

Lively while rather narrow-based pluralism provides an explanation for the rather significant voicing of fundamental rights issues in contexts where the securitization frame is either dominant – as in the US during the Brush Administration – or very influential but 'diffused' by the still prevailing civilian discourse in the EU. In both contexts, surveillance technologies can be seen as a 'soft', mainly 'civilian', security measure; the case of biometrics and PNR specifically points to the paradox of an arguably 'soft' – basically, non military – security measure with potentially very 'hard' implications on fundamental rights. Here issues of proportionality, assessments on whether and how the measure actually helps combating terrorism, provision of legal safeguards and accountability procedures, review of errors and improvements in the application of surveillance technologies, pluralistic information and debate are crucial in making them overall relatively 'soft' or very 'hard'. The case of extraordinary rendition raises the issue of covert military operations being pursued through civilian facilities (planes, airports), in countries not at war, with the support of profiling and surveillance not submitted to democratic scrutiny and with significant impacts on fundamental rights.

Fundamental Rights, Rule of Law and Exceptions

The cases of biometrics and PNR illustrate the complex search of multiple compatibilities: enhancing security and safeguarding privacy and other fundamental rights, boosting the biometrics market or protecting the aviation sector and ensuring the accountability of public and private organizations handling sensitive data, guaranteeing non-discrimination between EU citizens and third country nationals and problems of reciprocity of measures.

The search for compatibility is well illustrated by the metaphor of 'balance'. This metaphor is widely used in legal and political discourse, and is based on two basic assumptions: that different policy goals and/or rights are comparable and relative rather than absolute, and that normally both (or more) of those should be guaranteed rather than having a zero-sum-game where one is completely abandoned in name of the other. This means that the metaphor does not apply when a policy goal or a right are considered as absolute. For example, according to the European Convention on Human Rights, the protection against torture is considered an absolute, fundamental right for which there can be no exceptions, while some derogation on ground of state security is permitted with regard to other rights such as fair trial or privacy. On the other hand, security goals have been invoked to justify exceptions even in the case of 'absolute' rights, such as the prohibition of torture; therefore, attention needs to be paid to the process that enables or forbids the undue resort to 'exceptionalism'. In short, we need to differentiate between exceptions provided *by* law, and exceptions *to* law; the first case poses important dilemmas, but it is the latter that radically challenges the rule of law as such and raises the issue of unconstraint power. Summing up, we can distinguish – following Nikiforos Diamandouros (European Ombudsman 2004) – substantive and procedural aspects of balancing, as well as ordinary and exceptional balancing. Surveillance technologies may have less dramatic impacts than direct resort to force – for example in terms of loss of lives, but they raise crucial issues nevertheless with regard to the process by which exceptions are granted, by whom, why, for how long.

In the case of measures such as biometric identification, the driving factor in 'setting the balance' is security – eventually linked with competitiveness, possibly the most important 'driver' in the EU. Fundamental rights are also strongly advocated and some of them (for example data protection) are provided for not only in the Charter but also in previous and binding Community law: they proved important in the decision to postpone the issue of a centralized database and are likely to influence – but very unlikely to prevent- future developments of biometric identification. The PNR case indicated how the sheer urgency and priority that characterize security discourses led to the attempt to find a quick 'fix' of accountability procedures and to the EP appeal to the ECJ and the subsequent ruling concerning the wrong choice of legal basis. Extraordinary renditions go much further by infringing both democratic process and substantive fundamental rights – among them, the prohibition of torture for which no exception is granted by law and thus can only be pursued as an exception to law.

Exceptions granted *by* law pose serious enough problems in national law contexts in terms of the proper working of checks and balances to assure – among other aspects – that proper safeguards against abuse of fundamental rights and clear time limits are respected by executives and law enforcement agencies. The matter takes specific features in the EU context due to the fact that measures taken in the second and third 'pillar' are not rooted in Community law, the non-binding nature of the Charter of Fundamental Rights, as well as the diversity of judicial systems and related issues concerning mutual recognition. These aspects could facilitate intentional or unintentional exceptions *to* law, for example concerning the rightful legislative procedure (the European Parliament resort to the European Court of Justice on the PNR case being an illustration of such type of concerns) or the infringement of fundamental rights in the case of renditions. In the US context, the ruling of the Supreme Court *Rasul vs Bush* on the right of Guantanamo prisoners to accede to trial was a landmark in the re-establishment of limits to a seemingly unconstrained state power.

Democratize Expertise, Expertise Democracy

One of the factors that may facilitate abuse of power is the concentration of knowledge and its fencing from contestation and verification. As persuasively argued by Kaufmann (2004), the inflation of threat before the Iraq War can be interpreted as a failure of the 'marketplace of ideas', a market that should weed out unfounded, mendacious, or self-serving arguments.

Indeed knowing what one is talking about is usually considered a precondition for his or her credibility and surely being able to master some 'basics' and/or also the more complex technological, legal and other issues pertaining to biometrics, PNR or threat assessment is a pre-requisite for being able to participate in the policy debate concerning their robustness, usefulness, suitability and impacts. Expertise in these fields is still quite narrowly based in some technological communities, plus some practical expertise (for example of border guards, police, airport personnel) and secret intelligence. However a broadening of expertise on surveillance technologies and their implications, and also on threat assessment is taking place, adding legal, social and institutional expertise to the technical one, with critical perspectives being developed within the expert communities and 'counter-expertise' being provided by non-governmental organizations. This broadening could allow a 'democratization of expertise',[10] in the sense of pluralistic and open debate, and quality control, on the knowledge available, and mitigate the risk of unaccountable and secretive 'guardianship'.

In turn the democratization of expertise can enhance the 'intelligence of democracy', a term used by Charles Lindblom (1965) in connection with his incrementalist analysis of policy making. While different in its focus on how to

---

10 European Commission 2001b, Liberatore and Funtowicz 2003.

distribute and diffuse expertise to inform public debate and legislative bodies, the notion of 'expertising democracy' shares with the 'intelligence of democracy' the fact that they offer a way of coming to terms with the complexity of decisions at stake by incorporating a plurality of knowledge sources and their confrontation. An interesting and actual example of expertising democracy are some institutions such as the Parliamentary offices for the assessment of science and technology options; some of these offices intervened quite early and competently in discussing the features and the pros and cons of biometric identification and are intervening on issues such as data retention, DNA databases and so on. Similarly, data protection authorities appear among the authoritative sources of knowledge to advise democratic institutions in the field of biometrics, PNR and other technological applications.

These examples point, in turn, to different stages and types of accountability. Borrowing from Philippe Schmitter (2003) these include ex-ante and ex-post parliamentary oversight, as well as vertical (rulers to parliaments to citizens) and horizontal (checks-and-balances model) forms of accountability. Parliamentary offices, data protection authorities, internet consultations, and so on are mainly resorted to in the ex-ante stage, but could be usefully mobilized also in the ex-post stage to evaluate policy performance; in addition, they could assist both vertical and horizontal accountability by enhancing the expertise of citizens, representative institutions, executives and judiciary. This can only work, however, on the premise of genuine commitment to accountability, including in cases of emergency and the pursuit of security.

Conclusions and Perspectives

The analysis offered in this contribution leads to two main conclusions.

Firstly, transatlantic cooperation is characterized by both convergence and divergence. Convergence in relation to the commitment to massive surveillance as a perceived suitable measure to fight terrorism (and –at the same time– enhance some business sectors) which costs in terms of privacy and integrity are considered proportionate to the stated security objectives. Divergence is to be noted with regard to the resort to force, the belief in unilateral action and the endorsement of practices like extraordinary renditions as governmental policies by the US Administration versus the commitment to multilateralism and international rule of law and the preference for civilian means in the EU context, with however an ambiguous stance on fundamental rights as indicated by some collusion on extraordinary renditions.

Secondly, the relations between security and democracy are not to be taken for granted. When torture is allowed by military troops or police of democratic countries it is clear that democracy is not in good health; similarly when exceptions tend to become the rule, the very core of rule of law is jeopardized. The largely used metaphor of the balance in the EU context leaves open where the balance tips, and the cases discussed above show that significant costs in terms of privacy and possibly other rights are seen as acceptable. At the same time, it is good to hear from a representative of Homeland Security that there is no matter of balancing liberty and security because liberty is paramount (personal conversation during a conference in Brussels), but many practices post 9/11 point to the strong dominance of security objectives and discourses in the US while with significant debate due to the pluralistic feature of the American society.

In terms of future perspectives, some points of attention need to be considered.

Firstly, the infringement of fundamental rights by democratic countries call into question the their very normative/value basis, possibly their internal social cohesion (with certain social groups submitted to profiling, stereotyping and discrimination on ethnic, religious or other ground), and also their credibility in the eyes of people outside –eventually in those countries where democracy should be 'promoted', let alone imposed. The role of international human rights law and criminal justice need to be strengthened to allow for international – on top of national – rule of law to be applied, and exceptions or abuses limited or punished.

Secondly, multipurpose measures and technologies can be useful and justified in some case – for example to assist victims in cases of human-made as well as natural disasters. However massive surveillance intended to fight terrorism – and eventually illegal migration or trafficking – raises question about its effectiveness (will biometrics really deter skilled terrorist or *mafiosi?*) and side effects (how many bona fide travellers are avoiding to travel to the US to avoid the complex checks?). Pervasive surveillance is a quite sensitive and controversial issue in democratic societies as indicated by the popularity of the novel by Orwell *1984*, the literature on Foucault's conceptualization of social control,[11] or the public and media attention devoted to the *Echelon* case.[12]

Thirdly, and related to the previous, the paradox of surveillance technologies needs to be addressed. Surveillance techniques such as census and civil registration developed as means of granting civil rights and, at the same time, as potential means for states to gain informational power over citizens. This paradoxical character is retained with globalization (Lyon 1994), leading to unprecedented surveillance capacities by public and private actors at global scale, and this needs to be regulated accordingly.

---

11 In Orwell's novel *1984*, the world is divided into three countries that include the entire globe: Oceania, Eurasia, and Eastasia. Oceania, and both of the others, is a totalitarian society led by Big Brother, which censors everyone's behaviour and thoughts. Concerning diverse perspectives on Foucault's work – especially *Surveiller et punir '(1975)*, translated in English as 'Discipline and punish' – see, Lianos 2003, Mathiesen 1980.

12 In December 1997 a report on *An Appraisal of the Technologies of Political Control* (European Parliament 1997) was presented to the STOA -Scientific and Technological Options Assessment – Panel of the EP. The report addressed various technologies: closed circuit television networks, vehicle recognition systems, bugging and tapping devices, national and international communication interception networks. The latter received most attention by MEP and media, especially in connection with Echelon, a US/UK surveillance system comprising the activities of intelligence agencies such as CIA in the US and MI6 in UK. The system had been uncovered already in the 1970s by researchers in UK but only in 1997 public attention was raised to the fact that non-military targets such as governments and business were subject to electronic spying in virtually every country. Echelon possibly benefited the US in crucial trade negotiations with the EU.

Fourthly, security tends to be an area where 'knowledge is power' in its basic sense of potentially excluding those outside intelligence circles, and also one where mistakes in analysis can cost lives as well as other tangible and intangible assets. It is thus reasonable to argue that security is an area where democratizing expertise and having a working marketplace of ideas is of paramount importance.

Finally, some implications for the international order should be considered. A more stable international order can be expected through an increased convergence between the EU and the US, for example in terms of setting of international standards and strengthening the related international networks and institutions. But such order will only be legitimate if international law and protection of fundamental rights are taken seriously. In particular, the application of double standards in protecting such rights (for example by the US or EU governments towards their own citizens and towards other people within or outside their territory) or in complying with international agreements and conventions (including the Geneva Conventions, the UN resolutions on the Middle East, and so on) would make the international order be normatively contradictory. In turn, this could make it also less effective – rather than being the price to be paid to effectiveness; anyone could indeed free-ride from basic norms that should underlie international order and cooperation if the US or Europe do so, and nobody – including the very international institutions that can hardly work without major countries' contribution – would appear as credible guarantors of such norms. In short, increased transatlantic convergence cannot afford being purely instrumental to security (and economic) considerations. In this regard it can be argued that 'speaking truth to friends' – including powerful friends – is a crucial aspect of international cooperation in general and of transatlantic relations in particular; it is an ingredient of mutual and cumulative monitoring of the state of democracy and – eventually – of its further consolidation and diffusion.

Acknowledgments

Thanks to Peter Burgess, Christine Chwaszcza, Kyriacos Revelas, Yannis Stivachtis and Mario Telò for useful comments.

References

Barber, Benjamin (2003), *Fear's Empire: War, terrorism and Democracy* (New York, London: W.W. Norton & Company).

Brodeur, Jean Paul *et al.* (eds) (2003), *Democracy, Law and Security: Internal Security Services in Contemporary Europe* (Aldershot: Ashgate Publishing).

Chryssochoou, Dimitris (1998), *Democracy in the European Union* (London: Taurus Academic Studies).

Council of Europe (2006), Committee on Legal Affairs and Human Rights, Alleged secret detentions and unlawful inter-state transfers involving Council of Europe member states, 7/6/2006.

Council of the EU (2005), Press Release 6228/05.

Dahl, Robert (1985), *Controlling Nuclear Weapons: Democracy versus Guardianship* (Syracuse: Syracuse University Press).

Data Protection WP (2004), *Opinion 7/2004 on the inclusion of biometric elements in residence permits and visas taking account of the establishment of the European information system on visas.*

De Vries, Gijs (2004), Terrorism, Islam and Democracy, EurActiv, http://www.euractiv.com/en/justice/gijs-vries-terrorism-islam-democracy/article-136245.

Dewerpe, Alain (1994), *Espion. Une anthropologie historique du secret d'etait contemporain* (Paris: Gallimard).

EC (2004), *Council Regulation on standards for security features and biometrics in passports and travel documents issued by Member States* EC n.2252/2004, OJ L 385/1 of 29.12.2004.

EC (1995) *Directive 95/46/EC on the protection of individuals with regard to the processing of personal data and on the free movement of such data* of 24 October 1995, OJ N L281, 23.11.95

European Commission (2006) –Newsroom 16 June 2006 –The Commission adopts two initiatives to comply with the ruling of the ECJ on the transfer of PNR to the US.

European Commission (2004), COM (2004) 116 final, 'Proposal for a Council Regulation on standards for security features and biometrics in EU citizens' passports.

European Commission (2004), COM (2004) 190 final, Draft Decision on adequate protection of personal data contained in the PNR, 17 March 2004.

European Commission (2001), Report of the working group *'Democratizing expertise and establishing scientific reference systems'*, in preparation of the White Paper on Governance, Brussels: http://europa.eu.int/comm/governance/areas/index_en.htm (accessed 16/5/2005).

European Council (2004a), *Declaration on Combating Terrorism*, http://ue.eu.int/ueDocs/cms_Data/docs/pressData/en/ec/79637.pdf (accessed 16.5.2006).

European Council (2004b), *The Hague Programme. Strengthening freedom, security and justice in the EU*,http://europa.eu.int/comm/justice_home/news/information_dossiers/the_hague_priorities/doc/hague_programme_en.pdf (accessed 16/5/2006).

European Council (2003a), *A secure Europe in a better world – the European security strategy*, http://ue.eu.int/cms3_fo/showPage.ASP?id=266&lang=EN&mode=g (accessed 16.5.2006).

European Council (2003b), Council Conclusions, Thessaloniki: http://ue.eu.int/ueDocs/cms_Data/docs/pressData/en/ec/76279.pdf (accessed 16/05/2006).

ECJ (2006), Judgement of the Court of Justice in Joined Cases C-317/04 and C-318/04.

ECJ (2005), Opinion of Advocate General Lèger, delivered on 22/11/2005, Case C-317/04 Eureopan Parliament v Council of the European Union and Case C-138/04 European Parliament vs European Commission.

European Ombudsman (2004), *Balancing the obligations of citizenship with the recognition of individual rights and responsibilities – the role of the Ombudsman*, <http://www.euro-ombudsman.eu.int/speeches/en/2004-09-09.htm>.

European Parliament (2006), Draft Interim Report on the alleged use of European countries by CIA for the transport and illegal detention of prisoners, 2006/2027 (INI).

European Parliament (2004a), *Report on the Commission's proposal for a regulation amending regulation laying down uniform format for visa and residence permits*, by C.Coelho A6-0029-2004.

European Parliament (2004b), *Report on the Commission's Proposal for a regulation on standards for security features and biometrics in EU citizens passports*, by C.Coelho A6-0028/2004.

European Parliament (2004c), Report by MEP Johanna Boogerd-Quaak, A-0271/2004.

European Parliament (1997), *An Appraisal of the Technologies of Political Control*, STOA PE 1666.499.

EUROPOL (2006a), Organized Crime Threat Assessment, http://www.europol. eu.int/publications/OCTA/OCTA2006.pdf.

EUROPOL (2006b), Overview of Counter-Terrorism activities 2006 http://www. europol.eu.int/publications/SeriousCrimeOverviews/2005/overview_SC5. pdf.

EUROPOL (2005), published by Statewatch, Terrorist activity in the EU: Situation and Trends Report 2004–2005, http://www.poptel.co.uk/statewatch/news/2006/ may/europol-terr-rep-2004–2005.pdf.

Furedi, Frank (2002), *Culture of Fear: Risk Taking and the Morality of Low Expectation* (London: Continuum Int. Publishing Group).

Harty, Maura (2005), 'US Visa Policy: Securing Borders and Opening Doors', in *The Washington Quarterly*, Spring 2005, 28: 2, 23–43.

Kaufmann, Chaim (2004), *Threat Inflation and the Failure of the Marketplace of Ideas*, International Security, 29: 1, 5–48.

Kohler-Koch, Beate and Eising Rainer (1999), *The Transformation of governance in the European Union* (London-New York: Routledge).

Koopmans, Ruud and Erbe, Jessica (2004), 'Towards a European Public Sphere? Vertical and horizontal dimensions of Europeanized political communication', *Innovation*, 17, 97–118.

Koslowsky, Rey (2005), 'Toward Virtual Borders: Expanding European Border Control Policy Initiatives and Technology Implementations, paper at the Conference', *An Immigration Policy for Europe?*, NYU Florence and RSCAS, March 13–15.

Laffan, Brigid, O'Donnell, Rory and Smith, Michael (2000), *Europe's Experimental Union. Rethinking integration* (London-New York: Routledge).

Lianos, Michalis (2003), 'Social Control after Foucault', *Surveillance & Society* 1: 3, 421–30.

Liberatore, Angela (2004), 'Governance and democracy: reflections on the European debate', in *Good Governance, Democratic Societies and Globalization*, edited by S. Munshi and B.P. Abraham (New Delhi: Sage).

Liberatore, Angela and Funtowicz, Silvio (eds) (2003), 'Democratizing expertise, expertising democracy', Special Issue of *Science and Public Policy* 30: 2, June 2003.

Lindblom, Charles (1965), *The Intelligence of Democracy: Decision making through mutual adjustment* (New York: The Free Press).

Lipchutz Ronnie (ed.) (1995), *On Security* (New York, Columbia University Press).

Lyon, David (2004), 'Globalizing Surveillance. Comparative and Sociological Perspectives', *International Sociology* 19: 2, 135–49.

Nelson, Lisa (2004), 'The Making of Policy: Biometrics, Privacy and Anonymity', *Chicago Policy Review* 8: 1, 19–36.

Nomikos, John (2004), 'European Union Intelligence Agency: a necessary institution for Common Intelligence Policy?', in V. Koutrakou (ed.), *Contemporary Issues and Debates in EU Policy: The EU and International Relations* (Manchester: University Press).

Rothschild, Emma (1995), 'What is Security?', *Daedalus* 124: 3, 53–98.

Sandel, Michael (ed.) (1984), *Liberalism and its Critics* (Oxford: Blackwell).

Schmitter, Philippe (2003), 'The Quality of Democracy: The Ambiguous Virtues of Accountability', <http://www.iue.it/SPS/People/Faculty/CurrentProfessors/PDFFiles/SchmitterPDFfiles/Accountability.pdf>.

Sjursen, Helene (2003), *Security and Defence*, ARENA Working paper 10/03.

Solana, Javier (2004), 'Terrorism and Intelligence Co-Operation', <http://europa-eu-un.org/articles/en/article_3558_en.htm>.

Telò, Mario (2006), *Europe: A Civilian Power?* (Palgrave: Macmillan).

The White House (2002), The National Security Strategy of the United Sates of America, Washington.

Wallace, Helen and Wallace, William (eds) (2000), *Policy-Making in the European Union* (New York: Oxford University Press).

Chapter 8

Transatlantic Intelligence Cooperation, the Global War on Terrorism, and International Order

John M. Nomikos

The end of the Cold War more than a decade ago created a world in which the relative stability between the two superpowers has disappeared. During the Cold War, a country's every action was conducted in the light of the adversary relationship between the United States and the Soviet Union. The cataclysmic changes that took place in Central and Eastern Europe inevitably changed the face of politics in Europe and in the Western world as a whole. The civil war in Yugoslavia was, and continues to be, the first case of ethnic conflict in Europe in the post-Cold War order.

On 11 September 2001 (9/11), the international community was introduced to a new type of terrorism, one that was truly global in its organization and its impact. In both the European Union (EU) and the United States (US), it was immediately clear that an effective response would require new levels of cooperation across the Atlantic and around the world. The post 11 September 2001 era has challenged governments, policymakers, religious leaders, the media and the general public to play both critical and constructive roles in the war against global terrorism (Nomikos 2005, 191). The process must be a joint transatlantic partnership which emphasizes shared beliefs, values, and interests; addresses more constructively the differences and grievances; and builds a future upon the recognition that all face a common enemy, one that can be effectively contained and eliminated only through a recognition of mutual interests and the use of multilateral alliances, strategies, and action.

The purpose of the chapter is to identify the relevance of global terrorism as a new threat both to national security and to international peace and security. A multitude of specific transatlantic initiatives, to protect everything from cargo to infrastructure, have gone from mere ideas to being operational programs in the US as well as in the European Union Member States. At the same time, entire new bureaucracies in US, such as Department of Homeland Security (DHS) and the Transportation Security Administration, have emerged into large functioning organizations. The argument of this chapter is that the focus needs to be on speeding up means of practical exchange on operational matters, not on building elaborate new structures in the EU and US. Moreover, the sense of urgency generated by the terrorist acts in New York, Madrid and London is accelerating measures that will have important consequences for wider transatlantic intelligence cooperation against drugs, organized crime, people trafficking, border security, terrorist financing and other security issues. But equally important was the decision by both the European Union and the United States to boost the capacity of their domestic law enforcement agencies (Europol, FBI, DHS) and judiciary (US Department of Justice, Eurojust) to respond to global terrorism and to look for ways to cooperate in counterterrorism policies regardless of their own differences in processing intelligence-sharing among the EU Member States and the US. This chapter also focuses on the significance of the EU mechanism such as Europol and the Situation Center, which are intended to build intra European cooperation in law enforcement, and it goes further to point out the necessity of an EU Intelligence Service similar to the Central Intelligence Agency in US as a necessary tool for transatlantic intelligence sharing cooperation in order to combat prospective international terrorist acts. Today, it is almost impossible for a nation state to deal with terrorism alone, regardless of the efficiency of its intelligence service, without international cooperation with other intelligence services. Finally, this chapter concludes with the strategic role of the military intelligence using NATO capabilities to deal with global terrorism. NATO patrols in the eastern Mediterranean have increasingly become an information and intelligence-based operation through the sharing of data gathered at sea by NATO allies and Mediterranean-rim countries. The level of military intelligence achieved to date provides a sound formation upon which to build in the future. The international dimension of intelligence fits the modern patterns of increased international specialist contacts necessary for preventing terrorist acts in the 21st century.

Post 9/11 Transatlantic Partnership in Counterterrorism Cooperation

After 9/11, Western nations were left with no choice but to closely cooperate in terms of intelligence, know how and even sometimes procedures. But this is without doubt one of the most difficult areas for cooperation between nations (Guitta 2006, 1–5). Indeed, in order to be effective, this cooperation must be very discreet, often touching on sensitive, 'sovereign' areas like intelligence and justice. Most importantly, collaboration must also focus on operational issues – such as on how to prevent terrorist attacks in the planning process.

Transatlantic partnerships on counterterrorism have improved tremendously since the 11 September attacks. Certain individual partnerships are flourishing and there is reason to be optimistic that many European nations and United States will continue to enjoy long-term alliances, based on reciprocal approaches to security matters. In 2003, the US State Department reported on Patterns of Global Terrorism by stating:[1]

> European nations worked in close partnership with the United States in the global counter terrorism campaign and have continued to strengthen their legal and administrative ability to take action against terrorists and their supporters, including freezing their assets. The contributions of European countries in sharing intelligence, arresting members of terrorist

---

1   Read the US Department of State Report on Patterns of Global Terrorism 2003 at http://www.state.gov/s/ct/rls/pgtrpt/2003.

cells, and interdicting terrorist financing and logistics continued to be vital elements in the war on terrorism

The European Union as a whole also has been a useful ally in some areas in the war on terror. As US Secretary of State Condoleezza Rice noted that 'all countries benefit from US intelligence gathering and counterterrorism measures, because US is not the sole target of Islamic extremism'. Having experienced devastating attacks in Madrid (11 March 2004) and London (7 July 2005), the European Union has awakened to the fact that financial networks are often a terrorist's key asset. In several communiqués since then, the European Commission has proposed measures to stop terrorists from gaining access to financial resources. Similarly, the European Commission stated that Member States are the best intelligence gatherers for this information, but for this information to be used effectively, it must be shared among European Union partners and followed up on more thoroughly.[2]

Furthermore, the European Commission has called for greater transparency in the non-profit sector, which is often used by terrorists to acquire and funnel funding for their operations. This approach also has the endorsement of the European Court of Justice, which ruled in September 2005 that the European Union legally has the power to freeze suspected terrorists' assets, in response to a challenge by defendants in Sweden whose funds were frozen in 2001. While only time will tell whether all this 'action' amounts to real change or effective results, the European Union is finally showing a more cooperative side to the United States (Guitta 2006, 2).

European Union: From Coordinator to Actor in Counterterrorism?

Since the Madrid and London bombings, the European Union has had mixed results in improving counterterrorism policies. It has made some progress in encouraging governments to improve their police and judicial cooperation, and to review how they should collectively respond to emergencies and protect critical infrastructure from terrorist attacks. But national police often collaborate with their peers in other countries on an informal basis, rather than through European Union channels.[3] In addition, the European Union's focus has been mainly on internal law enforcement policies; but international cooperation is crucial in the fight against terrorism, and there is considerable scope for the European Union to make counterterrorism more of a priority for its foreign policy.

However, there is a paradox in the European Union's role in counterterrorism. On the one hand, the governments agree in principle that cooperation at the European level is a good thing because of the cross-border nature of the terrorist threat. On the

---

2 Read the Report on EU Response to London Bombings adopted by extraordinary Council meeting at Justice and Home Affairs, (13 July 2005) at the European Council (25 March 2004) and Council Document – Plan of Action on Combating Terrorism 10586/04 of 15 June 2004.

3 Read the European Union's role in counter-terrorism coordination and action, Strategic Comments, Vol. 11, Issue 2, International Institute for Strategic Studies, March 2005, pp: 1–2.

other, they are slow to give the European Union the powers (such as investigation and prosecution) and resources (such as intelligent agents and money) it would need to be truly effective. This is because security policy – especially protecting citizens – goes to the core of national sovereignty, and governments are reluctant to give the European Union powers that could interfere with their existing laws and national security practices. Currently, the European Union coordinates national anti-terrorism policies rather than pursuing its own.[4]

Finally, the terrorist attack in Madrid on 11 March 2004, produced a new level of urgency in the EU's efforts against terrorism. The Commission decided to appoint Gijs de Vries as the EU Counter Terrorism Coordinator to maintain an overview of all the instruments at the Union's disposal in the fight against terrorism (EU Council, Report on Terrorism 2004).

Furthermore, Americans are right to point out the differences in ideology, tactics and weaponry between al-Qaeda style terrorists (Keohane 2005, 1–38) and long standing European terror groups. It is also true that, until the terrorist attacks in Europe, the only EU state that had much previous experience of Islamist terrorist activity was France. However, even though there are sometimes differences in emphasis, both the American and European methods mix judicial, police, diplomatic and military means with a long-term political approach to tackling terrorism. The real difference between Europeans and Americans is that the United States has mainly chosen to fight its war on terror abroad, whereas the Europeans have focused primarily on the threat at home.

Transatlantic Attitudes and Differences towards Counterterrorism Policies

Despite the differences in American and European attitudes, counterterrorism cooperation across the Atlantic is very strong. US officials state that they are happy with the assistance they have received from European capitals – especially from Paris – in sharing information on al-Qaeda cells. The German government has even allowed a US prosecutor and some FBI agents to carry out investigations with a German federal prosecutor across Germany (Keohane 2005, 1–38). The US not only works with EU governments, but also with EU bodies. In the past year, the US and the EU have signed numerous agreements on sharing airline passenger data, screening shipping cargoes, and on procedures for extraditing terrorist suspects, and the US Department of Homeland Security has sent an attaché to the US delegation in Brussels.

Container Security Initiative (CSI)

Aside from these issues of implementation, there have also been some difficult disputes over specific matters. At times, these have seemed to threaten the overall atmosphere of cooperation, but there has usually been a shared determination to find some sort of resolution, even if only temporary. The two most notable issues that

---

4   Ibid., op. cit.: pp. 1–2.

have caused tensions in transatlantic cooperation against terrorism are the 'Container Security Initiative' and Passenger Name Records (PNR).

The Container Security Initiative (CSI) by the US Customs Service (which later became part of the Department of Homeland Security) in January 2002, allowed containers that had been pre-screened at foreign ports to have priority in unloading at US ports. The US government soon began negotiations with countries with major ports over the required equipment and procedures, including the stationing of US Customs officials at those ports (Aaron 2004, 8–12). As these bilateral talks proceeded with EU Member States (France and the Netherlands), the European Commission voiced objections, arguing that ports participating in CSI would have unfair competitive advantages over other ports; this would distort trade and was contrary to the EU Single Market. Nevertheless, in January 2003, the European Commission initiated legal action against EU Member States participating in the CSI, eventually eight Member States. A few months later, negotiations began between the US Customs Service and the European Commission Directorate for Taxation and Customs Union. A new bilateral agreement was reached after only eight months and finalized in March 2004. The previous bilateral agreements between the United States and the European Union Member States were subsumed under this new arrangement, and implementation of the screening and inspection procedures began.

Passenger Name Records (PNR)

The Passenger Name Records dispute originated, like CSI, in a desire to enhance screening and make transport more secure, although this time it required information about airline passengers rather than shipping containers. Under the Aviation and Transportation Security Act of 2001, the US government began to require airlines flying into the Unites States to provide certain information on all passengers before landing (Aaron 2004, 9). The Advance Passenger Information System (APIS) collected information from each passenger's reservation (the PNR), including name, address, date of birth, and payments details. The information varied according to what was required by each reservation system. By supplying this information, however, European carriers allegedly put themselves in violation of the European Union's privacy directive, which maintains strict controls over how private companies may maintain and share information on individual customers. European companies thus faced either fines in the United States or fines in Europe. After considerable difficulty, the Department of Home Security in the US and the European Commission managed to reach an agreement in principle that allowed data to be collected without violating the privacy directive. A final agreement between the US and EU was signed in May 2004.

Terrorist Financing List and Hizbollah

It is often observed that Europeans are far less convinced about terrorism as a fundamental and global threat than are American leaders and citizens. Since the 2001 attacks, European leaders have made clear repeatedly that the fight against global terrorism is a top priority. Following the attacks in Madrid and London and the revelation that these were perpetrated by al-Qaeda, (Aaron 2004, 11) the importance of global terrorism has escalated in European eyes. But European and US approaches do differ in their judgments as to the most appropriate and effective response; and as to whether the overall strategy in responding to terrorism should be one of war-fighting or risk management.[5] The initial US response to 11 September was military in nature – the invasion of Afghanistan and the toppling of the Taliban. A more comprehensive approach involving law enforcement quickly developed, as demonstrated by the speedy passage of the US Patriot Act, but responding to global terrorism has continued to be a high priority mission for the US military. The emphasis on a military response has been reinforced by the war in Iraq, which has been justified in part as an element in the war on global terrorism.

In the European Union Member States, terrorism is first and foremost a crime, which can best be addressed by crime-fighting procedures and tools, rather than overt military methods. In addition to traditional law enforcement methods, a number of EU Member States (including Britain, France, Spain, and Italy) have had special procedures for terrorist investigations and prosecutions, including permitting lengthy detentions). Responding to global terrorist networks requires greater emphasis on cross border collaboration, especially in sharing information and collaborating on investigations and eventual prosecutions.[6] Although some European counter-terrorist units and specialist police forces can certainly be considered para-military, the overall orientation is far more weighted toward law enforcement as the appropriate response to terrorism rather than action by military forces. One result of this difference in US and European approaches has been a disconnect over the potential role of NATO in fighting global terrorism. While some US policymakers see NATO as having role in assisting coordinate military training and doctrines relevant for fighting global terrorism, many Europeans greet such suggestions with skepticism – not surprisingly given their doubt about a military response to terrorism generally.

Secret Intelligence Services, State Sovereignty and Global Terrorism

The leading elements in the effort to counter terrorism are the most secret. These are the civilian intelligence and security services of the larger states in North American and Europe. Secret intelligence exchange between these organizations is a world within a world, governed by its own diplomacy and characterized by elaborate agreements, understandings and treaties (Aldrich 2004, 731–53). The main substance of these agreements focuses upon the security of intelligence rather than intelligence exchange itself, and reflects concern over how that intelligence will be circulated

---

5　Many European experts view terrorism as a risk that can be managed through a combination of law enforcement techniques, political negotiation, and selective-limited military action. Most of US political leaders have regarded terrorism as a topic of the utmost daily urgency since September 2001. The stated goal has been to eradicate terrorism, not manage it, and the threat of imminent danger – of being truly at war – has given rise to a willingness to bend the normal rules in order to protect the country.

6　Ibid., op. cit.: p. 12.

within each national system. This, in turn, fosters an attitude of intense caution towards the idea of sharing, and especially towards multilateral sharing. Moreover, in the US and Europe, secret intelligence services are often close to the core executive and so associated with ideas of sovereignty. States will happily place some of their military forces under allied command, but hesitate to act similarly in the area of intelligence, where coordination rather than control is the most they will accept. This resistance to the multilateral pooling of very sensitive data, on security grounds and wider concerns about sovereignty, will prevent both an unhealthy agglomeration of secret data (Aldrich 2004, 737) and the rise of a federal super secret service. What we are seeing instead is a focused effort to cooperate more quickly on specific cases or to exchange limited data more effectively.

The most remarkable example of cooperation is the English-speaking effort in the realm of signals intelligence (SIGINT) known as UKUSA. Sharing in this realm between the US, the UK, Australia and Canada is so complete that national product is often indistinguishable (Andrew 1994, 95–109). But this is an Anglo-Saxon rather than a transatlantic partnership; moreover, the institutional linkage between UKUSA and continental European states has diminished, rather than grown, over the last decade. The United States has withdrawn some SIGINT assets from Germany and relocated them within the UK. The Netherlands have advocated a stronger national SIGINT (Jane Intelligence Review 2003) capability after a disappointing experience with multinational sharing in the Balkan states.

Unsurprisingly, intelligence cooperation is partly building confidence and the time line is necessarily long. Western security services have often developed their associations for decades and these are now growing in importance. These security networks exchange less sensitive data, background studies, scenario analyses and policy views.

Past and Present Intelligence Sharing Networks: 'Kilowatt, Megatonne and the Berne Club'

The war against international terrorism in the 1970s brought about two more institutionalized multilateral cooperation frameworks, Kilowatt and Megatonne.

Kilowat and Megatonne Networks

Kilowatt was the code-name for multilateral intelligence cooperation efforts among European states aimed at expanding the exchange of information in the fight against global terrorism (Nomikos 2005, 03–112). Kilowatt was the first truly European intelligence forum, comprising representatives of intelligence services from the UK, France, West Germany, Italy, Belgium, the Netherlands, Switzerland, Denmark, Ireland, Norway, and Israel. Megatonne intelligence network reported as a network for sharing intelligence on the activities of radical terrorists in Europe. Megatonne was sponsored by France and aimed mainly at countering the threat of Islamic Algerian terrorists on the European mainland, activities that escalated in the early 1990s.

The Berne Club

The Berne Club is a cooperation framework among Western European internal security services. It is based on periodic meetings attended by the heads of relevant security services, including the German BfV, the British MI5, the French internal security services (DST) and the Swedish SAPO. It now numbers 17 members, the most recent adherent being the Greek intelligence service (NIS-EYP). The Berne Club operates in an informal way, with meetings being conducted in different locations and organized by each country in turn (Shpiro 1995, 1–21). In recent years, meetings by the Berne Club have dealt with a range of internal security issues, including global terrorism, illegal immigration, and cross border forms of organized crime. Berne Club has analysed past and present European intelligence cooperation framework.

Little publicity has been given to successful European security intelligence cooperation immediately preceding 9/11. In early 2001, intelligence indicators suggested that Osama bin Laden was planning a campaign of bomb attacks in Europe. Based on a well-functioning international exchange of information among the major security and intelligence services in Europe, a number of successful operations against persons within the bin Laden network were launched (Aldrich 2004, 738). By mid-April 2001, a total of eighteen individuals had been apprehended in a series of coordinated operations across Europe. During some of these, weapons and chemical intended for the manufacture of explosives were seized. In other words, the long-established Berne Group was functioning fairly well.

However, the Berne Group is not transatlantic and the US is not a member. Accordingly, following 9/11 the Berne Group created a new organization called the Counter-terrorist Group (CTG). This is a separate body with a wider membership of European Union (EU) intelligence and security services, (Aldrich 2004, 739) together with the US, Switzerland and Norway. The first meeting was held in November 2001 at the Hague and was chaired by the Belgian security service. The main product of this group is a common threat assessment in the field of Islamic terrorism. Although CTG is not an EU organization and reports through national security services to each capital, the national chair of CTG rotates in synchronization with the EU presidency and its threat analyses are made available to some high-level EU committees. During 2002 and 2003, CTG devoted considerable energy to institutional matters and the problems of multilateral data exchange. CTG does not have a geographical headquarters, but is probably the most important focus of day-to-day cooperation. At its meeting in Switzerland on 21 April 2004, the Berne Group decided that CTG should play the major role in implementing intelligence-related aspects (Aldrich 2004, 739) of the European Council's Declaration on Combating Terrorism that followed the attack on Madrid.

Similarly, the US intelligence community has long been noted for its lack of communal identity. Ingrained reluctance to share, together with incompatible data systems, was a key factor in explaining intelligence problems preceding 9/11. Washington has sought to counter this problem by the establishment of the Terrorist Threat Integration Center (TTIC). Created in May 2003 to remedy the failure of US intelligence and law-enforcement agencies to communicate, the TTIC is an analytic center (Aldrich 2004, 741) tasked with collating data from more than a dozen American intelligence agencies and since June 2004 has enjoyed its own independent headquarters in Washington DC. However, the Central Intelligence Agency retains its own rival Counterterrorism Center, while the Department of Defense likes neither.

European Union Intelligence Service: A Necessary Institution for Transatlantic Intelligence Cooperation

The tentative European intelligence cooperation that developed during the 1990s fell short of a common policy necessary for an effective Common Foreign and Security Policy (CFSP) and autonomous defense capability. European intelligence cooperation to date has been hampered by emphasizing national sovereignty over sharing intelligence. Institutional obstacles also stand in the way of increased intelligence cooperation (Nomikos 2005, 191–203). Intelligence organizations generally believe that no other organization's analysis is as reliable as their own, which leads them to place more faith and confidence in their own work. These organizations also tend to view International Relations as a zero-sum game, and may not agree with a cooperative approach to security and defense integration.

The Treaty of Maastricht negotiated by the European Union in 1991 helped set the agenda, establishing as EU objectives the implementation of a Common Foreign and Security Policy as well as the eventual framing of a Common Defense Policy. No means were established to implement a CFSP, however, nor did the Treaty of Maastricht (Nomikos 2005, 197–98) make any specific mention of increasing intelligence cooperation with the CFSP framework. The Persian Gulf and Yugoslavia crises proved more of an impetus to a common European Union intelligence cooperation policy than did Maastricht. Dependence on the US for intelligence during both crises convinced the Europeans that they needed improved intelligence collection capabilities, especially with regard to space-based assets.

Although some EU Member States such as Belgium and Austria, have recently made public calls for the creation of a Europe-wide Central Intelligence Agency (CIA). With little doubt, the European Union should establish the proposed permanent European Union Intelligence Service in order to enhance intelligence sharing with North American on the war against global terrorism.

To be effective, a European Common Intelligence Policy cooperating with American intelligence institutions, under the umbrella of a European Union Intelligence Service (Vest 2006, 90–91) must be able to swiftly and accurately disseminate intelligence information to military forces. The ability to do so is crucial to the development of a European Intelligence Policy, as well as the multinational corps agreed upon in Helsinki.[7]

---

7 European Union leaders meeting in Helsinki, in December 1999, and a follow up meeting in Sintra, Portugal in February 2000 agreed to major changes in European security and defense policy, many of which had been initially suggested in Cologne, Germany. Three additional bodies have already been established to support the European Union Defense Policy: a Political and Security Committee, composed of ambassadors with an advisory

The comparison has been made with the Central Intelligence Agency. The US had little experience with intelligence prior to World War II. Then the Americans were suddenly put in the position of a superpower. Such inexperience is also largely the case for the European Union concerning the war on global terrorism. The European Union Intelligence Service should be mobilized on what the CIA was originally supposed to be – an organization focused not on covert operations, but analysis. The European Union Intelligence Service will be an independent intelligence outfit that would initially focus on providing the European Commission and European Council with strategic insights based on open sources and information contributed by EU member intelligence services. To be sure, spy chiefs (Vest 2006, 91) are usually leery of sharing or leaving their organizations open to penetration. But casting such a service as primarily analytic and focused on global terrorism is hard to disagree with on practical grounds.

However, liaison between European security services and the US remains problematic.[8] In the wake of 9/11 a large number of the FBI agents arrived in Germany and began independent investigations, to the chagrin of their German hosts. There are now almost as many FBI as CIA personnel in the European Union. The French have displayed sensitivity about the FBI's interest in extending its influence in Eastern Europe through its International Law Enforcement Academy in Bucharest (Romania) interpreting this as encroachment into EU's backyard (Wirtz 1993, 85–9). Each state has its own peculiarities. Germany finds sharing security intelligence difficult because of awkward constitutional limitations and its federal structure. France has been beset by internal infighting between its own secret services. These complexities translate into myriad complex interfaces with the many competing American agencies located around Washington's beltway.

Intelligence and Law Enforcement: Borders and Infrastructure

The 9/11 terrorist attacks were a factor for dramatically increasing judiciary and police cooperation in Europe. Within Europe, efforts have focused on the so-called Third Pillar areas of justice and home affairs. That impetus, however, was limited to the Third Pillar: for the past four years, all policies developed by the European Union have been influenced in one way or another by the fight against terrorism. In fact, soon after the Madrid seismic shock, heads of state and government met in Brussels to adopt a 'new' action plan against terrorism. It is symptomatic to note that the fight against terrorism, which had been downplayed for a year, ultimately became the challenge for the next decade within less than one week. Once more, European streets had to be drenched in blood before this topic was placed at the top of the political agenda. The European Union (Mathieu 2005, 112–113) nevertheless

---

role to the EU Council of Ministers; on EU Military Committee of senior officers; and a Multinational Planning Staff. While details of the intelligence support to be provided to the multinational force are not yet available this level of support is likely to require significantly increased intelligence cooperation.

8   Read the Critics inside Intelligence Community say that post 9/11 agencies still not sharing intelligence, NEWSWEEK, No. 28, March 2004.

recognized its weakness in this respect. It thus adopted a solidarity clause, and created a coordinator and an integration of an information exchange cell within the European Council. European leaders have expressed a will to increase cooperation between European police forces and intelligence agencies.

The kind of intelligence that relates to law enforcement issues often appears pedestrian alongside some of the intelligence service activities discussed above; however, it can not be overemphasized that dutiful collection and exchange of rather mundane data, sometimes merely open data such as names and addresses, (Aldrich 2004, 741–42) often produces important results. Moreover, names and addresses are one thing; private information is quite another. Some of the most recent transatlantic agreements have permitted too much access to personal data by categories of officials that are extremely widely defined. This is a substantial threat to privacy that points to future trouble.

Since September 2001, law enforcement authorities in the US and EU have been pushed to abandon their traditional local or traditional orientation, with only mixed results. As with information collection, the US and European efforts have moved in parallel but largely separate tracks, with the emphasis on building collaboration within the US and the EU, rather than reaching out across the Atlantic. In the US, the Federal Bureau of Investigation (FBI) has given increasing emphasis to an antiterrorist mission; an evolution which has been reinforced by the recommendation of the 9/11 Commission. In the EU, there have been efforts to revitalize institutions[9] – such as EUROPOL, the SITUATION CENTER, FRONTEX, and EUROJUST – intended to build intra EU cooperation in law enforcement.

These European organizations are intended to facilitate the building of an effective network of national judicial authorities and prosecutors, and eventually the harmonizing of judicial policy and practice across a wide range of cross border crimes, including terrorism. However, these efforts have been hindered by persistent tensions over whether bilateral or multilateral arrangements are most effective, as

---

9   European Union has created four agencies for a better cooperation towards combating organized crime, human trafficking, and other criminal and terrorist acts. EUROPOL (European Police Office) based in the Hague and it was created in 1992 to handle Europe-wide criminal intelligence. EUROPOL supports EU States by: a) facilitating exchange of information; b) providing operational analysis; c) providing reports and crime analysis; and d) providing expensive and technical support for investigations and operations. – THE SITUATION CENTER is part of the EU Council Secretariat. Its mission is to provide EU decision makers with synthesized strategic assessments on security and terrorism. – FRONTEX is the European Agency for the management of operational cooperation at the External Borders of the EU States. It was created in June 2005, based in Warsaw. FRONTEX supports the European coordination in combating threats, in particular international terrorism, human trafficking and illegal immigration. – EUROJUST is the judicial cooperation unit of the European Union. This permanent body was established in 2002. It is a permanent network of judicial authorities. EUROJUST's mission is to enhance the effectiveness of actions when EU States are facing serious cross-border and organized crime. EUROJUST aims to improve the coordination between competent authorities by facilitating; investigating and prosecutions; the extension of international mutual legal assistance; and the implementation of extradition requests.

well as shortages of understanding and resources. US Law enforcement has long had a bilateral relationship with equivalent agencies in individual EU Member States, for example, between US Customs and Immigration and Naturalization Service officials, and the Department of Justice Joint Terrorist Task Forces and several national European police forces (Aaron 2004, 17–19). These tensions over bilateral vs. multilateral approaches have been reinforced by a general lack of understanding among US officials about European law enforcement traditions and procedures, as well as EU processes and institutions. The traditional US legal attaché system has not been able to provide enough individuals with adequate training and knowledge to be effective liaisons in the evolving context of European law enforcement. The US Department of Justice has not been able to provide regular liaison with EUROJUST. On the European side, limitations in financial and personnel resources are hindering the development of more effective Europe wide institutions and thus perpetuating the bilateral emphasis. Despite these differences, however, this is an auspicious time to push for greater transatlantic cooperation in law enforcement and judicial policy. The attacks on Madrid (2003) and London (2005) have strengthened the connections between many European law enforcement agencies and demonstrated to everyone that a stronger 'European level' structure is essential.

Another area of transatlantic cooperation – tracking the financial aspect of terrorism – has been placed high on the agenda. The priority resulted in a series of measures to freeze the assets of terrorist organizations. Within the European Union, the operational activities are undertaken by a small working group, based in Brussels, in bilateral cooperation with Member States. Despite the creation of new frameworks for cooperation (Qudrat 2003, 163–176) and better electronic databases of targeted persons, this work remains complex, detailed and slow. Although officials have worked hard in this area, the instruments remain unequal to the task. The fundamental framework remains the Financial Action Task Force set up by the G7 in 1989, which ideally should be replaced by a properly resourced international organization. There are already signs that suspects are moving towards informal financial transfers that will deny investigators valuable paper trails in the future.

The most significant achievement is the European Arrest Warrant (EAW), which was introduced by the Council Framework Decision 2002/584/JHA of 13 June 2002.[10] Its basic aim is to abolish extradition procedures between Member States and replace them by a system of surrender between judicial authorities. As the European Union fact sheet on the fight against terrorism emphasizes, the European Arrest Warrant reduces the ability of terrorists and other criminals ' ... to evade justice by exploiting differences in national legal systems'.[11] The 25 EU Member States have

---

10 Read Vasillios Grammatikas, After London: The Impact on EU counter-terrorist policies and upon the fundamental rights of citizens, PACIS, Issue 17, (Defense Analyses Institute), 2005, pp. 31–64.

11 See also http://ue.eu.int/uedocs/cmsUpload/3counterterrorfinal170605.pdf and see also the Annex to the EU Plan of Action on Combating Terrorism where the implementation status for the various instruments listed in the Declaration on Terrorism is displayed for each EU Member State – http://ue.eu.int/uedocs/cmsUpload/WEBad02.en05.pdf.

already enacted national legislation to implement the Framework Decision on the European Arrest Warrant.

Another practical step was taken by the Framework Decision 2002/465/JHA of 13 June 2002 on 'Joint Investigation Teams' (EU Official Document OJL 162 2002, 1; and OJL 16, 2003, 68) which aims to institutionalize bilateral police cooperation in cases of criminal investigation into terrorism, drugs and human trafficking. This should be seen in combination with the Council Decision 2003/48/JHA of 19 December 2002 on the implementation of specific measures for police and judicial cooperation to combat global terrorism. The latter document introduces specific measures to facilitate and speed up cooperation between the judicial and police authorities of the Member States, providing inter alia, for the designation of special units or persons within the police and judiciary of the EU Member States to deal with issues of terrorism, the exchange of information and evidence relating to terrorist offences.

Finally, the Austrian Presidency (1 January 2006) endorsed the European Council on a draft Decision on the European Evidence Warrant (EEW) for obtaining objects, documents and data for use in proceedings in criminal-terrorist matters. The aim of this proposal is to establish a mechanism to facilitate the obtaining of evidence in cross-border cases based on mutual recognition principles. Before sending a EEW, the issuing authority has to assess that the objects, documents or data can be obtained under the law of the issuing Member State in a comparable case if they were available on the territory of the Issuing Member State, even though different procedural measures might be used. Eventually, the EEW will cover the following issues: (EU Council Doc 2732, Justice and Home Affairs, 01/06/2006).

- To conduct interviews, taking statements or initiating other types of hearing involving suspects, witness, experts or any other party;
- To carry out bodily examinations or obtain bodily material or biometric data directly from the body of any person, including DNA samples or fingerprints;
- To obtain information in real time such as through the interception of communications, covert surveillance or monitoring of bank accounts.

So far, the approach of the US and EU, as it derives from the various documents of either a political or legal nature, considers terrorism as a very serious form of criminal activity and introduces measures that will effectively counter terrorism and minimize the operational capability of terrorists by denying them access to funding and other aspects essential for their operations.

Military Intelligence and NATO Capability

Defense is one area where divergent alliance policies and priorities have a direct impact on the potential for transatlantic intelligence cooperation against global terrorism. The United States sees military intervention as the dominant component of the war against terror and intelligence spending focused on supporting defense activity accordingly remains at the forefront of the American effort; European approaches are rather different. The American defense industry, in contrast to European firms, has been strongly encouraged to develop C4I (command, control, communications, computers and intelligence). Moreover, the US Department of Defense is able to draw further (Gury and Callum 2002, 765) strength from advances in commercial and civilian technologies in which the United States is a world leader. This predominance has profound consequences for the future of transatlantic military cooperation.

These consequences are already visible. During the first Gulf War in 1991, French forces encountered severe difficulties with allied interoperability in the area of command and communications. In Bosnia and Kosovo, the UK encountered similar problems. When planning Operations Enduring Freedom in Afghanistan in 2001, the US received many offers of military assistance from European partners but rejected most of them, preferring to avoid the restraints of a wide coalition and the burden of supporting weak allies in the field. Currently, decisions as to whether the US acts unilaterally or multilaterally (Yost 2001, 97–128) are still partly political; in ten years' time they will be largely determined by technology. As a result of the revolution in military affairs, the US will find itself unable to interoperate with lesser forces, and NATO will find itself providing various forms of follow-on support, from medical services to military policing. In other words, the information and technology gap will relegate NATO to washing the dishes.

From the American perspective, the US was the prime target of the jihadists and, therefore, more acutely in need of actionable intelligence. While this attitude has some grounding in fact, the profound inclination of the US Department of Defense to militarize counterterrorism – despite clear demonstrations of the limitations of the military as a counterterrorism instrument – has given US allies and partners special pause. The 2006 Quadrennial Defense Review, for example, envisages special-operations forces engaged in both kinetic and indirect low-visibility operations around the world as the United States' principal instrument for winning the Global War on Terror.[12]

Indeed, the US has apparently already assumed such risks in executing so-called 'renditions' of terrorist suspects on European soil. The US employed the practice very sparingly and selectively in the 1990s, but steeply increased its use after 11 September. The UK parliament is investigating whether the British government allowed the CIA to use British airspace for renditions. Suspected CIA planes have also been spotted in Finland, Hungary, Iceland, Poland, Portugal, Romania and Spain as well as the three countries conducting the investigations. These revelations have made European governments less inclined to coordinate military intelligence operations with the US. They fear adverse public reaction that could have disruptive political consequences and jeopardize intergovernmental intelligence cooperation even further. At the same time, there is gathering momentum in the US intelligence community towards re-prioritizing missions. If

---

12 Read the analysis 'Cooperative Intelligence – Renewed Momentum?', at the Strategic Comments, Vol. 12, Issue 4, 4 May 2006, International Institute for Strategic Studies, (UK), pp. 1–2.

the Cold War was the era of collection, the post-Cold War years may have become the era of processing.[13]

Similarly, on the NATO side, changes in the security environment at the end of the Cold War obliged NATO to revise its indications and warning methodology. As a result of reduced risk of armed conflict between states and increased risk of conflict within states, NATO has broadened its approach to early warning in a number of ways (Kriendler 2006, 1–8). Firstly, the range of potential risks addressed has been extended well beyond the threat of direct aggression to NATO territory to encompass non-military risks and even unconventional threats such as terrorism. Secondly, increased interaction with members of the Euro-Atlantic Partnership Council (EAPC)[14] further contributes to early warning. And thirdly, NATO has developed a new Intelligence Warning System (NIWS). The recent establishment of the Terrorist Threat Intelligence Unit (TTIU) at NATO Headquarter is a reflection of the importance that allies attach to sharing military intelligence related to terrorism. The TTIU analyses threats by drawing on information from NATO member nations. It also provides its own forward-looking assessments. The unit has a permanent staff of seven plus additional experts and analysts on loan from nations. It is expected to play an important role in ensuring NATO decision-makers are well informed about terrorist activities.

Furthermore, NATO is also seeking to develop additional technical capabilities to enhance its ability to deal with global terrorism. For example, among the capabilities explicit in the approach by the Conference of National Armaments Directors (CNAD) is a 'Joint Military Intelligence, Surveillance, and Reconnaissance' (Kriendler 2006, 1–8). In the CNAD program for Defense Against Terrorism, one item is 'New Technology for Intelligence, Reconnaissance, Surveillance and Target Acquisition of Terrorists' (ISRTA of Terrorists), which describes thoroughly that one of the toughest challenges in fighting terrorism is finding and tracking the terrorist, whose tools are anonymity and secrecy. To increase our ability to do so, we have set three main goals: to obtain a detailed understanding of how to determine characteristic features of terrorists organizations; to develop method and tools for early warning identification of terrorists activities; and to identify promising future research areas.

At last, NATO was one of the very first institutions to declare itself part of the campaign against terrorism with its invocation of the collective defense clause on the day following the September 2001 attacks.[15] Even though, in March 2003, the European Union and NATO signed an agreement on the security of information, a prerequisite for the exchange of intelligence between the two organizations (Lefebvre 2003, 527–42), but NATO's ability to cooperate with the European Union Member States in the anti-terrorism effort is constrained by restrictions

---

13 Ibid., op. cit.: pp. 1–2.

14 The Euro-Atlantic Partnership Council (EAPC) brings together 46 NATO partner states for dialogue and consultation on political and security-related issues.

15 Many nations have used their NATO membership to obtain assistance and support in challenging times. After the attacks of 11 September, 2001, for example, the United States invoked Article 5 of the treaty, its mutual defense clause, meaning that an attack on one NATO Member was an attack on all – http://www.nato.int/docu/basictxt/treaty.htm#Art5.

imposed by EU Member States. They seem concerned that NATO might eclipse the EU in this area, despite their very different talents and mandates. Even once these specific differences are resolved, NATO's involvement will still be hampered by distinctly different US and European views on the utility of military force in combating terrorism. However, NATO does have some distinctive strength (Aaron 2004, 24–5) that it could bring to full engagement in the struggle against global terrorism. NATO patrols in the eastern Mediterranean have interdicted shipments of contraband and generally made the shipping lanes safer from attack.

Over the years, Active Endeavor has increasingly become an information and intelligence-based operation through the sharing of data gathered at sea by NATO allies and Mediterranean-rim countries. The level of military intelligence achieved to date provides a sound foundation upon which to build in the future. [16] The aim is to develop a much more effective information collection and analysis system and to change the character of the operation from one that is intelligence-supported to one that is intelligence-driven. The experience that NATO has acquired in Active Endeavor and other maritime interdiction operations has given the Alliance unparalleled expertise in this field. This expertise is relevant to wider international efforts to combat global terrorism and, in particular, the proliferation and smuggling of weapons of mass destruction. As a result, countries involved in the Proliferation Security Initiative, a US-led partnership aiming to assist halt flows of dangerous technologies to and from states and non-state actors of concern, are currently seeking to learn the lessons of NATO's maritime operations.

Active Endeavor has proved to be an effective tool in countering terrorism at and from the sea in the Mediterranean. There are, of course, many aspects of combating terrorism that would gain little or nothing from the involvement of a military alliance, including most of the law enforcement and homeland security issues covered in this article. But engaging NATO more fully and appropriately will make the transatlantic intelligence cooperation that much stronger and better prepared if circumstances arise in which a military response is required, and it will remove an element of contention at the core of that partnership.

International Order in a World Threatened by Global Terrorism

Global terrorism has emerged as a horrifying reality and forceful phenomenon of the 21st century. Its rise as a major challenge to the nation-state has occurred in the context of the post-Cold War international order, characterized by the absence of a major power rivalry and near unipolarity, (Hecht 2006, 1–5) with the United States as the dominant power. While no nation state is currently capable of directly challenging the US dominance on a global scale, the subnational global terrorist networks with asymmetric strategies have adopted this mantle. This challenge is not an easy one to detect or defeat.

---

16 Read at the Vice Admiral Roberto Cesaretti, 'Combating Terrorism in the Mediterranean', NATO Review, No.3, Fall 2005, www.nato.int/docu/review/2005/issue3/english/art4.html.

With the demise of the Cold War, the situation has changed. As the possibility of a major power declined dramatically, large military organizations with the primary mission of fighting interstate wars became somewhat redundant. The new security challenges that arose, be they global terrorism, drug trafficking, illegal migration, or ethnic conflicts, all required new or modified instruments to combat them. States seem to be driven by the assumption that, although the Cold War has ended, the potential for new systemic and subsystemic rivalries exists (Aydinli and Rosenau 2005, 49–64). Major powers proceeded as if they should always be prepared for the eventual arrival of a challenger or challengers. In the US case, the general expectation has been that China would emerge as the most powerful rising challenger to American dominance. The US has also been focusing on a small group of regional challengers (Iraq, Iran, Syria, and North Korea) with ambitions to acquire weapons of mass destruction while preparing to fight in two different regional theaters simultaneously.

The price of non-cooperation, or only partial cooperation, for international order could be enormous. Further terror outrages could have major destabilizing effects in numerous regions, sending shockwaves that will affect moderate secular Islamic regimes and directly affecting international economies through rising energy prices.

Recent arrests of terror networks in the United Kingdom and in Germany amply demonstrate the ability of small, local al-Qaeda cells to gear towards terror attacks on a massive scale. The arrests of over 30 people in the UK suspected of planning to blow up ten transatlantic flights by using liquid explosives is but one example of the level of sophistication achievable by such cells negating much of the conventional means of terror prevention. It also shows the dogged determination of small radical Islamic terror cells to inflict horrendous casualties through relatively small attacks, easy to plan and carry out.

Modern terrorists are flexible in their movements and in their operational planning. They easily change location, transfer money and people across borders and conduct a range of preparatory activities before every attack. The leading 9/11 suicide kidnappers; for example, lived in Germany and regularly traveled both to Asia and America while planning their attacks. Such patterns of travel, movements of funds, communications and interpersonal relations can only be analysed and effectively monitored by multinational intelligence cooperation and extensive information sharing. Only by pooling intelligence resources can Western security authorities hope to surmount the inherent flexibility of terrorism and effectively determine intent for active prevention.

However, to have the United States and the European Union cooperate in reconstructing international order in an era of global terrorism should be easy in principle. There are differences in their foreign policy role concepts. For the United States, the role concept contains strong doses of unilateralism and an inclination to seek solution through military force. For the European Union Member States, (Hecht 2006, 1–5) a strong commitment to multilateralism and international institutions in principle is marred by lack of cohesion and an inclination by Member States in practice to put other, national considerations first. Therefore, a transatlantic alliance for world order will not only require, on both sides of the Atlantic, the ability to agree on a common vision, a clear shift of political priorities away from domestic preoccupations, and the political will to mobilize the necessary resources; but also, and most importantly, changes in role concepts on both sides of the Atlantic that would enable the US and EU to cooperate efficiently. While Europeans have become concerned after terrorist outrages in Madrid and London, they do not look to the US to protect them. Europe continues to believe in conflict resolution using logic and reason, while failing to recognize the very lack of logic or reason when dealing with ideological and religious fanatics.

The US hegemony has been an especially vexing problem for Europeans because there is so little they can do about it. Hopes for a multi-polar international regime have faded since the 1990s. It is clear today that the United States' political, economic and military power will be impossible to match for decades. The war on terror (Hecht 2006, 5) has also introduced the doctrine 'pre-emption.' Europe continues, with the exception of Tony Blair in the UK, to oppose this policy even after the London events of 7 July, 2005. Most of Europe still regards preventive action as characteristic of a super power and a breach of international law and legitimacy.

Thinkers as diverse as Henry Kissinger and Kofi Annan have recently suggested that changes in the UN Charter must consider new criteria legitimizing pre-emptive measures in addressing particular types of threats. These may include actions against terrorists and the states that protect them, such as Syria or Iran with long histories of conspiracy, as well as terror itself. There may even be provisions that could legitimize the use of force in occupying the oil fields of Saudi Arabia in case of an al-Qaeda takeover, to save the world (Hecht 2006, 5) from economic disaster. Some theorists claim that the legitimacy for action depends on creating wide international consensus, but determining the width and composition of the required consensus is problematic.

Therefore, global terrorism presents multifarious problems for the nation-state. These problems arise from the global reach of terrorist networks, the religious connection, the ability of terrorists to wreak havoc on key economic centers of the advanced world, and the asymmetric strategies that they follow that are difficult to confront using traditional national security approaches (Aydinli and Rosenau 2005, 49–64). Any effort to solve the problem of terrorism purely through a traditional state-centric military approach is not likely to succeed. The consequences of war are generally unpredictable, this time in a more profound way, as the nation-state is fighting an invisible enemy who adapts his asymmetrical strategies continuously and has operational bases spread across the globe.

Although elements of a military approach may be relevant in some situations, they will most likely give more political and ideological legitimacy to the 'martyrs.' On the other hand, not taking any military action also holds risks as groups may become emboldened by their 'victory' (Aydinli and Rosenau 2005, 49–64) and pursue even greater terrorism. Either way, the stability of the regions in question is at considerable risk. The challenge for national security planners is to find balanced short-term and long-term policies that effectively address the military, diplomatic, economic, and political dimension of the problem. The battle against global terrorism needs to be fought on different fronts – political, ideological, economic, intelligence and military. Any quick-fix solutions and scapegoating, however tempting, will breed further terrorism and insecurity and challenge to the international order.

Conclusion

Intelligence cooperation is the most important weapon in the battle to contain the global terrorism, but its significance is even greater than that. The first few years of the twenty-first century have witnessed a change in the role of secret intelligence in international politics. Intelligence and security issues are now more prominent than ever in Western political discourse as well as the wider pubic consciousness. Much of this can be attributed to the shock of the terrorist acts in US (2001), Spain (2003) and London (2005).

In our insistence on the concept of "world order", we do not view international relations solely as the struggle for power between competing states or the consequences for the international system of the distribution of power between states; but rather, as suggested by Hedley Bull, as a relationship between order and anarchy in a more fundamental sense (Bull 2002, 4–19). This means that international relations must be viewed from a perspective of values, which considers interpretations of morality, freedom, justice, civilization and individuality in an understanding of the relationship between law and power on the national as well as the international level.

By placing emphasis on order, the intention is to focus on levels below (transnational figures of identification) as well as beyond state level (the regional level, but also for instance conceptions of the Western, the Islamic and the Arab world), and to examine their significance in terms of the potential for political action of the state as well as in terms of regional relations, and, finally, the interaction between regional circumstances and non-governmental actors (such as Al Qaeda, Hizbollah, the Muslim Brotherhood and so on). Moreover, the fact that some of Bull's pluralist assumptions have been embraced by policy makers is an indication of the continuing salience of his ideas.

Across a range of post-Cold War issues, globalization has undermined many of the familiar mechanisms by which states formerly provided their populations with security. Indeed, organized crime, drug-trafficking, money-laundering and immigration (Aldrich 2004, 752) have become securitized precisely because of their increasingly transnational character. With the erosion of the familiar national border post, states have turned the more proactive measures to protect their populations, and these efforts are more intelligence-led.

Modern intelligence is a multinational activity. National intelligence power is a function not only of national capabilities but also of the foreign cooperation and product they obtain (Herman 1996, 217–18). Governments' intelligence needs are met by varying mixtures of national and foreign efforts. The international dimension of intelligence fits the modern patterns of increased international specialist contacts. In the field of intelligence, international exchanges are a necessity for international society.

However, regarding transatlantic intelligence cooperation as a tool combating global terrorism, Richard J. Aldrich has remarkably pointed out that:

> Transatlantic intelligence cooperation has achieved some remarkable things over the years, but it is not about to deliver greater alliance cohesion. Moreover, across an increasingly diverse western alliance, (Aldrich 2004, 752–53) the interface between

strategic intelligence analysis and the core executive is changing at different speeds. In some places analysis is still kept at arm's length from the policy process; in others, objective intelligence reporting is likely to sit increasingly awkwardly with presidential styles of governance which prefer subjective policy advice.

Finally, in the 21st century, the war against global terrorism requires more than ever collective action among the intelligence services depended on shared intelligence and common assessments in order to prevent once again prospective major terrorist acts in United States and the European Union Member States.

References

Aaron, David L., *et al.* (2004), *Post 9/11 Partnership: Transatlantic Cooperation against Terrorism* (Washington DC: The Atlantic Council Press).

Aldrich, J. Richard (2004), 'Transatlantic Intelligence and Security Cooperation', *International Affairs* 80: 4, 731–53.

Andrew, Christopher (1994), 'The Making of the Anglo-American SIGINT Alliance', in *In the Name of Intelligence: Essays in Honor of Walter Pforzheimer*, Hayden B. Peake and Samuel Halpern (eds) (Washington, DC: NIBC Press).

Aydinli, Ersel (2005), *Globalization, Security and the Nation-State* (Albany, NY: State University of New York Press).

Bull, Hedley (2002), *The Anarchical Society*, 3rd edition (New York: Columbia University Press).

Cesaretti, Roberto (2005), 'Combating Terrorism in the Mediterranean', NATO Review, 3: 1–3.

EU Council (25/03/2004) and Council Declaration on *EU Response to London Bombings*.

EU Official Document (20/06/2002), OJL 162, on *Police Cooperation Joint Investigation Teams*.

EU Official Document (22/01/2003) OJL 16.

Grammatikas, Vasillios (2005), 'After London: The Impact on EU counter-terrorist policies and upon the fundamental rights of citizens', *PACIS Journal* 17: 31, 64.

Guitta, Olivier (2006), *Homeland Security in a Global Context: An Overview of European-US Cooperation* (Washington DC: American Legislature Exchange Council Press).

Gurry, T. (2002), 'The transformation and future prospects of Europe's defense industry', *International Affairs* 78: 4, 765.

Hecht, Thomas (2006), 'Defining a New International System in a World Threatened by Jihad: The Danger of a Transatlantic Divide', Begin-Sadat Center for Strategic Studies (BESA) Perspectives, 16: 1–5.

Herman, Michael (1996), *Intelligence Power in Peace and War* (London: Cambridge University Press).

Keohane, Daniel (2005), *The European Union Counter Terrorism* (London, Center for European Reform Press).

Kriendler, John (2006), *NATO Intelligence and Early Warning* (London: UK Ministry of Defence).

Lefebvre, Stephen (2004), 'The Difficulties and Dilemmas of International Intelligence Cooperation', *International Journal of Intelligence and Counterintelligence* 16: 4, 527–42.

Mathieu, Raphael (2005), The *European Union and the Fight Against Terrorism* (Paris: Euro-future Press).

Nomikos, John (2005), 'A European Union Intelligence Service for Confronting Terrorism', *International Journal of Intelligence and Counterintelligence*, 18: 2, 191–203.

Nomikos, John (2005), 'Eastern Mediterranean Intelligence Cooperation', *PACIS Journal* 17, 103–112.

Oudraat de Jonge, C. (2003), 'Combating Terrorism', *Washington Quarterly*, 26: 4, 163–76.

Shpiro, Shlomo (1995), 'European Mediterranean Intelligence Cooperation: A Hidden Element in Regional Security', Research Institute for European and American Studies Paper, 20: 1–21.

Stekee Menno, and Major General Bert Deddeb, (2003), 'Analysis on SIGINT in Europe', *Janes Intelligence Review* (December 2003).

Vest, Jason (2006), 'Artificial Intelligence', *Foreign Policy*, 90–91.

Wirtz, J. (1993), 'Constraints on intelligence collaboration: the domestic dimension', *International Journal of Intelligence and Counterintelligence* 6: 1, 85–99.

Yost, David (2001), 'The NATO capabilities gap and the European Union', *Survival* 42: 4, 97–128.

PART III
International Order: Normative Issues

Chapter 9

Normative Development of Self-Defence and Pre-emptive Action: Implications for International Order

Muge Kinacioglu[1]

The United States (US) decision to undertake a military action in Iraq, not only without Security Council authorization but also in defiance of overwhelming opposition of the majority of the Security Council as well as its NATO allies, was a turning point in terms of commitment of the world's dominant power to the normative underpinnings of international order regarding the use of force. The most controversial issue has become the Bush administration's conception of the pre-emptive use of force as formulated in the National Security Strategy (NSS) of 2002. Admittedly, the concept of pre-emption has long been a contentious doctrine in international law. However, the Bush administration's articulation of the concept has added a more divisive dimension to the debate. While in traditional international law, the claim to pre-emptive use of force can be invoked where there is imminence of an attack, the NSS argued for adjustment of the concept of the imminent attack to 'the capabilities and objectives of today's adversaries'. It asserted that '[t]he greater the threat, the greater is the risk of inaction – and the more compelling the case for taking anticipatory action to defend ourselves, even if uncertainty remains as to the time and place of the enemy's attack' (NSS 2002, 15). Likewise, President Bush's second term NSS, released on 16 March 2006, preserves 'pre-emption' as part of the US national security strategy in countering terrorism and proliferation of weapons of mass destruction (WMD). It reiterates that the US 'does not rule out the use of force before attacks occur' grounding the right to do so on 'long-standing principles of self defense' (NSS 2006, 23).

This essay addresses the question whether the US conception of pre-emptive action has led to any fundamental change or modification of the international regulation of the use of force in general and rules of self-defence in particular. More specifically, it inquires whether such reading of Article 51 of the United Nations (UN) Charter and customary international law has expanded the scope of permissible use of force. In this context, the paper aims to extrapolate the normative trends of legitimization regarding admissibility of the pre-emptive action by looking at the UN's application of the right of self-defence.

---

1   The author would like to express her thanks to Ms. Ebru Ilhan for her assistance in the research of parts of this chapter.

The notion of legitimacy in this paper largely draws on Inis Claude's seminal work on the collective legitimization function of the UN. As Inis Claude observes, politics is not only 'a struggle for power but also a contest over legitimacy'. That is not to imply that power and legitimacy have an 'antithetical' relationship. In fact, legitimacy supplements power, as the 'obverse of the legitimacy of power is the power of legitimacy' (Claude 1966, 368). Thus, actors seek legitimization to bolster their policies. Inis Claude identifies two aspects of the discussions of political legitimacy, namely law and morality. Lawyers are inclined to define legitimacy as a mere translation of 'legality'. Moralists, in a similar way, tend to approach the issue of political legitimacy as a question of moral justification. Claude argues that although both law and morality stand as powerful grounds for legitimization, in the final analysis legitimization is a political process, which is not entirely governed by legal rules and moral principles (Claude 1966, 369). Moreover, he contends that as much as law and morality may reinforce each other in some cases, they may also come into conflict in other cases. Hence, what is significant from this perspective is the agency of legitimization, that is, who is accepted as 'the authoritative interpreter of the principle', and how the process of legitimization takes place rather than the principles of legitimacy themselves (Claude 1966, 370). In other words, principles of legitimacy may change or their application may be uncertain and ambiguous, but what gains greater significance is the nature of the process itself.

In the light of the above presuppositions, the UN appears as the most prominent international organization undertaking a function of collective legitimization and setting a hallmark of approval. Although it can be argued that the UN hardly represents the world society, it would be reasonable to assert that it embodies a critical mass of actors. In addition, it is recognized by states as the most respected forum for the representation of global general will. Thus, as Claude observes, the UN has unique advantages 'for playing the role of custodian of the seals of international approval or disapproval' (Claude 1966, 371–2).

A few remarks should also be made concerning norms in order to underline their significance in explaining state behaviour. Norms of legitimacy comprising legal, political and moral elements constitute one of the main determining factors in international politics. They set a 'standard of appropriate behaviour for actors within a given identity' (Finnemore and Sikkink 1998, 891) and they function as constraining and enabling frameworks for state behaviour. 'Shared ideas, expectations and beliefs about appropriate behaviour' in return provide for 'structure, order and stability' (Finnemore and Sikkink 1998, 894). In this respect, one can question the power of norms in international politics by pointing out the discrepancy between the acceptance of norms in principle and the instances of their breach in practice. Proponents of Realist School in International Relations for example would portray the US invasion of Iraq as an extension of power politics. From this point of view, international law and international institutions are reduced to means through which the dominant powers maximize their political gain. By implication, normative frameworks have little explanatory power in analysing state behaviour. However, whether the actor is genuine or not is beyond the point, for what matters is the need felt by the actor to legitimate its behaviour and to take actions compatible with the declared principles. From the perspective of this article, consistent endorsement of certain justifications is essential in the evolution of standards of behaviour of state conduct.

Within this framework, the essay first overviews the law of self-defence and examines the concept of the anticipatory self-defence in international law as well as under the UN Charter paradigm. It then explores cases whereby states invoked the right to self-defence in order to discern the cumulative impact of repeated UN endorsement/disapproval of a specific position. After examining pre-emptive action as developed in the 'Bush Doctrine', the paper inquires whether the UN responses amount to normative change regarding the scope of self-defence and the prohibition on the use of force. It ends with a discussion of the implications of such normative developments for international order and institutions of international society.

Prohibition on the Use of Force

Being a product of the desire to prevent recurrence of the conflicts that had given rise to the Second World War, the UN Charter established a normative order that sternly restricts the use of force in international relations. The ban on the use of force is laid down by Article 2(4) of the Charter, which requires that states 'refrain in their international relations from the threat or use of force against the territorial integrity or political independence of any state, or in any other manner inconsistent with the Purposes of the United Nations'.

The prohibition of the use of force was a rule of pre-Charter customary international law. However, permissible forms of self-help[2] had relatively a wider base in the pre-Charter period (for detailed exploration of the concept, see Kelsen 1952, 8–9). Read together with the authoritative General Assembly resolutions, such as the *Declaration on Principles of International Law* (GA Res. 2625 XXV 1970) and the *Definition of Aggression* (GA Res. 3314 XXIX 1974), it is clear that Article 2(4) prohibits all unilateral use of force – employed directly or indirectly. As such, Article 2(4) stipulates a general proscription of the use of force. More precisely, it extends the prohibition of force beyond war to include other types of unilateral use and threat of force. It therefore endows the prohibition of force as a general and authoritative principle (Henkin 1991, 38). The substantial majority of legal scholars attribute the norm contained in Article 2(4) a *jus cogens* character (see for example, Shaw 1991, 686; Cassese 1994, 141). The *jus cogens* status of Article 2(4) is also confirmed in the *Nicaragua* judgment of the International Court of Justice (ICJ), whereby it referred to statements by government representatives who considered the prohibition of force in Article 2(4) as not only a principle of customary international law but also 'a fundamental and cardinal principle of such law' (ICJ Reports 1986, para. 190). The Court also inferred the *opinio juris* of states from the consent given to numerous General Assembly resolutions that reiterated the norm of the prohibition of force,[3] in particular the 1970 *Declaration on Principles of International Law*, which was adopted by consensus. In addition, the Court referred to the views of

---

2 Self-help may generally be defined as forcible measures to redress violations of the law.

3 See for example, GA Resols. 290 (IV), 1 December 1949; 378 (V) A, 17 November 1950; 380 (V), 17 November 1950; 2625 (XXV), 24 October 1970; 3314 (XXIX), 14 December 1974; 42/22, 18 November 1987.

the International Law Commission on the *jus cogens* character of the provisions of Article 2(4) (ICJ Reports 1986, para. 190).

Thus, Article 2(4) presumes the illegality of any unilateral use of force. The norm it establishes has universal and imperative applicability in that it is consistently reaffirmed in a number of international documents as well as in General Assembly and Security Council resolutions. Notwithstanding, the Charter allows for two exceptions to the general prohibition on the use of force in international law: individual and collective self-defence under Article 51, and enforcement measures authorized by the Security Council in response to 'any threat to the peace, breach of the peace or act of aggression' under Chapter VII (and for the regional organizations under Chapter VIII).

The Charter is fairly open-ended regarding the Security Council's power to authorize force 'to maintain or restore international peace and security', (Article 42) when it determines there is a 'threat to the peace, breach of the peace, or act of aggression' (Article 39). It does not furnish explicit definitions as to what constitutes a threat to peace, a breach of the peace, or an act of aggression. It leaves this completely to the judgment of the Security Council. Thus, as one scholar notes, 'a threat to the peace is whatever the Security Council says is a threat to the peace' (Akehurst 1984, 181). In contrast, the UN Charter is restrictive with respect to the use of force by states. It considerably confines the legitimate self-help measures by allowing for only one condition as an exception to the prohibition of the use of force, and in fact attaching it back to Security Council by stipulating in Article 51 that the unilateral measures in the exercise of the right of self-defence 'shall be immediately reported to the Security Council'.

Self-Defence as an Exception to the Unilateral Use of Force

Self-defence is a kind of self-help 'against a specific violation of the law, against the illegal use of force, not against other violations of the law' (Kelsen 1952, 60; Thomas and Thomas 1956, 79). In this sense, it can be defined as 'coercive self-help as a response to a forceful wrong' (Higgins 1963, 199). Since there exists a general agreement in the legal scholarship on the permissibility of the use of force in self-defence, the appeal to self-defence constitutes the most frequently invoked justification for the use of force.

Under the UN Charter, Article 51, which contains the right to individual and collective self-defence, provides for the only exception to the proscription of the unilateral use of force, specifying the conditions under which individual states may resort to force. It states:

> Nothing in the present Charter shall impair the inherent right of individual or collective self-defence if an armed attack occurs against a Member of the United Nations, until the Security Council has taken measures necessary to maintain international peace and security. Measures taken by Members in the exercise of this right of self-defence shall be immediately reported to the Security Council and shall not in any way affect the authority and responsibility of the Security Council under the present Charter to take any time such action as it deems necessary in order to maintain or restore international peace and security.

There has been considerable controversy regarding Article 51, since the scope of self-defence and the circumstances under which the right of self-defence may be exercised are ill defined. This is especially the case with regards to what is meant by *armed attack.* In this respect, the most contentious issue pertains to whether the use of right of self-defence is confined to the circumstances whereby an armed attack has already occurred or whether this right can be invoked in anticipation of such an attack.

On the one hand, there are those who argue that Article 51, read in conjunction with general prohibition of the use of force set out in Article 2(4) and interpreted in the light of the drafting history of the Charter, limits the invocation of such a right to cases where an actual armed attack has actually occurred (Brownlie 1963, 265; Kelsen 1951, 797–8; Lauterpacht 1955, 299; Henkin 1979, 140–43). This view accepts no other circumstances under which the right to self-defence may be raised. The concept of *inherent right* is taken to imply the undeniable nature of this right to members and non-members alike, and to indicate that the UN may provide assistance to a non-member in their defence against an armed attack. Hence, it is argued that the term *inherent* was intended to underline that defence against an armed attack is a right of every sovereign state (Kelsen 1951, 792).

On the other hand, there are legal scholars who argue that Article 51 should not be interpreted as excluding the right to anticipatory self-defence in the case of an imminent danger of attack. This view rejects the restrictive interpretation of the word *if*, as it is employed in Article 51, as meaning *if and only if* These scholars point out that by qualifying the right of self-defence as *inherent* the article indicates the existence of a right of self-defence in pre-Charter customary international law, according to which preventive measures are permitted. Consequently, it is argued that the word *inherent* does not signify an intention to restrict the pre-existing customary right. In this sense, the argument goes, by the term *armed attack* Article 51 refers merely to one situation, whereby a state could invoke the right of self-defence (Bowett, 1958, 185; Higgins 1963, 201). Supporters of this view refer to the legal criteria for permissible self-defence as formulated by US Secretary of State Daniel Webster, in the *Steamer Caroline* incident,[4] (for details of this case, see Lauterpacht 1955, 300–301; Pratt *et al.* 1980, 78–80; LaFeber 1994, 109–10) as reflecting the authoritative customary law (Jennings 1938, 92; Schachter 1991, 151; Arend and Beck 1993, 72; McCormack 1996, 247). Upon the invasion of American territorial waters, Webster set out the elements of self-defence that provided the philosophical basis for the right to use force in self-defence and the limits to the exercise of that right. According to this formulation, anticipatory self-defence is admissible, when 'the necessity of that self-defence is instant, overwhelming, and leaving no choice of means and no moment for deliberation'.[5] Thus, the two conditions for anticipatory self-defence are necessity and proportionality: First, the state resorting to use of

---

4   *Caroline* incident refers to the British attack in 1837 to a vessel owned by US nationals, *Caroline*, on the basis of its alleged support to the anti-British insurgency in Canada and with a claim to right to self-defence.

5   See note of Webster to British authorities, 27 July 1842, quoted in McCormack 1996, 183.

force in self-defence needs to demonstrate that the use of force by the other state is imminent and that there is no available remedy other than use of force to prevent the attack. Second, the state using force in self-defence is required to take action proportionate to the threat in question. In this respect, Webster maintained that in order for such a forcible action to be permissible, 'the act, justified by the necessity of self-defence, must be limited by that necessity, and kept clearly within it'.[6]

There has been no authoritative decision in international litigation on the question of anticipatory self-defence. In the *Nicaragua* case, the ICJ left the question open, by stating that '... the issue of the lawfulness of a response to the imminent threat of an armed attack has not been raised. Accordingly the Court expresses no view on that issue' (ICJ Reports 1986, para. 194). The Court's position on this issue is unclear, given that Judge Schwebel in his dissenting opinion in the *Nicaragua* case, argued that Article 51 does not circumscribe self-defence to a situation *if, and only if armed attack occurs* (ICJ Reports 1986).

One other problem related to the exercise of the right of self-defence arises out of the subjective character of the decision to resort to force in self-defence. Because of the nature of the international system, each state is, by this right, entitled to judge on its own whether to resort to force to defend itself (Shaw 1991, 694). However, a legal question remains whether circumstances merit the legitimate exercise of self-defence (Brierly 1942, 257; McCormack 1996, 259). Under Article 51, the exercise of right of self-defence is permissible 'until the Security Council has taken the measures necessary to maintain international peace and security'. As such, Article 51 recognizes that there may be pressing situations, which requires an immediate defensive response. Thus, the language of the article allows states to temporarily judge the urgency of the situation and decide to act in defence, but at the same time by stipulating 'measures taken in the exercise of self-defence shall be immediately reported to the Security Council', it also subjects the state's reasoning to international review (Higgins 1963, 205, 207). International precedent demonstrates that an action of defensive nature is not necessarily considered legitimate based solely on the judgment of the state taking that action. For example, Japan maintained that its action in Manchuria in 1931 was defensive. But the Assembly of the League of Nations concluded that the Japanese action could not be considered as a legitimate exercise of the right of self-defence (Lauterpacht 1955, 302–303). In the same vein, the judgment of the International Military Tribunal in Nuremberg in 1946 rejected the German Nazi leaders' argument that Germany acted in self-defence and that every state must be the judge of whether a given situation yields to the exercise of the right of self-defence, by asserting that 'whether action taken under the claim of self-defence was in fact aggressive or defensive must ultimately be subject to investigation or adjudication if international law is ever to be enforced'.[7]

As a result, due to the lack of an objective criteria for assessing the alleged imminence of an attack and the consequent potential for abuse, the dominant view

---

6   Letter from Mr. Webster to Mr. Fox of 24 April 1841, 29 British and Foreign State Papers 1129, 1138 (1857), quoted in Lori F. Damrosch *et al.* (eds) (2001), 923.

7   Judgment of the Military Tribunal at Nuremberg, 1946, *Trial of German Major War Criminals Before the International Military Tribunal*, quoted in Schachter (1991), 137.

among legal scholars – who make reference to the UN's aspiration to restrict the use of force by the individual state inasmuch as it is possible – reads Article 51 as ruling out the use of force for self-defence, other than that in response to an armed attack (Brownlie 1963, 227–75; Henkin 1979, 141–5; Akehurst 1984, 222–3; Simma 1994, 666–7).

State Practice and the UN Response

In almost all cases of unilateral use of force, states have claimed a defensive character. Where there was an actual armed attack, there was little controversy on the right of states to self-defence. However, practice illustrates that the circumstances under which states have raised the claim of individual self-defence do not necessarily involve an armed attack as such.

When India launched a full-scale attack against Pakistan on 3 December 1971 (for the background of the conflict see, Wheeler 2000, 55–9), its justification was self-defence against an earlier Pakistani attack and against the threat posed to Indian economy and security by the massive inflow of refugees caused by the repressive Pakistani policies in East Pakistan (UN Documents A/PV.2003 1971; S/PV.1611 1971). Although not expressly condemning the intervention, the UN considered Indian use of force as an immediate threat to international peace and security (GA Res. 2793 XXVI 1971; SC Res. 307 1971). The absence of condemnation in the related resolutions can be interpreted as the admission of the Indian claim that the situation in concern constituted a threat to its vital security interests, whereby the target state is unable or unwilling to act. However, it can also be inferred from the reference to Article 2(4) and repeated calls for withdrawal of troops and cease-fire in the resolutions that the claim is not admitted as one providing basis for self-defence. Although the Indian intervention might be considered to fulfil the conditions of necessity and immediacy, the UN did not qualify it as an act of self-defence due its disproportionate scale and consequence in relation to the aims allegedly pursued.

In December 1978, an estimated 100,000 Vietnamese troops entered Kampuchea, joined by some 20,000 United Front troops – a resistance organization, which was founded in the 'liberated area of Kampuchea'. After two weeks of fighting, the capital Phnom Penh fell, and a provisional government was created by the Front with the assistance of Vietnam.[8] During the Security Council's consideration of the matter, the Vietnamese representative asserted that Vietnamese action was a response to the persisting aggression of Pol Pot's regime against Vietnam (UN Doc. S/PV.2108 1979, 11–14). Apart from the Soviet Union, most states[9] including some communist countries[10] condemned the Vietnamese intervention.

---

8   For the course of events, see 'Vietnamese Invasion of Cambodia – Uprising led by United Front – Fall of Phnom-Penh', *Keesing's Record of World Events* 25 (May 1979).

9   For reactions of the members of ASEAN (Association of South East Asian Nations) for example, see 'Reactions in ASEAN Countries', *Keesing's* 25 (May 1979).

10 Among the communist countries that condemned the Vietnamese intervention were China, Romania, Yugoslavia and North Korea. For reactions of these countries, see 'Reactions

They stressed the need to observe the Charter's principle of non-interference in the internal affairs of states, respect for their independence, sovereignty and territorial integrity, and the settlement of disputes by peaceful means; and called for a cease-fire and the withdrawal of all foreign forces from Kampuchea. A number of states, among which were France, the United Kingdom, Norway and Portugal, argued that Pol Pot government's human rights violations could not justify intervention by another state (UN Documents S/PV.2108–2112 1979; S/PV.2114–2118 1979; S/PV.2129 1979). The United States, on the other hand, asserted that Vietnam's dispute with Kampuchea could not give Vietnam a right to take over that country (UN Doc. S/PV.2114 1979, 3). A draft resolution, which would call upon all foreign forces to withdraw from Kampuchea, failed due to the Soviet veto (UN Doc. S/13027 1979). Another draft resolution to the same effect sponsored by the five countries of ASEAN also failed for the same reason (UN Doc. S/13162 1979). Notwithstanding the Council's failure to take a position, the General Assembly adopted a resolution, by which the Assembly deeply regretted the armed intervention by outside forces in the internal affairs of Kampuchea and called for the immediate withdrawal of all foreign forces from Kampuchea (GA Res. 34/22 1979). In the following considerations of the situation, the Assembly stressed the need for all states' commitment to the principles of respect for the independence, sovereignty and territorial integrity of all states; non-intervention and non-interference in the internal affairs of states; non-recourse to the threat or use of force and peaceful settlement of disputes. It also deplored the continuation of the armed intervention (see GA Resolutions 35/6 1980; 36/5 1981; 37/6 1982; 38/3 1983; 39/5 1984; 40/7 1985; 41/6 1986; 42/3 1987; 43/19 1988, 44/22 1989). Judging from the debates and draft resolutions that were put to vote in the Council as well as the Assembly resolutions, it can be maintained that the majority of the Member States of the United Nations did not perceive the Vietnamese intervention in Kampuchea as an act of self-defence, despite the general recognition in the draft resolutions and the decisions of the Assembly of the conflict between Vietnam and Kampuchea. Notwithstanding the repeated Vietnamese complaints of Kampuchean aggression, the absence of an actual armed attack did not render its action as one of self-defence. In addition, Vietnamese action did not stop as soon as its alleged aim was realized and it retained an army of occupation in Kampuchea.[11]

In stark contrast to Vietnam's intervention in Kampuchea, Tanzania's intervention in Uganda in the same year[12] justified with similar terms was met with general indifference. In the vein of Vietnamese intervention, Tanzanian intervention also led to the overthrow of the existing Idi Amin regime and a change of government in Uganda. However, unlike Vietnam, Tanzania did not explicitly invoke the right of self-defence, although President Nyerere of Tanzania presented the Tanzanian military action as a defensive one in response to Uganda's

---

in Communist Countries', *Keesing's* 25 (May 1979).

11 Vietnam did not withdraw its forces from Kampuchea until the late 1980s.

12 For the events leading to Tanzanian intervention see, 'October 1978 Invasion of Tanzanian Territory by Uganda – International Reactions' and 'Tanzanian Military Action Against Uganda', *Keesing's* 25 (June 1979).

earlier invasion of the Tanzanian territory and occupation of Kagera Salient.[13] The Tanzanian intervention never came before the Security Council, nor was it debated by the General Assembly. The general lack of interest in the Tanzanian intervention may be contrasted with the Vietnamese one, which was justified on similar grounds and resulted in a similar outcome – the overthrow of the existing regime. The difference in reactions can be explained by the considerable agreement among states with Tanzania's claim that Uganda had attacked first (for further elaboration of the international reactions, see Wheeler 2000, 122–32).

When Israel launched a military operation to Lebanon in June 1982, it also justified its action on the basis of individual self-defence against the attacks across its northern border from PLO (Palestinian Liberation Organization) bases in southern Lebanon (UN Yearbook 1982, 435). The reactions to Israeli intervention were overwhelmingly negative. At various Security Council meetings held during 1982, all countries except the United States regarded the Israeli action as an act of aggression and condemned it (UN Yearbook 1982, 433–40, 452–7, 466–70). However, the United States veto prevented the Council to adopt a resolution to that effect (UN Doc. S/15185 1982). Nevertheless, the resolutions of 5 and 6 July, adopted unanimously, expressed concern for the violation of the territorial integrity, independence and sovereignty of Lebanon, and called for a cessation of all military activities and unconditional Israeli withdrawal from Lebanon (SC Resols. 508 1982; 509 1982). The following Security Council resolutions confirmed the Council's demand for an immediate cease-fire and withdrawal of all Israeli forces (SC Resols. 515, 1982; 516 1982; 517 1982; 518 1982). It was only in its 17 September resolution that the Council openly condemned unanimously the subsequent Israeli incursions into Beirut in violation of the cease-fire agreements and of Security Council resolutions (SC Res. 520 1982). The general disapproval of Israeli action was most notably reflected in the General Assembly resolutions. In its seventh emergency special session, the General Assembly, calling for withdrawal of Israeli troops, condemned Israel for its non-compliance with the Council resolutions of 5 and 6 June (GA Res. ES-7/5 1982). During the consideration of the matter, Israel's claim to have acted in self-defence was rejected by a number of states.[14] Virtually all states pointed out that Israeli allegations were unconvincing, and that its action was one of aggression and invasion (UN Yearbook 1982, 440–47, 458–66, 470–74). By a resolution adopted on 19 August, the Assembly once again condemned Israel for its non-compliance with the Council's resolutions (GA Res. ES-7/6 1982). In the subsequent resolutions on the matter, the Assembly expressed full support for the Council's demands for an immediate cease-fire and unconditional Israeli withdrawal from Lebanon, and called for strict respect of the territorial integrity, sovereignty, unity and political independence of Lebanon (GA Resols. ES-7/9 1982; 37/123 E 1982). As such, the Israeli action raised extensive

---

13 'Continued Mediation Efforts', *Keesing's* 25 (June 1979).

14 The countries, which pointed out that the Israeli claim of self-defence was a pretext for its aggression included Iraq, Pakistan, Poland, Belgium on behalf of the EC members, Indonesia and Zaire. *UN Yearbook* 1982, 442. Among other states rejecting the Israeli claim to have acted in self-defence were Mexico, Mongolia, Nigeria, Senegal and Uganda. *UN Yearbook* 1982, 460.

negative reactions from the international society.[15] It was condemned widely in the absence of an actual armed attack and due to the extensive character of the operation, which led to military occupation of half of Lebanon, including Beirut.

Thus, the UN response to the above cases of uses of force in self-defence has conformed to the restrictive interpretation of Article 51 and the customary requirements of necessity and proportionality in the exercise of the right of self-defence. Although there were prior acts of aggression involved in these cases, the absence of an actual armed attack together with the disproportionate magnitude of the military responses led to the UN's decline to consider those military interventions as acts of self-defence.

As to the right to anticipatory self-defence, the most representative case is Israel's bombing of the nuclear reactor under construction in Iraq in 1981 with the claim that the nuclear reactor in question would be producing nuclear material, which would be used in building nuclear weapons to attack Israel. Justifying the action on the basis of anticipatory self-defence, the Israeli ambassador to the UN stated that 'Israel was exercising its inherent and natural right of self-defence, as understood in general international law and well within meaning of Article 51 of the Charter' (UN Doc. S/PV. 2280 1981, 16). During the Security Council debates, taking a restrictive position on Article 51 by confining the right to self-defence to cases where there is an actual armed attack, several states, among which were Syria, Guyana, Pakistan, Spain and Yugoslavia, condemned the Israeli action. While some other states did not argue against a right of anticipatory self-defence, they pointed out that Israel failed to meet the necessity requirement. The representative of Sierra Leone, for example, making reference to the Webster formula, maintained that 'the plea of self-defence is untenable where no armed attack has taken place or is imminent' and deemed the Israeli action as an act of aggression(UN Doc. S/PV.2283 1981, 56). In the same vein, the British representative held that Israeli attack 'was not a response to an armed attack' and that '[t]here was no instant or overwhelming necessity for self-defence'. He expressed that the Israeli use of force could be positioned neither in international law nor in the Charter (UN Doc. S/PV.2282 1981, 42). Consequently, the Security Council unanimously condemned Israeli action and found 'the military attack by Israel in clear violation of the Charter of the United Nations and the norms of international conduct' (SC Res. 487 1981). Expressing the US view in the aftermath of the adoption of the resolution, the US Ambassador asserted that the Israeli action had violated the UN Charter o, particularly because Israel did not exhaust peaceful means for the resolution of this dispute (UN Doc. S/PV.2288 1981, 14). Thus, by implication, the US view also underlined the Israeli failure of fulfilling the conditions of necessity and immediacy.

---

15 For example, at the end of the 23rd European Council meeting in Brussels, which was held on 28–29 June 1982, the European states agreed that they had maintained 'their vigorous condemnation of the Israeli invasion of Lebanon'. Also, Yugoslavia asserted that military activities of Israel against the Palestinian forces in Lebanon were an act of aggression which ran 'counter to the principles of the United Nations Charter and the wishes of the entire international community'. See '23rd European Council Meeting in Brussels', and '12th Congress of League of Communists', *Keesing's* 28 (August 1982).

To sum up, the UN reaction to these individual cases of unilateral use of force on self-defence grounds has been in conformity both with the restrictive interpretation of Article 51 and the customary requirements of the exercise of the right of self-defence.

Bush Doctrine of Pre-emption

In the months leading up to March 2003, the Bush administration argued for a doctrine of *pre-emptive self-defence* far more extensive than traditionally understood, as a ground for invasion of Iraq under international law. At the 2002 West Point Commencement, President Bush stated that 'not only will the United States impose pre-emptive, unilateral military force when and where it chooses, but the nation will also punish those who engage in terror and aggression an will work to impose a universal moral clarity between good and evil'. He maintained that, 'If we wait for threats to fully materialize, we will have waited too long' (Bush 2002). The NSS of 2002 further articulated this conception of pre-emption by stating 'as a matter of common sense and self-defence, America will act against such emerging threats before they are fully formed' (NSS 2002, ii). It advanced the idea of pre-emptive American action in order to prevent hostile acts by adversaries (NSS 2002, 15). Referring to the legal ground for advocacy of such policy, the NSS asserted:

> For centuries, international law recognized that nations need not suffer an attack before they can lawfully take action to defend themselves against forces that present an imminent danger of attack. Legal scholars and international jurists often conditioned the legitimacy of pre-emption on the existence of an imminent threat – most often a visible mobilization of armies, navies, and air forces preparing to attack.
>
> We must adapt the concept of imminent threat to the capabilities and objectives of today's adversaries (NSS 2002, 15).

There are several problems with this assertion in relation to international order. First, this formulation of anticipatory self-defence is far broader than any previously claimed. In essence, it is based on the idea of prevention rather than pre-emption insofar as it conceives responses to non-imminent threats. It is the removal of the element of immediacy, which in turn dilutes the criterion of necessity, of this articulation that lies at the heart of the recent discussion. Where there is a credible evidence of an imminent threat and hostile intent, and that the threatened state has no alternative remedy, there is little objection to a state's use of force both as a matter of common sense and law. Given the changed nature of the threats, in particular emergence of new threats such as proliferation of WMD and terrorism, it is possible to conceive of threats that are real but not imminent. Indeed, these threats were identified not only in the American security strategy but also in the European Security Strategy of 2003 as the main challenges facing the international order and stability today. The problem with the expansive formulation of anticipatory self-defence, however, is less with the requirement of immediacy *per se*, when there is credible evidence of the reality of the threat in question – determined by capability and hostile intentions – and when there is no alternative course of action (Evans 2004, 65). The controversy arises as to the agency of the decision – whether the decision of a preventive offensive war can be taken unilaterally. In this sense, as the UN Secretary-General Kofi Annan asserted, the right to use force pre-emptively sets precedents for a 'proliferation of the unilateral and lawless use of force, with or without justifications' (Annan 2003b). As mentioned above, the Security Council is broadly empowered by the general language of Article 39, to deem such circumstances sufficient to authorize force. Further, the UN practice in the field of international peace and security is replete with instances of the Security Council's innovative means to deal with new challenges and threats. These include the development of peacekeeping forces, expansion of the concept of *threat to peace* from interstate conflict to internal matters such as human rights violations, and delegation of authority to national forces to carry out Chapter VII enforcement measures. Most recently, the Security Council's expansion of the scope of *armed attack* to include terrorist attacks by non-state entities stands as yet another example of the degree of UN's adaptability to the changing threats (see SC Res. 1368 2001). Thus, the point is that it is possible to conceive a multilateral action in order to tackle the emerging threats to international security without undermining the constitutive principles of international order.

Second, such loose understanding of pre-emptive action not only considerably removes the restraints on 'when states may use force' but also 'undermines the restraints on how states may use force' (O'Connell 2002, 19). A subjective determination of a possible attack logically leads to a subjective determination of the amount of force required for pre-empting a possible attack. Thus, not only the immediacy and necessity criteria but also the proportionality component of the traditional understanding of anticipatory self-defence becomes troublesome.

Finally, what is also problematic about the pre-emptive action contemplated in the NSS for international order is not only its unilateral character but also its total US focus (Roberts 2003, 47). The fact that the conception of extended anticipatory self-defence in the NSS does not entail a discussion of the limits and criteria of pre-emptive action as a possible resort by other states suggests that invocation of such a right is reserved to the US only. Hence, the lack of any reference to the norm of non-intervention underpinning international order together with the failure to discuss the repercussions of such aggressive unilateralism or widespread acceptance of such a right for international relations constitutes another flaw in the Bush doctrine of pre-emptive action. Admittance of such a broad right would amount to legitimization of potential future preventive strikes, possibly in the most conflict-ridden regions, such as Middle East, South and East Asia. In essence, it would lay the legal ground for any state to attack another regime with the claim of a possible future threat regardless of the evidence, which would in turn seriously undermine the international order and stability.

Collective Legitimization of Self-Defence after 9/11

The day after the September 11 events, the Security Council unanimously passed a resolution, which recognized 'the inherent right of individual and collective self-defence in accordance with the Charter', condemned the terrorist attacks of 9/11 and stated that it 'regards such acts, like any act of international terrorism, as a threat to international peace and security'. It also expressed the Council's 'readiness to take all necessary steps to respond to the terrorist attacks of 11 September 2001, and to combat all forms of terrorism', and recognized that Article 51 self-defence extended to use force against 'those responsible for aiding, supporting or harbouring the perpetrators, organizers and sponsors of these acts will be held accountable' (SC Res. 1368 2001). NATO assumed a similar stance by invoking collective defence clause of the Washington Treaty (Article 5) (North Atlantic Council 2001). A clear position was also taken by the European Council. On 21 September, affirming its solidarity with the United States, the EU stated that a US response was legitimate on the basis of Security Council Resolution 1368. The Member States declared that they were prepared to undertake actions that 'must be targeted and may also be directed against abetting, supporting or harbouring terrorists' (European Council 2001). A week later, the Security Council adopted Resolution 1373 of 28 September 2001. Reiterating main points of Resolution 1368, Resolution 1373 put a number of requirements on states to prevent the financing of terrorist acts and the recruiting of terrorists. Although these resolutions were not direct authorizations of force, by admitting a right of self-defence in this context, they nevertheless established a legal ground for the following US-led intervention in Afghanistan (Roberts 2003, 37). In addition, these resolutions and related statements recognized the right of self-defence to attack the terrorist bases on the territory of states that are unable or unwilling to prevent terrorist actions, and established regime responsibility for failure to prevent or punish such actions. Thus, once the US established the Taliban government's substantial involvement in providing support to the activities of Al Qaeda through credible evidence, the members of Security Council concurred with the US presumptions. Further, after the fall of the Taliban regime, the UN authorized the establishment of an International Security Assistance Force (ISAF) for maintenance of security in Kabul and in surrounding areas. By the same resolution, the Security Council also authorized participating states 'to take all necessary measures to fulfil its mandate' (SC Res. 1386 2001). The Security Council responses and resolutions together with wide state support evince that the US military campaign in Afghanistan was widely regarded legal as well as legitimate. Thus, one may point to a normative trend regarding the scope of self-defence towards extending the concept of *armed attack* to include acts of terrorism by non-state terrorist organizations, and by extension, the permissibility of the use of force against those regimes that have failed to prevent terrorist attacks.

The reactions to the US-led invasion of Iraq stand in stark contrast to the military intervention in Afghanistan. Although the US argued for a right of pre-emptive self-defence under international law against the threat of WMD and terrorism during the months preceding the war, it is notable that it did not employ this line of legal reasoning for its military action against Iraq. Instead, the US asserted that its action was authorized under existing Security Council resolutions (for detailed legal basis of the invasion argued by the US, see UN Doc. S/2003/351), most notably by Resolution

678 of 1990.[16] Similarly, the UK and Australia did not invoke self-defence (for UK's legal analysis, see Goldsmith 2003). They argued that Iraq's failure to uphold the 1991 cease-fire obligations of Resolution 687 (1991) had revived the authority to use force under Resolution 678 (UN Documents S/2003/350; S/2003/352). Merits of the US legal case – that there was no need for another resolution authorizing force after Resolution 1441, which determined that Iraq was in material breach of its obligations to authorize force (SC Res. 1441 2002) – and the issue of whether or not revival of the previous authorization of force is viable are out of the scope of the present study. This said, it has to be noted that there was explicit opposition at the UN to the US legal theory for the invasion. During the Security Council debate after the military action against Iraq, convened on 26 and 27 March 2003, the overwhelming majority of states condemned the US attack as 'violation of international law and the United Nations Charter', and called on the Security Council to 'end the illegal aggression' (UN Press Release SC/7705 4726th mtg. 2003). The Russian representative stated that none of the Security Council decisions 'authorizes the right to use force against Iraq outside the Charter of the United Nations', while Syrian delegate noted the following:

> the verbatim record of the meetings of the Security Council include comments by those members that are hastening to wage war against Iraq, confirming their belief that that resolution does not allow for international law to be circumvented or to permit a strike against Iraq without first reverting the Security Council (UN SCOR 58th Sess. 4726th mtg. at 26–8).

Indeed, at the Security Council debate after the adoption of Resolution 1441, the UK representative held that there was no *automaticity* in Resolution 1441, and stated that if there was a further Iraqi breach of its disarmament obligations, the matter would return to the Council for discussion as requires in paragraph 12 (UN Doc. S/PV 4644 2002, 5). Similarly, the US representative affirmed that the resolution embodied no *hidden tigers* or *automaticity* with respect to the use of force (UN Doc. S/PV 4644 2002, 3).

Many other states strongly objected to the intervention on legal grounds. Among them were Algeria, Belarus, Brazil, Cuba, India, Indonesia, Iran, Lebanon, Libya, Malaysia (as Chair of the coordinating bureau of the non-aligned movement), Sudan, Switzerland, Vietnam and Yemen (UN Press Release SC/7705 4726th mtg. 2003).

Further, the Council of the League of Arab States adopted a resolution on 24 March 2003, calling for immediate cessation of acts of war and withdrawal of foreign forces from Iraq (UN Doc. S/2003/365 2003). The UN Secretary-General Kofi Annan also expressed his concern prior to invasion that '[i]f the US and others were to go outside the Council and take military action it would not be in conformity with the Charter' (Annan 2003a). Later, he warned in his address to the General Assembly on 23 September 2003 that if states 'reserve the right to act unilaterally, or in ad hoc coalitions', this would be 'a fundamental challenge to the principles on which, however imperfectly, world peace and stability have rested for the last fifty-eight years' (Annan 2003b). Finally, there was significant public opposition to the war in

---

16 Resolution 678 authorized a coalition of states to repel Iraq from Kuwait and to restore international peace and security.

many states.[17] Consequently, the US action in Iraq was largely considered not only unlawful but also illegitimate to the extent that it lacked an explicit authorization from the Security Council and was undertaken despite strong expression of disapproval.

Conclusion

Article 2(4) of the UN Charter lays down the illegality of any unilateral use of force not authorized by the UN. The norm it establishes is consistently reaffirmed in a number of international documents as well as in the General Assembly declarations. The only exception to the general ban on the unilateral use of force is the right of self-defence as stipulated in Article 51. By allowing for only one condition as an exception to the prohibition of the use of force, the Charter has considerably limited the scope of legitimate self-help measures.

The UN reaction to the forcible actions in the post-UN Charter period unequivocally reflects that unilateral use of force on the basis of self-defence is subject to meticulous international review with a view to maintain international order and security. In the cases examined, the UN's application of self-defence as a legal ground for military actions has been contingent on whether the action taken was a response to an actual armed attack and on the principles of immediacy and proportionality.

Notwithstanding, after the devastating attacks of 9/11, a normative trend is discernible with regards to the scope of *armed attack*. The US was widely supported in its claim to defend itself against terrorist attacks mounted from Afghan territory. In addition, the subsequent Security Council resolutions affirmed the acts of terrorism by non-state entities might provide a permissible ground for states to use force in self-defence. Further, the right of self-defence against regimes that are unable or unwilling to prevent terrorist activities operating from their soil was also admitted.

The recent debate raised by the NSS is concerned with the preventive actions where the threat is not imminent. Nonetheless, the key element of the asserted US legal theory for military operation against Iraq was the Security Council mandate for enforcement of measures as it previously commanded, rather than an expansive understanding of self-defence as contemplated by the Bush doctrine. Central to the US and also UK legal justification was Iraq's failure to abide by the Security Council resolutions. Consequently, by justifying the invasion within the scope of the UN Charter and the Security Council previous resolutions, the US in fact demonstrated its respects to the Charter paradigm and confirmed the relevance of the Security Council to the maintenance of peace and security. By extension, the US decision not to raise the doctrine of pre-emption as a legal basis for its action can be presumed to indicate the concern with setting a potential precedent which could impair the UN Charter system. Thus, one can infer that the expanded notion of self-defence to include preventive military action has not led to a normative shift regarding the scope of self-defence. To the degree that the US sought collective blessing and adopted the

---

17 See for example 'Across Europe, Millions Protest a War in Iraq', *Washington Post*, 15 March 2003, at A17.

prevailing normative code in its discourse, international norms of self-defence as stipulated by the UN Charter and formulated in the customary international law, as well as UN's role in collective legitimization remain intact. As ICJ asserted in its *Nicaragua* decision:

> If a State acts in a way *prima facie* incompatible with a recognized rule, but defends its conduct by appealing to exceptions or justifications contained within the rule itself, then whether or not the State's conduct is in fact justifiable on that basis, the significance of that attitude is to confirm rather than to weaken the rule (ICJ Reports 1986, para 185).

In addition, the reluctance of the overwhelming majority of the Security Council to authorize use of force against Iraq demonstrates the international society's persisting conviction that the prohibition on the use of force is the primary safeguard for the preservation of international order and the peaceful coexistence among states. It follows that in the aftermath of 9/11, there has been a willingness to adapt the UN to deal with new kinds of threats, as exemplified in the extension of Article 51 self-defence to use force against non-state terrorist organizations as well as 'those responsible for aiding, supporting or harbouring the perpetrators, organizers and sponsors of ... acts' of terrorism (SC Res. 1368 2001).Nonetheless it is unlikely that the UN will apply a broad interpretation of Article 2(4) and Article 51 to unilateral preventive interventions in anticipation of a threat in cases where there is no credible evidence of the immanence of the threat both in terms of capability and specific intent. While deviations from the rules on the use of force can be expected, the US asserted doctrine of pre-emption has not generated general assent so as to lead a normative shift in the rules governing use of force. Further, the failure to find WMDs in Iraq as claimed, together with the sustained and violent reaction in Iraq following the invasion have not only underlined the international reluctance for a self-affirmed right of pre-emption, but also indicated that power lacking normative foundation cannot attain legitimacy and may yield to persistent and fierce resistance.

Finally, one can appraise the possible consequences of the repeated exercise of the US policy of pre-emption for the institutions of international society, specifically the balance of power, international law, diplomacy, war, and great power management (Bull 1977, 101–233). To begin with, as Bull argues, the existence of a general balance of power prevents 'the system from being transformed into a universal empire' (Bull 1977, 106). Moreover, stable balances of power are instrumental in removing the incentive to resort to preventive war and serves to maintain the system of states (Bull 1977, 107). Given the current dominance of the US in the international system and its unilateral policies, the existing system of states can hardly be conceived as at *balance*. In such a state, one might expect a growing endeavor by other powers to countervail the US pre-eminence. At the same time, such standing of the international system does also carry with it the danger of gradually undermining the conditions of effective functioning of other institutions on which international order depends – international law, diplomacy, war, and great power management (Bull 1977, 107). These institutions require a state of affairs whereby no one power is prevailing (Bull 1977, 117).

Further, the US exercise of pre-emptive action without proper application of the key elements of the customary international law would deeply impair the rules laid down by the society of states to confine reasons for which a state can legitimately resort to force, and would bring with it 'the threat of breakdown of international society itself into a state of pure enmity or war of all against all' (Bull 1977, 187). Arbitrary interpretation of the central principles of international law by the most dominant power in the international system would not only heavily undermine the efficacy of international law in international relations, but would also severely weaken the role of diplomacy. As Bull explains, diplomacy can perform no role 'where foreign policy is conceived as the enforcement of a claim to universal authority, the promotion of the true faith against heretics, or as the pursuit of self-regarding interests that take no account of the interests of others' (Bull 1977, 170–71).

On the other hand, the possible positive role war can play as Bull suggests – the enforcement of international law, preservation of the balance of power and advancement of a just change (Bull 1977, 188–9) – would also be eliminated by a widespread feeling that the use of force is self-serving and uninhibited rather than in the interests of the common values, rules and institutions of the international society as a whole, and with a degree of legitimacy. As a result, great powers' effective management of their relations with one another and their consequent contribution to international order would become problematic as well. Unless the US overcomes its crisis of international legitimacy, the vast gap in military capabilities between the US and the rest of the powers will remain a potential irritant and generate increasing unilateral tendencies on the part of the US and counterbalancing policies in return.

References

Akehurst, M. (1984), *A Modern Introduction to International Law* (London: George Allen and Unwin).

Annan, K. (2003a), Press Conference, The Hague, The Netherlands, 10 March 2003, <http://www.un.org/apps/news/infocusnewsiraq.asp?NewsID=421&sID=7>.

Annan, K. (2003b), 'The Secretary-General address to General Assembly', 23 September 2003, <http://www.un.org/webcast/ga/58/statements/sg2eng030923>.

Arend, A.C. and Beck, R.J. (1993), *International Law and the Use of Force, Beyond the UN Charter Paradigm* (London: Routledge).

Bowett, D.W. (1958), *Self-Defense in International Law* (New York: Frederick A. Praeger Inc. Publishers).

Brierly, J.L. (1942), *The Law of Nations, An Introduction to the International Law of Peace* (London: Oxford University Press).

Brownlie, I. (1963), *International Law and the Use of Force by States* (Oxford: Clarendon Press).

Bull, H. (1977), *The Anarchical Society, A Study of Order in World Politics* (London: Macmillan Press).

Bush, G.W. (2002), Graduation Speech, United States Military Academy, West Point, New York, 1 June 2002. <http://www.whitehouse.gov/news/releases/2002/06/20020601-3.html.>.

Cassese, A. (1994), *International Law in a Divided World* (New York: Oxford University Press).

Claude, I.L. Jr. (1966), 'Collective Legitimization as a Political Function of the United Nations', *International Organization* 20: 3, 367–79.

Damrosch, L.F. *et al.* (eds) (2001), *International Law: Cases and Materials* (St. Paul, Minn.: West Group Publishing).

European Council (2001), Conclusions and Plan of Action of the Extraordinary European Council Meeting on 21 September 2001, <http://ue.eu.int/ueDocs/cms_ Data/docs/pressData/en/ec/140.en.pdf>.

European Security Strategy (2003), 'A Secure Europe in a better world', 12 December 2003. <http://ue.eu.int/uedocs/cmsUpload/78367.pdf>.

Evans, G. (2004), 'When is it Right to Fight?', *Survival*, 46: 3, 59–81.

Finnemore, M. and Sikkink, K. (1998), 'International Norm Dynamics and Political Change', *International Organization* 52: 4, 887–917.

Goldsmith, P. (2003), UK Attorney General, 'Legal Basis for Use of Force against Iraq', 17 March 2003, <http://www.number10.gov.uk/output/Page3287.asp>.

Henkin, L. (1991), *Right v. Might, International Law and the Use of Force* (New York: Council on Foreign Relations Press).

Henkin, L. (1979), *How Nations Behave: Law and Foreign Policy* (New York: Columbia University Press).

Higgins, R. (1963), *The Development of International Law Through The Political Organs of the United Nations* (London: Oxford University Press).

Jennings, R.Y. (1938), 'The Caroline and McLeod Cases', *American Journal of International Law* 32, 82–99.

Kelsen, H. (1952), *Principles of International Law* (New York: Rinehart & Company).

Kelsen, H. (1951), *The Law of the United Nations* (London: Stevens & Sons Limited).

LaFeber, W. (1994), *The American Age, US Foreign Policy At Home and Abroad, 1750 to the Present* (New York: W.W. Norton & Company).

Lauterpacht, H. (ed.), Oppenheim, L. (1955), *International Law: A Treatise, Vol. I – Peace* (London: Longmans, Green & Co.).

McCormack, T.L.H. (1996), *Self-Defence in International Law, The Israeli Raid on the Iraqi Nuclear Reactor* (New York: St. Martin's Press).

National Security Strategy of the United States (2006), <http://www.whitehouse. gov/nsc/nss/2006/nss2006.pdf>.

National Security Strategy of the United States (2002), <http://www.whitehouse. gov/nsc/nss.pdf>.

North Atlantic Council (2001), Press Release, 12 September 2001, <http://www. nato.int/docu/pr/2001/p01-124e.htm>.

O'Connell, M.E. (2002), 'The Myth of Preemptive Self-Defense', ASIL Task Force Papers, <http://www.asil.org/taskforce/oconnell.pdf>.

Pratt, J.W. *et al.* (1980), *A History of United States Foreign Policy* (USA: Prentice-Hall, Inc.).

Roberts, A. (2003), 'Law and the Use of Force After Iraq', *Survival*, 45: 2, 31–56.

Schachter, O. (1991), *International Law in Theory and Practice* (Dordrecht, the Netherlands: Martinus Nijhoff Publishers).

Shaw, M.N. (1991), *International Law* (Cambridge: Grotius Publications Limited).

Simma, B. (ed.) (1994), *The Charter of the United Nations, A Commentary* (Oxford: Oxford University Press).

Thomas, A.V.W. and Thomas, A.J. Jr., (1956), *Non-intervention, The Law and Its Import in the Americas* (Dallas: Southern Methodist University Press).

Wheeler, N.J. (2000), *Saving Strangers, Humanitarian Intervention in International Society* (Oxford: Oxford University Press).

Chapter 10

Legitimacy, International Order, and Political Theory[1]

Scott G. Nelson

The extent of a man's, or a people's, liberty to choose to live as he or they desire must be weighed against the claims of many other values, of which equality, or justice, or happiness, or security, or public order are perhaps the most obvious examples. For this reason, it cannot be unlimited (Berlin 1998, 240) – Isaiah Berlin.

The fact that democracy continues to be invoked in American political rhetoric and the popular media may be a tribute, not to its vibrancy, but to its utility in supporting a myth that legitimates the very formations of power which have enfeebled it (Wolin 2004, 601) – Sheldon S. Wolin.

The quest for international order amidst dramatic political change was, until recently, a challenge stemming from the accelerated flux of a globalizing world. Today order is sought amidst growing regional violence sparked by a superpower state provoked by strikes and threats of asymmetric power. This power acquires its strength in large part by exploiting the networks and vulnerabilities of globalization. But international order is threatened by more fundamental vulnerabilities that lie at the heart of the liberal doctrines that undergird globalization's logics and processes. To get at these vulnerabilities, this chapter probes two foundational concepts that serve as crucial supports for the discourses and practices of international order in a perilous time: legitimacy and democracy. The ambiguous and uncertain role these concepts play in domestic spheres is rarely acknowledged and deserves critical elaboration. Unreflective appropriations of such concepts in international relations carry implications for stabilization and conflict mediation in many parts of the world.

1 Author's note: A version of this paper was presented at the Comparative Interdisciplinary Studies Conference in The Hague, 1–3 July 2006. Angela Liberatore won't recognize the paper that follows here, but her insightful comments on the earlier one make the considerably revised version much better. I would like to thank my colleagues Timothy W. Luke, Edward Weisband, and Laura Zanotti for providing feedback and making suggestions on improving some of the arguments; Stephen K. White gave me valuable suggestions for extending the analysis. I owe a lot to my colleague Yannis Stivachtis with whom I have had many conversations about the importance of legitimacy in international relations. I thank him for provoking me at many turns and for sharing his own work-in-progress that has been important to my thinking.

Most if not all of the prevailing notions of politics are what W. B. Gallie (1962) famously referred to as 'essentially contested concepts,' and by this he meant they are subject to endless disputes over their proper and intended uses and meaning. International order is certainly such a concept, as the papers in this volume attest. What order is and how it obtains – whether system- or structural-level constraints and dispositions are at work; whether and how ideas and ideals play a role; whether the age-old struggle for power gives rise to balancing and thus contributes to system stability; whether market forces and an integrating world economy are contributing factors; and finally, whether eternal *fortuna* has a hand – all of these aspects and so many more present enormous questions for our understanding of order and how it should be analysed. Not least among the set of concerns one has when grappling with such a concept is that the very notion of order itself assumes that any political *form* that could be said to embody or constitute 'the international', 'the world', or 'the system', is meant to function as a bounded, coherent, representable *whole* with its own self-representable strategies that govern how the *form* should be understood and meaningfully analysed. Is the *form* of politics to which order refers and defers considered to be orderly or is it anarchical, and to what degree? Is the *form* even political, and in what sense? Such questions, in fact, require at least two prior questions: what, exactly, is the essence of order if what it amounts to is something less than 'it all', and how does the very *idea* of a bounded 'system' presuppose the notion of some condition or 'rule' of order (over, say chaos or anarchy or war) itself?

Such concerns as these remind us that we are all, for good or worse, indebted to Hobbes' famous assumption that the state of nature is strictly a non-political domain, and that order (and by this Hobbes meant stability and peace) is made possible only after a common power is imposed (1994). Also worth remembering is that order, in Hobbes' mind, is only said to obtain within a well-bounded space. And perhaps what is most important of all, the power which installs order is the only power capable of giving things, entities, and actions within that space their intended meaning. Only after a common set of meanings is adopted (or imposed) does order become possible, and can politics itself begin.

Hedley Bull (2002) resisted the strict Hobbesian view that politics requires a sovereign power capable of holding all actors to account. Cooperation and regulated intercourse among states happen in the absence of such a power, and under the right circumstances an ethos of cooperation installs itself, grows, and matures over time, delivering the system of states from anarchy to something that looks more like a commodious society with its diffusion of ideas, culture, technology, capital, and goods. Bull was a close reader of Hobbes, and he learned from other close readers of Hobbes, including Kant, who saw the inconsistencies and (perhaps intentional) ambiguities in Hobbes' great theory. Bull saw that Hobbes fashioned a thought experiment that would allow him to say a lot more about political life than history would let him get away with. Hobbes admitted, again it is worth remembering, that the state of war that obtained in the state of nature never actually existed as a real, historical condition, much less as a permanent 'order of things', in any society. Contrived though it was, the state of nature as a condition of 'a war of every man against every man' was a powerful starting point for theorizing a political life. Bull wondered though, what this life was made to constitute, what it represented, and what was the cost to our conceptions of the politically possible as a result of these particular assumptions and definitions, and not others.

Assumptions, definitions, and the many concepts we use to theorize international politics mattered profoundly for the development of the great schools of international theory. The English School abounded in concepts that theorists like Hedley Bull, Martin Wight, Adam Watson and others developed and elaborated in rich, textured analyses. But for the student of international relations today it seems the fascination of discovery and analysis may not be found within the schools, paradigms, or great debates of the discipline, so much as it lies with the very concepts of theoretical analysis themselves, concepts like order and realism and morality and security and democratization and many others that must be unpacked with fresh eyes. Today, thanks in part to the likes of the English School theorists, we seem to have a greater appreciation of perspectives and analytical approaches not found within the accepted schools and traditions of the discipline, and it may pay to look closely at recent theorisations of seminal concepts to understand how and why reaching beyond accepted schools and traditions can illuminate some hidden redounds of order and war in the late-modern international imagination.

For the past five years political theorists have become prominent spokespersons in public discussions of foreign policy, security strategy, diplomacy, international law as well as several offshoots of these principal scholarly fields of world politics. At the time of this writing the momentous military and diplomatic failures in Iraq, North Korea, Iran, Sudan, Israel-Lebanon-Palestine and elsewhere, as well as what can only be regarded as a calamitous (often called neo-conservative) doctrine of engaging perceived enemies through hard-asset military confrontation or the threat thereof, have thrust a once-specialized vocabulary and grammar of thinking into public discussions bearing upon the nature, appropriate use, and limits of American power. What is immediately noteworthy is that this vocabulary and grammar have been so widely dispersed, occupying non-specialized fields and at times reaching into popular media venues that comprise much of mainstream American political discourse. In academic settings, scholars in such fields as geography, economics, religious studies, history, and cultural studies among others, regularly weigh in on ongoing foreign policy debates, many of which are pitched at a theoretical level. Sovereignty, realism, neo-conservatism, Islamic-fascism, liberal internationalism, human rights, national identity structures, democracy, freedom, benign dictatorship, colonialism, sectarianism – these and concepts like them increasingly populate the political rhetoric and drive debates. These have become the defining concepts of the times. They are the concepts everyone feels the need to speak, to pronounce in some authoritative gesture, as if to probe the heart of the orders and logics of world politics after 11 September 2001.

The many people speaking on these themes, scholars in any number of fields and commentators from none of them, often find themselves talking with (and in some cases *as*) scholars of international relations theory in what might be called the classical sense. In using the term 'classical' I do not mean to propagate the idea, firm in many practitioners' minds, that international relations is a wholly autonomous field of expertise with a well-bounded history, a proven claim to a well-defined system of 'core' knowledge, a firm research agenda, and highly specified and widely practiced methodological protocols. Still less do I pretend that theories pertaining to world politics themselves constitute a single, autonomous knowledge or analytical domain.[2] True, analyses offered by specialists do carry a certain weight. Also true, in public discussions the voices of 'the classicists' often rise above, although more often of late they have been drowned out by commentators with no special training in the histories and theories of international relations. The volume, the vitriol, and not least the sheer number of people speaking in public forums on the subject of world politics today gives us reason to pause and ask, what explains the attraction of time-honored concepts and what might be called *the draw of theory?* What do the experts know about political theory, and why should we look to them for guidance vis-à-vis the signal international crises of our time?

It can be regarded as a platitude that expertise usually derives in part from a critical facility with the presuppositions and assumptions governing a field of knowledge. Also of first-order importance is an understanding of historical vicissitudes that offer up ontological 'constants' as basic entities with pride of place in theoretical analyses – entities such as an account of human nature, or assumptions dealing with the 'fact of anarchy', state behavior, the security environment, or the 'communal virtues' that fuel state cooperation. True, expertise should not become so specialized that theoretical presuppositions or the long arch of history gets forgotten or sublimated. Just the same, theoretical explorations risk becoming so diffuse that rhetorical insistence trumps analytical depth. Theory should infuse the specialist's work and not merely in terms of serving as a guide for empirical study. Theoretical analysis is a method or a resource of *critical* interrogation. It allows the practitioner to separate out contingency from necessity, asking how the products of human choices come to be regarded as natural and necessary, and additionally, asking how things might be otherwise than they are, how relations among people or states might be improved, how relations might effect non-violent change amidst the fitful and all too violent march of large-scale forces like global capitalism and the politics of superpower.[3]

This chapter argues that one of the more interesting intellectual developments bearing upon world-political discussions of late – again, speaking only of the past five years – is the turn to *theory*. More precisely, what is noteworthy is the return of a form of inquiry utilized by scholars in disciplines well outside the officialdom of international relations, scholars concerned with the state of the world-political and America's role in dictating or effecting change therein. Needless to say, the 'state' of international relations at the present time is structured and delineated by the global war on terrorism. But the terrorist imaginary defers to a host of other potent theoretical signifiers and some extremely dense theoretical doctrines and debates. Freedom, democracy, and the limits to American power, are examples. In relation to this time and the terms and concepts in use today, scholars must grapple with the

---

2 For a discussion of the history of international relations in terms of the construction of an analytical field amidst the forces of consolidation in the social sciences, Jim George (1994) is still useful.

3 I am adopting Sheldon S. Wolin's use of the term 'superpower'. See Wolin (2004), chapter seventeen: 'Postmodern Democracy: Virtual or Fugitive?'

very nature, the task, if not the obligation, of theoretical analysis and the perspective it affords. The obligation pertains to a labor that theoretical analysis is meant to perform, one could even say is *duty-bound* to perform, bearing upon dramatic events and transformations now so fiercely underway. As will be shown, the labor that theory undertakes has implications not only for *understanding,* but also for the forms of political community that are pursued.

The voices of theory heard today were present prior to September 2001; many existed long before the end of the Cold War.[4] But something has changed in the urgency as well as the complexity of those analyses that are probing the policies now under such intense public scrutiny in so many parts of the world. Urgency, it might be said, is one with our time. Danger is the distance that separates order and chaos; danger is also the timbre of the times, a consciousness of the frailty of 'our time', a *sense* of urgency and immediacy that takes the form of a *conscience* as well as a *consciousness,* a moral temperament and a way of knowing bearing upon *a* time and *a* space for politics. Fear intervenes in this moral economy. As Hobbes well knew, fear presides over the politics we endeavor to craft into some manageable work of art that for the last four hundred years has taken two dramatic forms, both of which are the work of a uniquely *modern* artifice: the sovereign state and the international order.

What kinds of criticism are today being offered in theoretical idioms? What new insights might revisiting a few theoretical concepts and concerns – as well as their attendant paradoxes, ambiguities, and uncertainties – afford? Might we become better attuned to arguments they disclose not heard before – to new ways of phrasing old questions, new temperaments and nuances of elucidation, to novel logics that challenge current modes, one could even say *styles,* of thinking?[5] What is the distance that separates the scholar or a disciplinary field laboring in international or political theory from the insights being sought? Those who find themselves called upon to speak of history's lessons – economic contingencies that merit mention, violent cultural generalizations bandied about, religious fissures that are pronouncing themselves anew – all of this and so much more is done today in the service, it would seem, of apprehending new dangers in a world escaping our control. What might theoretical analysis contribute just here?

The turn (or *return*) to theory bearing upon recent world-political events and the trends they have helped set in motion has good and bad causes, and good and bad consequences. This chapter will speak briefly to aspects of both, but its principal concern involves speaking to some neglected theoretical redounds of the modern imagination where some important lessons, or in any case *teachings*, might help one grapple more skillfully with critical choices today. As we watch in terrified

---

4   Among the many voices which have become so very prominent are Mearsheimer and Walt (2006), Barber (2004), Kateb (2006). Among the less prominent but nonetheless penetrating analyses is Wolin (2003); (2004); and Butler (2004).

5   The word 'styles' in this context is adapted from Edward Said's *Orientalism* in which the discourses of Orientalism are understood as *stylized* expressions of thought, discourses and networks of interests that are put to work in the service of interpreting, dominating, structuring and having authority over (Said 1994, 2–3).

fascination the onset of what so many have claimed is a radically new era of world politics, an era as of yet unnamed which gestures to a reality so opaque, so ill-timed, and turning ever-more violent, we must assess the prospects for order through political imaginaries that are increasingly taking on global forms the nature and terms of which remain profoundly unclear. Indeed, the very nature of change itself makes the task of sighting humane orders that can be achieved all the more difficult. The work of theory, then, must grapple with the increased pace of world-historical trends and transformations. In front of emerging realities (perhaps) not of our choosing but certainly of our making we find ourselves in a condition much like Walter Benjamin's 'Angel of History', the figure inspired by Paul Klee's 'Angelus Novus.' A figure *of* history, inescapably contingent, thrown backward, his wings collapsed as the storm of history hurls 'wreckage upon wreckage' in front of his feet, Benjamin proscribed a condition that was also our only hope. In a word, theoretical analysis must concern itself with the status of what appears a single 'chain of events' out of which catastrophe is necessarily produced (Benjamin 1955, 259–260).

On the Status and Power of Theory

I want to concentrate on a sphere of theory that deals mainly with domestic political experience. This may strike the reader as curious given the fact that I have been calling attention to theoretical work in international relations. The long tradition of reflections on politics – invoking such concerns as the just community, the exercise of authority by right as opposed to decree, the ideal of autonomy, the limits to the legitimate exercise of power and so forth – all of this is itself very much constitutive of international political theory. We might observe that what might be called 'domestic theory' pre-frames, as it were, what has come to be called international relations theory; knowledge of the manner in which it does so is critical to current debates. We might call the sphere of domestic theory 'Sphere 1'. 'Sphere 2' refers to the theory of international relations. Neither sphere is as singular and distinct as is often assumed – each has long been intertwined with the other, though never in exactly the same ways at the same times. Nevertheless, the fact that overlap exists does not mean we should dispense with two unique and distinct *categories* of analysis (as long as awareness that such categories are historically produced is itself subject to interrogation). Each sphere has its own history, and each historical recounting provides a glimpse as to how efforts in each sphere have tried to shore the one up against the other, against that which threatened to intrude, intervene, and overcome. We might consider the forms of political experience each sphere elucidates, reworks and refines. If experience typifies a character attributable to a community, and if the community has finite, if elastic boundaries, then perhaps the Western tradition's reflections on what it is possible to achieve as a community is relevant for the United States' (and ultimately also Europe's) experience in Iraq and elsewhere in the Middle East. It may also be relevant to the type of international community nations might work together to advance.

What does it mean to foundationalize our assumptions about politics? Does a commitment to basic entities that account for a political life, human nature for example, shield some entities, adjacent ones, from critical questioning? Certainly no one in this 'critical age' wants to leave anything unexamined, and yet the need to secure an unquestioned fundament for our claims, empirical and normative, persists. In conceptualizing world politics, the need to destabilize an unquestionable fundament (sovereignty, for example) can be suddenly revoked, especially when the destabilizing question is issued from outside the domain which lays claim to a privileged understanding of survival itself. Political realism in a Morgenthauian gloss, for example, elaborates a doctrine of foreign policy which reserves the basic right to stand in need of foundational assumptions – for example, the state – and every actor in the international system is said to regard recourse to this right as necessary, given as it is in the one sure universal of political life, what Machiavelli termed *necessita*. Still, political and international theory proceeds much of the time as if the right to issue foundational assumptions will *not* be exercised. International institutions are erected on the faith that much can be achieved when various, competing interests seek ways to share the burdens of global governance and imbue these institutions with trust and an ethic of mutuality. Think of the values embodied in the UN Charter and the Universal Declaration of Human Rights, or the WTO's principles of reciprocity and non-discrimination. The state is a foundational concept or entity, but its existence as a conceptual entity is determined in part by a *system* of states with a foundational ontology uniquely its own. Yet, in crucial respects the system's ontology is contingent upon the notion of statehood itself. The state and the system, then, share an identity of mutual, relational affinity.

Do theorizations of foundational concepts yield tensions and paradoxes lodged at the heart of our motives which issue these concepts into intellectual circulation? Certainly they do, at least by measure of the concepts that figured prominently in Machiavelli's writings. Think of the manner in which he engages the concepts of *virtu* and *fortuna* in *Il Principe* and *Discorsi*. Skill, intelligence, wit, sagacity, knowledge and strength served as the primary characteristics of successful leadership. But as effective instruments of statecraft they invariably encountered the winds of *fortuna*, she who 'demonstrates her power where precautions have not been taken to resist her [*dove non e ordinata virtu a resisterle*]' (Machiavelli 1994, 75). Or in his *Leviathan*, consider the emphasis Hobbes places upon human rationality, a characteristic he ascribes to all individuals who, as it happens, are also driven to take actions out of fear (Hobbes 1994). Or consider Kant's careful negotiation of the requirement of a benign, sovereign power capable of shoring up the borders in order to permit the free exercise of public reason which can only go so far in questioning the sovereign's legitimacy (Kant 1991). In each of these thinkers the foundational concepts are posited, delineated, and affirmed against others that threaten their viability. The flux of time is also at work as each thinker wrestles with the forces of history that threaten efforts to secure the orders – domestic and international – which the conceptual entities are designed to establish. Each theorist stresses that historical vicissitudes can be harnessed toward the task of establishing a workable, long-lasting polity, and yet the flux of time and the violent reordering of political space is what each most wants to guard against.

Contemporary theorists exhibit these same tensions and paradoxes. One could follow Robert Cox's thinking captured in his famous remark that theory 'is always *for* someone and *for* some purpose' as far as it goes (Cox 1981, 128). Cox rightly emphasizes the vested interests at work in any theory's articulation. However, one may ask if the interests which ground any theory are held and secured as stable, coherent, bounded interests for very long. One may be skeptical of the idea that interest are themselves coherent efforts to achieve a single, or even an amalgam of several, self-same *aims* for *particular* reasons that can be ascribed to definitive, unchanging *motives.* Such doubts about the coherence and status of vested interests do not invite paralysis, but instead introduce circumstance and distinction, space and time, into our theorizations about politics. Priorities shift over time because identities mutate and rework themselves as assertions of self and other are mediated by always-already-unfolding habits of thinking which *themselves* change and reorient interests and allegiances. Theory must therefore be a mobile strategy of thought and articulation. It is critical to be aware of the frames it imposes on whatever social reality it strives to constitute and illuminate against the force of time and the circumstance of place.

To put the idea in social science parlance, Sheldon Wolin has suggested on several occasions that political theory enjoys a certain status when it aspires to a *critical* analysis of the nature, terms, and direction of a political life that comprises many different spheres of human activity. A sense of judgment is necessary in order to discriminate among various spheres of life. A sense of appropriateness of judgment is as well.

> Appropriateness of judgment ... depends upon varied forms of knowledge for which there is no natural limit. This dependence is rooted in the basic quest of political and social theory for theoretical knowledge about the "wholes" made up of interrelated and interpenetrating provinces of human activity. Whether the primary theoretical task be one of explanation of critical appraisal, the theorist will want to locate "divisions" in the human world and embody them in theoretical form. For example, what aspects of that division which we call "religion" have a significant bearing on the activity called "economic"? Perforce, a political theory is, among many other things, a sum of judgments, shaped by the theorist's notion of what matters, and embodying a series of discriminations about where one province beings and another leaves off. The discriminations may have to do with what is private and what is public, or they may be about what will be endangered or encouraged if affairs move one way rather than another, or about what practices, occurrences, and conditions are likely to produce what state of affairs (Wolin 1969, 1076).

We often forget that theory works spatially to delimit a representable field of experience – it critiques the space that is, and it points to a space that might be. Wolin says that political theorists must recollect and restate what is common to that space, what might be termed the 'space of experience', what is rightly *shared*, in order to contrive ways of ordering that experience differently. Wolin's term for a common political experience is a rather obtuse notion called 'the political', a notion he distinguishes from 'politics'. If politics is the rough-and-tumble of vested power, party and interest-group politics, 'the political' 'signifies the attempt to construe the terms of politics so that struggles for power can be contained and so that it is possible to direct it for common ends, such as justice, equality, and cultural values' (Wolin 1988, 198). Theoretical labor positions itself just here, based as it is on a willingness to understand how and why such ends have been pursued historically, and an exploration of why and how certain ends might be adjusted to promote another politics, or recalibrated to better match the challenges of a time.

One payoff of this kind of analysis is that we might come to better understand more than *who* is doing the speaking, and with what *ends* in mind. We might come to better understand why we have developed the habits in thinking politics in the ways that we have, how we might think outside of known and familiar parameters – parameters established for what reasons, at what costs? – and how new possibilities and limits might be apprehended.

The Problem of Political Legitimacy

Political legitimacy is one of the more complex notions in Western political thought. It is complex as a *problem,* as a problematical *idea* that modern thought returns to again and again, concerned as it is to define, specify, or constitute justifiable grounds for government, civil society, and politics more generally. Political legitimacy is complex in its conceptuality, in the way it has been used to frame the problem of politics for moderns, to define and constitute the possibility of a politics of the experiential, of the communal in the sense of that which is *rightly* shared, an experience of the past that is valued and deserves to be advanced into the future. Of course, just what is meant by 'the communal' impacts the conception of legitimacy that is meant to serve as its ground. There are multiple ways in which legitimacy is essentially paradoxical, an unresolvable idea whose unresolvability, curiously, must be masked. Moreover, legitimacy is an essentially contestable notion which produces certain vulnerabilities in political thought, or infinitely unraveling contestations which produce a politics with which we are still, it seems, somehow unable to grapple.

If the concept, the idea, the *problem* of political legitimacy has been central to the modern political imagination, its mediation in modern theory has not often been placed at the center of political thought. There are exceptions. One does not have to read very far in Rousseau's *On the Social Contract* to see how his concern for legitimate power, the power of right, animates this foundational work of democratic theory. Right of law, says Rousseau, has no meaning in relation to force because when one is forced to act, when one acts out of necessity, one does not exercise will, one does not act voluntarily. According to Rousseau 'one is obliged to obey only legitimate powers' (Rousseau, 1987, 19–20). 'As soon as one can disobey with impunity, one can do so legitimately', he writes. The right of the social order does not come from nature, though he admits all power comes from God. So, he insists, does every disease. Rousseau worries, or suspects, that the strongest are capable of transforming 'force into right and obedience into duty' (19). He has already famously established that while man is born free, he finds himself everywhere in chains. He wonders how this change took place, and then he wonders what can render this change legitimate (17). Rousseau says that if slavery can be made to seem a legitimate condition that arises out of *necessity,* all hope for human liberty is lost.

All hope for morality is lost, in other words – for decisions motivated by a voluntary will capable of serving as the foundation stone of liberty. A will to obey, a feeling of duty, of being obliged – this will had a sacred status for Rousseau. In obliging, one exercises choice. Cowardice stands in the way of the will for Rousseau, much like it did for Kant. We will come back to Kant, but for now we should register this anxiety – how something that is arbitrary can come to be regarded as legitimate – of Rousseau's, an anxiety one does not find in Locke, a thinker to whom Rousseau owes quite a lot. The anxiety is certainly to be found in Hobbes. Hobbes recognized the problem legitimacy posed for politics, but his ultimate objective was not to call attention to its complexity for all to see, much less to illuminate how a condition can be made to *seem* legitimate when in reality it is not. Hobbes handled matters differently, wanting to offset the individual's natural inclination to question the legitimate nature of authority by providing proofs – visible, legible instantiations of stability and order – that could be observed as the necessary provisions of a just government. His hope, at least by some accounts, was to give people over to the idea that order was made possible through the unambiguous, rational formation of a civil commonwealth. Legitimacy would become the unquestioned order, the 'social convention' in Rousseau's terminology. For Hobbes, legitimacy was derived from the laws of nature, laws which are themselves derived from the natural condition of 'man.' So Hobbes' argument proceeded by and through convention as well, but he went to great lengths to conceal the arbitrariness of the conventionality.

In spite of differences in the constitution of political experience, it is legitimacy that founds the rule of law for a domestic polity. What links legitimacy to the rule of law is a *modern* orientation of politics itself: the social order can only be governed through convention as opposed to by God or by Nature, and yet it would not come to be regarded as necessarily frail in their light. Strangely, convention becomes linked to God or Nature by way of a *striving* that is itself critical to modern theory.[6] Kant, for example, in seeking to constitute a new God or a new Nature, pressed his ethical and political doctrines by willing human thought in a kind of outward elaboration of every human's innate reasoning capacity. According to William Connolly, the legacies of convention linger on today. A wide variety of political theorists, from Rousseau to Arendt to Derrida to Agamben concur, according to Connolly, that:

> a democratic state seeking to honor the rule of law is also one with a sovereign power uncertainly situated within and above the law. The rule of law in a state is enabled by a practice of sovereignty that rises above the law. Often the paradox of sovereignty is asserted with respect to the founding of a state, but those who locate a paradox in the founding act typically discern its echoes and reverberations in the state that results as

---

6 Sheldon Wolin speaks to this in his *Tocqueville Between Two Worlds: The Making of a Political and Theoretical Life* (2001). Chapters 1 and 2 are important in this context for the connections Wolin establishes between modern theory and modern power. His discussion of Hobbes on page 44 is especially important with respect to what is referred to here as 'striving'.

well ... For a polity of self-rule through law to emerge out of a nondemocratic condition, "effect would have to become cause." This is so because the spirit needed to nourish democratic self-rule can only grow out of [a] prior ethos of community already infused into the populace. The complication revolves around, first, whether these infusions exceed or express the self-rule of the people itself, and, second, how to wheel either condition, which depends upon the other, into place without first installing the other that depends upon it (Connolly 2004, 24).

Theorists like Connolly think it is important to explore the echoes and reverberations of such a paradoxical condition of politics. If legitimacy remains an interesting paradoxical condition or at least a problematical aspect of contemporary politics, these unintended but inescapable features, the *forces* we can attribute to discursive articulations within modern theory, are likely to produce political effects. Many of these will be swept under the rug because they come not from a genuine political *place*, not from expressly stated political concerns. Indeed, these political effects may acquire a certain *status* in the social order. *This* status just may combine with attempts one would presume are always being made to give people over to the idea of an unquestioned political ground, a truly *legitimate* political experience. The democratic experience, for example, or more accurately, what is made to count as its *ideal*. It is conceivable, too, that *these* attempts manifest themselves *discursively*, through rhetorics which embody a 'complex assemblage', to use Connolly's apt phrase (Connolly 2005), of intended and unintended meanings, articulations, signs, valorizations, cultural accoutrements, capital flows, and so forth. These factors are all part and parcel of what travels under the term 'world-political order' today, but precisely *how* they do, and how they issue from a paradoxical condition of modern politics is very difficult to grasp.

Think, for example, of all the meanings folded into the ideals of freedom and democracy today. One does not need to scratch very far below the surface of Bush administration rhetoric to see that free markets are granted primacy over and above other commodities of democratic societies, such as affordable health care, education, clean air and water, and so forth. But how is it that a discourse of freedom and democracy acquires its strength trumpeting certain values which benefit the few at the expense of the many? How does this discourse work? How does it offer up liberty as an unlimited commodity with no bearing upon other 'goods', such as equality, justice, security, or ecological sustainability?

The point here is to emphasize that prying open the terms, concepts, discourses, rhetorics and representations trafficked about reveal ambiguities and paradoxes with latent power. The ambiguities and paradoxes at the heart of Rousseau's democratic polity trigger efforts to mask the frail foundations upon which the experience is made to rest. Analyses of freedom and its delivery to other parts of the world must scratch below *this* surface; the outcome of such exercises will make us less sanguine about the virtues we have to bequeath. Why is it, we might ask, that we see ourselves in a position to offer *our* virtues to those beyond *our* borders who are thought to stand in need of an experience *we* are said to share and *they* are thought to not? Who is we and they, and what are the historical contingencies that effect both as a function, in part, of their imagined sacred, transcendental status?

Legitimacy and the Democratic Experience

Is it possible today to speak about democracy not in terms of its imagined ideal, but in terms of the impulse that triggers the term's discursive circulation? Can one attribute to the idea, and the idea in relation to the times in which it is invoked, a gravity or weight, a density? Indeed, we can, and we well *should*: an interrogation of the values we associate with the term must also concern itself with the times, broadly speaking, and the cultural dispositions that are said to be prevalent in those times and which help to trigger the term's entry into language. Consider, for example, a powerful cultural disposition at work today in the United States: nationalism. Nationalism has mixed of late with various Christian temperaments and tendencies, and together they hitch their wagon to a latent imperial attitude that has long seen America promoting democracy in the world with a missionary zeal. This is how the values ascribed to democracy, especially after 11 September 2001, acquire their cultural and historical density. But how does the concept of democracy operate in, as, and through *discourse* – through its appropriation in a rhetorical economy, a *political* economy, where various elements of its usage are all too readily spoken, and (perhaps) all too readily received?

There is thus good cause to scrutinize the *discourses* of democracy which find themselves in articulation in discussions of foreign policy today. By the term discourse I mean, following Kathy Ferguson, 'the characteristic ways of thinking and speaking that both constitute and reflect our experiences by illuminating certain roles, rules, and events while leaving others unnamed' (Ferguson 1987, 209). As Connolly writes, 'a mode of discourse does not merely describe a world that exists independently of it; it helps to constitute the character of the social world it delineates' (Connolly 1988, 34). Discourses of democracy, then, do more than serve as a beacon for our political hopes and aspirations. They also prepare the way for their uncritical acceptance. It is therefore crucial to examine the *discursive economy* of democracy by attending to what is and is not being said in those quarters where the concept is invoked to explain and, more importantly, legitimate democracy's spread as a foreign policy objective. One can invoke various idioms of foreign policy theory and explore their dimensions in time – say, the Cold War years, the Clinton-Bush decade, and after 11 September 2001. It is surely worth taking aim at some of the predominant ways in which the concept is invoked after the start of the second Iraq war, and in doing this we situate a highly specific discourse on democracy within an 'order' that lends it considerable power, providing what might be called 'democracy talk' with a series of cultural supports that help ease the concept's uncritical circulation. An analysis of the said and the unsaid of democracy with respect to what it is that allows the term to travel in our language with unusual ease allows us to study the limits which the saying experiences in all those cultural venues of American life the discourse has reached. These venues are no doubt lending power to the logic of neo-liberal politics that are part and parcel of the mechanisms and logics of globalization (Harvey 2005; Smith 2005).

If the 'great commodities' we associate with democracy are discursively produced, then the concept and the values to which it has recourse do not exist outside of history (Dunn 2005). They are inescapably bound to history, but more exactly they are also inescapably bound up with *accounts* of history and democracy's believed figuration in historical representation. That is to say, discourses of democracy in foreign policy proceed along different lines after Hobbes, after Kant, after Marx, Lenin, and after Fukuyama.[7]

What is also noteworthy about the discursive power of democracy today is, again, how it acquires traction through its association with dense cultural formations to which it is inextricably bound. By 'density' we mean the intersections of a plethora of cultural forces and impulses that activate what can be made to count as an already well-regarded, coherent, stable, bounded ethos of the democratic will. By virtue of the ways 'democracy talk' combines with nationalism, Christianity, and global capitalism, to name but a few potent cultural formations, it becomes an especially powerful force in American political culture. A host of other cultural forces intersect and are sometimes in fairly close alignment with these forces; sometimes they may be at cross-purposes before they are liquidated altogether. Religion, nationalism, patriotism, capitalist legitimation crises and so forth – all of these impinge upon the general discursive fields within which democracy figures so very prominently today.

We might take greater interest in two main economies that structure democracy's discursive production. The first concerns democracy as a realizable geo-spatial commodity, a commodity to which falls the task of securing the conditions for domestic freedom within a well-circumscribed space of political experience. Think of the geo-politics of the Middle East, specifically Iraq, Palestine, Syria and Iran. There is a temporal component to the domestic realization of democratic government that is intimately bound up with the spatial dimension. We should be probing the many ways in which it is so bound up. The second economy concerns democracy as *strategy,* specifically the pursuit of democratization through, say, the Bush administration's foreign policies which involve war as the initial mechanism of democracy's installment (Pickering and Peceny 2006). Spatial and temporal exigencies are at work here as well, but this second economy is concerned with democracy's promotion through the projection of power across state boundaries through hard-asset, military power.

As Dunn demonstrates (2005), democracy is not a stable, isolatable, inherently coherent concept or doctrine of thinking. As a concept received from the distant past it travels with considerable moral-ethical luggage derived from the endless affirmations of a sacred 'democratic experience' that are designed to do more than promote an already well-established, time-honored ideal of human freedom. We might wonder, then, in the company of Foucault (1980), why it is we feel this need to incite the many discourses of and on democracy, and those many ideals to which democracy gestures? What does all of this betray? Let us at least regard the discourses of democracy as a *labor,* a labor that is performed on us and a labor that we perform in turn on *ourselves,* that we *will* ourselves, at times incognizant of why

---

7   Francis Fukuyama's 'End-of-History' thesis has certainly had a long half-life if measured by the neo-conservative doctrines he once advanced as well as their uncritical acceptance by Bush administration officials. See Fukuyama (2006).

and at what cost. Doing so will require that we attend to the matter of foundations in political thought.

Weak Legitimacy and World Politics

In a recent book called *Sustaining Affirmation* Stephen White explores the problem of foundations in political theory in order to probe the status of the basic ontological entities of various theoretical traditions. White elaborates a flexible, accommodative, felicitous foundation or 'premise' for thinking about power, and especially those forms of power that inspire normative designs (White 2001). He argues that such a premise may actually be stronger than more rigid ideological foundations in any number of traditions of political thought. The field of International Relations would do well to consider White's arguments, for he is able to expose weaknesses in accepted doctrines and chart new political forms that do not strive for the kind of ontological stability and rigidity that have been the hallmarks of Western political thought and experience.

White is in conversation with postmodern and poststructuralist perspectives that have yielded much in the way of an understanding of the problem of foundations in the social sciences, including international relations. But he is uncomfortable with the reservations such theorists have about *affirming* an ethics or politics out of concern for resorting to a dangerous, exclusionary ontology of transcendence. White seeks to advance debates by shifting the 'intellectual burden ... from a preoccupation with what is opposed and deconstructed, to an engagement with what must be articulated, cultivated, and affirmed in its wake' (8). White asks if a critical perspective that has long been preoccupied with the contestability of foundations might wear a lighter burden, what might be called the onus of 'another justification',[8] an altogether different manner of engaging the always problematical turn to a timeless fundament for thinking about politics (Nelson 2004). White's aim, then, is to serve a philosophical purpose 'concerned with the constitution of, and reflection upon, the basic figures or portrayals that animate our thought and action'.

> Our figurations of self, other, and the beyond-human are never purely cognitive matters; rather they are also always aesthetic-affective. Wittgenstein captures something of this curious sense of basic 'beliefs' when he says: 'It strikes me that a religious belief could only be something like a passionate commitment to a system of reference. Hence although it's a belief, it's really a way of living; a way of assessing life' ... A 'felicitous' ontology would be one that offered a figuration of human being in terms of at least four existential realities or universals: language, mortality or finitude, natality or the capacity for radical novelty, and the articulation of some ultimate background source. The figures of weak ontology provide a 'rough cognitive and affective orientation'; they structure our perception of what is more or less significant in the ethical-political world and help to motivate us accordingly ... In sum, one does not so much derive principles as elicit an ethos from ontological figures (White 2005, 17).

---

8   White derives this in part perhaps from Michael Dillon's 'Another Justice' (1999). See also William E. Connolly (1993).

The quest for unchanging universals can only yield fabrications that will strive to mask the utter groundlessness of their claims to transcendence. What has so troubled modern theory is that various procedures are used to conceal the very absence of basic entities or properties in social life, clothing those procedures whereby the work of artifice is made to appear natural and inevitable. White's weak ontology inspires a different order of question that political theorists are now taking up with respect to domestic political concerns – for example, inclusion, equality, difference and otherness, and so on. But there is no reason these concerns should only apply to domestic political life, and the theoretical discourses of Sphere 1. They certainly have application in world politics, and the sphere, Sphere 2, where political notions like democracy and legitimacy are theorized. What follows is only a rough sketch of the line of thinking theorists of International Relations might begin to pursue.

Political space and the experimental aspect of political life within a well-circumscribed space is necessarily contingent upon what is beyond that space. It is also contingent upon the history through which it becomes possible to delineate a conception of the within that is distinguished from the without. These contingencies are powerful, and international relations theorists have remarked on them for some time.[9] These contingent aspects are often drawn upon to invoke and illuminate the violence that is done to otherness and difference when history and space are covered over rather than acknowledged and probed. Weak ontology points to the usefulness of such probes. White has remarked that weak ontology 'does not so much name a doctrine as gesture toward a thicket of philosophical issues' (White 2005, 11). The trouble, or the opportunity, is that these issues present themselves as problems to be overcome, when in fact they are ultimately irresolvable. Indeed, if they did not get configured as problems but as incitements for ongoing reflection, problematization,[10] and elucidation that did not strive to end in some unified Form-like conception, but which invited further questions and incitements to thinking, then perhaps another order of political possibilities might emerge. Indeed, the issues that White and others bring to the fore reflect a condition that is reflective of the very heterogeneity of *life itself.* A politics that is relational, mutually constitutive, and capable of forming another ethos of political identity and action does not rely upon transcendent hopes or an eternal will, but invests itself *laterally* in an outward (as opposed to inward) orientation of thought and action (White 2000, 11). It engages difference and otherness in another striving, in an 'aesthetic-affective' 'process of cultivation of oneself and one's disposition to the world' (11).

International Relations scholars might give more attention to the very restrictive vocabularies and grammars of political thought that mark their field and which predispose them to dismiss such forms of human striving. Would it not be worth exploring how the languages of International Relations are constitutive of, as well as

---

9   There are many works one might cite here. But one of the first provocations in this direction was the work of R.B.J. Walker. See, for example, Walker (1995).

10   I am borrowing Michel Foucault's use of this term in the introductory chapters of Foucault (1990).

always in the process of constitut*ing,* the anxieties that the long tradition of scholarship has insisted *must* intervene in all aspects of this life (Shaw 2004)? The task here, one could argue, would be to bring to bear other vocabularies and grammars of political thinking that are already very much at work, but which scholars at home in Sphere 2 have demonstrated such a profound unwillingness to see and understand.

Along with White, William Connolly has done much to introduce new vocabularies and grammars into this emerging picture.[11] Taking his cue from Nietzsche's reflections on 'Old Europe' [*sic*] and its history,' Connolly explores the significance of what he calls the 'politics of becoming':

> When the pace of life accelerates, nature ceases and becomes art. Inside this exaggeration is an insight. In an up-tempo world people readily become more 'cocky', experimental, and improvizational. That is, they become more democratic and less fixed and hierarchical. As these improvizations proceed, people can also become more alert to how 'accidents, moods, and caprice' have already shaped them. The connection between the shift in the experience of nature and the experience of identity is important, for unless essentially embodied human beings cast off the weight of a teleological experience of nature they are unlikely to come to terms with the element of contingency and fluidity in cultural identity (Connolly 2002, 157).

Further on in this work Connolly invites us to consider Nietzsche's contribution to democratic thinking, an unintended contribution that ran quite counter to Nietzsche's expressed affection for the nobility. Connolly explores some unintended ambiguities and ironies in Nietzsche that advance political thinking in quite new ways.

> To democratize the Nietzschean conception of nobility ... is to generalize the noble ethos he admires. It is to support a multidimensional pluralism of democratic life irreducible to the national or local pluralisms often associated with democracy; and it is to pursue the possibility of common action in that network through negotiation of an ethos of engagement between constituencies who fold into their relational identities the three qualities Nietzsche associates with the new nobility. The dissonant interdependence among these three elements – self-experimentalism, grace, and plurality – is precisely the condition of being appropriate to democracy in a fast-paced world (Connolly 2002, 165).

The accelerated processes of globalization are much on Connolly's mind as he searches for new reflective moments out of which an ethics and politics of 'critical engagement' can be cultivated. I would venture that there are affinities between Connolly's emerging *critical* democratic theory and cosmopolitan theories that are emerging from the likes of K. Anthony Appiah (Appiah 2006). Taken together, these rich discourses have seeped into public discussions bearing on the role of America in a post-2001 world. There are many other discourses which intersect these in turn (Sen 2006). Suffice is to say that this kind of labor is already being applied, but it deserves more exercise, and it also deserves more attention in policymaking communities.

---

11 Arguably Connolly's writings have mainly dealt with Sphere 1 theories, but a significant element of his work bears upon world-political issues. See Connolly (1991), especially Chapter 2, 'Global Political Discourse'.

Conclusion

The long tradition of Western political thought teaches, among many other things, that democratic governance and legitimate political order are achievable prospects located perilously close to chaos. The abyss of civil war was never far from the minds of the seminal thinkers.[12] In part what *theory* has been about is mediating democracy's proximity to chaos. If pronouncing what can come to be regarded as the boundary, border, inside, and outside in relation to a 'time' for legitimate democratic forms, democracy's exception – revolution, civil war, and so on – will serve as the powerful referent symbolizing the cost of *not* installing institutions that can enable real democratic practices to emerge and endure in their many forms. Why this rich tradition matters so profoundly for the task of insuring regional and global stability is too often assumed rather than re-examined, re-explained, and re-thought.

What is remarkable, and perhaps *originally* so, about core liberal-Enlightenment values we associate with democracy and legitimacy is this modern tradition's long preoccupation with pre-given limits and the resolve of some to do whatever is necessary, at whatever cost, to transcend them. Paraphrasing Kant's engagement of the limit, Isaiah Berlin observed that for this Enlightenment thinker knowledge of the limits that must be observed prevents one from attempting the impossible (Berlin 1998). Yet if political limits are not god-given, but are the expression of communal negotiations of the politically possible at a given time, then there can never be a final, fixed political form. Foucault may have been correct that modernity unleashed a human will that would forever engage the question of the limit – its arbitrariness, its temporal and spatial parameters, and experiments in what would be required to move beyond them (Foucault 1984). Perhaps modernity also provoked an anxiety and a restlessness, a willingness to question what could be made to be regarded as a way of escaping the limit by testing its spatial and temporal articulations through new political imaginaries, imagining another striving, other political possibilities that would serve as beacons, lighting other paths that history would one day show us as unmistakably advancing down.

References

Appiah, K. (2006), *Cosmopolitanism: Ethics in a World of Strangers* (New York: W.W. Norton).

Barber, B. (2004), *Fear's Empire: War, Terrorism, and Democracy* (New York: W.W. Norton).

Benjamin, W. (1955), *Illuminations* (New York: Harcourt, Brace and World).

Berlin, I. (1998), 'Two Concepts of Liberty', in *The Proper Study of Mankind*, Henry Hardy (ed.) (New York: Farrar, Straus and Giroux).

---

12 Hobbes certainly comes to mind. For an illuminating reading of Hobbes' appreciation of the especially devastating results of civil (as opposed to international) war, see George Kateb (1989). This essay deserves a public airing of its own as Iraq plunges deeper into the abyss.

Bull, Hedley (2002), *The Anarchical Society: A Study of Order in World Politics,* Third Edition (New York: Columbia University Press).

Butler, J. (2004), *Precarious Life: The Powers of Mourning and Violence* (London: Verso).

Connolly, W. (2005), 'The Evangelical-Capitalist Resonance Machine', *Political Theory* 33: 6 (December), 869–86.

Connolly, W. (2004), 'The Complexity of Sovereignty', in Jenny Edkins *et al.* (eds), *Sovereign Lives* (New York: Routledge).

Connolly, W. (2002), *Neuropolitics: Thinking, Culture, Speed* (Minneapolis: University of Minnesota Press).

Connolly, W. (1993), 'Beyond Good and Evil: The Ethical Sensibility of Michel Foucault', *Political Theory*, 21: 3 (August), 365–89.

Connolly, W. (1991), *Identity/Difference: Democratic Negotiations of Political Paradox* (Ithaca: Cornell University Press).

Connolly, W. (1988), *Political Theory and Modernity* (New York: Blackwell).

Connolly, W. (1984), *Legitimacy and the State*, William E. Connolly (ed.) (New York: New York University Press).

Cox, R. (1981), 'Social Forces, States and World Orders: Beyond International Relations Theory', *Millennium*, 10: 2, 126–55.

Dillon, M. (1999), 'Another Justice', *Political Theory*, 27: 2, 155–75.

Dunn, J. (2005), *Democracy: A History* (New York: Atlantic Monthly Press).

Ferguson, K. (1987), 'Male-Ordered Politics: Feminism and Political Science', in *Idioms of Inquiry: Critique and Renewal in Political Science*, Terence Ball (ed.) (Albany: State University of New York Press).

Foucault, M. (1990), *The Use of Pleasure: The History of Sexuality, Volume 2*, trans. Robert Hurley (New York: Vintage).

Foucault, M. (1984), 'What is Enlightenment?', in Paul Rabinow (ed.), *The Foucault Reader* (New York: Pantheon), 32–50.

Foucault, M. (1980), *The History of Sexuality, Volume 1: An Introduction*, trans. Robert Hurley (New York: Vintage).

Fukuyama, F. (2006), *America at the Crossroads: Democracy, Power, and the Neoconservative Legacy* (New Haven: Yale University Press).

Gallie, W.B. (1962), 'Essentially Contested Concepts,' in *The Importance of Language* (Englewood Cliffs, NJ: Prentice Hall), 121–146.

George, J. (1994), *Discourses of Global Politics: A Critical (Re)Introduction to International Relations* (Boulder: Lynne Reinner).

Harvey, D. (2005), *The New Imperialism* (Oxford: Oxford University Press).

Hobbes, T. (1994), *Leviathan*, Edwin Curley (ed.) (Indianapolis: Hackett Publishing).

Kant, I. (1991), *Kant: Political Writings*, H.S. Reiss (ed.) (Cambridge: Cambridge University Press).

Kateb, G. (1989), 'Hobbes and the Irrationality of Politics', *Political Theory*, 17: 3 (August), 355–91.

Kateb, G. (2006), *Patriotism and Other Mistakes* (New Haven: Yale University Press).

Machiavelli, N. (1994), *Machiavelli: Selected Political Writings*, trans. David

Wooton (ed.) (Indianapolis: Hackett Publishing).

Mearsheimer, J. and Walt, S. (2006), 'The Israel Lobby', *London Review of Books*, 28: 6 (23 March), 3–7.

Nelson, S. (2004), 'Sovereignty, Ethics, Community', *Philosophy and Social Criticism*, 30: 7, 816–41.

Pickering, J. and Peceny, M. (2006), 'Forging Democracy at Gunpoint', *International Studies Quarterly*, 50: 3 (September), 539–59.

Rousseau, J-J. (1987), *On the Social Contract*, trans. Donald A. Cress. (Indianapolis: Hackett Publishing).

Said, E. (1994), *Orientalism* (New York: Vintage).

Sen, A. (2006), *Identity and Violence: The Illusion of Destiny* (New York: W.W. Norton).

Shaw, K. (2004), 'Knowledge, Foundation, Politics', *International Studies Review*, 6: 4, 7–20.

Smith, N. (2005), *The Endgame of Globalization* (New York: Routledge).

Walker, R.B.J. (1995), *Inside/Outside: International Relations as Political Theory* (Cambridge: Cambridge University Press).

White, S. (2005), 'Weak Ontology: Genealogy and Critical Issues', *The Hedgehog Review*, 7.2 (Summer).

White, S. (2001), *Sustaining Affirmation: The Strengths of Weak Ontology* (Princeton: Princeton University Press).

Wolin, S. (2004), *Politics and Vision*, expanded edition. (Princeton: Princeton University Press).

Wolin, S. (2001), *Tocqueville Between Two Worlds: The Making of a Political and Theoretical Life* (Princeton: Princeton University Press).

Wolin, S. (1988), 'On the Theory and Practice of Power', in *After Foucault*, Jonathan Arac (ed.) (New Brunswick: Rutgers University Press).

Wolin, S. (1969), 'Political Theory as a Vocation', *American Political Science Review*, 63: 4 (December), 1062–82.

Conclusion

Sai Felicia Krishna Hensel

A good deal of human behavior can be understood and indeed predicted, if we know a people's design for living – Kluckhohn, *Mirror of Man.*

The process of transformation and change in the international system has been an ongoing cumulative process whose origins lie far back in the annals of history. Many of the watershed events in the history of mankind, whether they be related to conflict, technological innovations, or new ideologies have contributed to what we now recognize as globalization – a process with political, economic, and social implications for all societies. Globalization is both an integrative force and one which exposes both the existing and the newly emerging divisions between societies and cultures, as well as between nations and states. Globalization has caused us to confront the fundamental assumptions about boundaries, space, and time that inform our perspective of the international system. It is challenging to speak of an international order in such an environment and to portray it accurately.

The principal challenge of the post-modern world has been to adapt our vision to incorporate the changing spatial dimensions of the interconnected world. The contemporary international system is distinctive in that the boundaries of the state are transcended by global issues, such as terrorism, environmental degradation, Internet communication, commerce, and security, leading to the need for transnational organizations and global strategies to confront the new threats.

International relations theory offers paradigms for understanding the international system, as well as instruments for transformation of the system. We can construct models, define concepts, and explore inter-state relations in an efficient and systematic manner. Theoretical frameworks provide an effective medium for organizing our knowledge-base and adding to it or modifying it in response to our findings. Perspectives and theories have emerged in response to the need to explain changes in the international order and the present discourse contributes to this dialogue. The 'international society' or English School proponents presaged many of the elements of the current discussion. Their emphasis on societal values, norms, and instruments, such as diplomacy, humanitarian law, and human rights, provides a unique approach to the question of power relations.

Will universal problems substantively impact the way in which we approach inter-state relations? The answer may lie in whether the threat perception is shared by the relevant actors responsible for drafting solutions. International regimes often appear in response to a collective process of lobbying and interpreting of scientific data. This is a process that generally exemplifies a constructive interaction between states and non-state actors representing interest groups that may have a transnational structure. Global health, environmental standards, and humanitarian principles are some examples where international regimes are seen as both essential and effective in dealing with problems. Cooperative structures and collaborative enforcement are also seen as crucial in dealing with issues, such as global warming, toxic emissions, and disease prevention. Governments enter into strategic partnerships to employ their resources and institutions to enforce and monitor regulations and assume responsibility for ensuring the success of these agreements.

International regimes have become more important as the definitions of security in the international environment have expanded to include areas that are not conflict-related. There is a growing recognition that sustainable development should be seen as a security issue in itself, as it has broad and serious implications for the survival of societies. NGO's, interest groups, corporate bodies, and other transnational coalitions have greatly contributed to promoting awareness of such global problems as the spread of disease and environmental issues. The significant role of these new actors in the policy-making arena is being widely acknowledged and some of these groups have been accorded permanent positions in the new institutional structures. The implementation of policies, however, continues to be the responsibility of states.

Our understanding of transnational crises has been greatly enhanced by our knowledge base and by the communications network that conveys information to a global audience. The result is that populations and governments are able to (in most cases) comprehend the nature of the crisis as it impacts them and take suitable actions. The existence of communities of practice, such as the ICRC, CDC, INTERPOL, and so on, facilitates professional cooperation during natural disasters, pandemics, and terrorist incidents (Global Cooperation Framework 2, 2000, 10). The realization that this is an interconnected environment in which events in one region can, in many instances, impact other regions through trade disruption, atmospheric pollution, and other means is gradually becoming central to policy planning.

The transformation of the geo-political environment, driven in some measure by issues originating in the virtual world, presents a tremendous challenge for governance. These challenges exceed the capacity of any one state or group of states and require cooperative institutions, policies, and enforcement mechanisms. This has led some analysts to envisage a multi-level governance structure, based on multiple identities and loyalties held by the population (Toffler, 1987).

The debate on the new world order has coalesced primarily around two perspectives, one proclaiming the continued relevance of the nation-state and its institutions and the other anticipating the eventual development and strengthening of supra and transnational bodies which would, in some instances, supersede the authority of the individual state. The argument for the continued relevance of the nation-state in setting policy rests, in part, on the premise that if technologies are the driving force behind the development of supra-national institutions, then the lack of access to these technologies by a large proportion of the global population will continue to give the upper hand to national elites that control access to technology. This perspective reinforces the argument for the continuing supremacy of the state in the international order.

The transformation of world politics by technology has long been predicted by many professionals. Technological advances have provided us with the means to realize our vision of a desirable world, but there is a sense of apprehension that our knowledge exceeds our ability to control it and understand its consequences. The concern that technology is a driver of change, rather than a reflection of change, and that technological determinism is destroying traditional concepts of humanity is a growing concern among scholars.

The discussion on global strategic initiatives is increasingly focusing on global norms and values. Normative values are being seen as central to the character of the twenty-first century international order. The normative standards of a community are critical for predicting their behavior in responding to the challenges of a changing world and their ability to form cooperative alliances. The multipolar world particularly requires shared norms and values – fundamental values that are based on a 'web of expectations' and which require continual reinforcement to remain effective (Raymond, 1997).

The reality about the changed nature of world power is that military might and economic strength alone may no longer be totally effective in influencing states. Instead, new micro-challenges are matters of increasing concern, such as the suicide bomber, the improvized explosive device (IED), and the bioterrorist. If the primacy of 'hard power' is being challenged by micro-disruptors, then what is our hope for the future? The answer might lie in 'soft power', the knowledge-based ability to influence policy (Keohane and Nye, 1998). The microchip has dispersed power and knowledge amongst countless small units and enabled both constructive and destructive forces.

Cooperative strategies involving private and public enterprise and local and supra-national institutions are forming the basis of collaborative networks that are engaging in collective action to meet the environmental and economic challenges that are preventing societies from their access to a good life. In the ongoing crises of global warming and environmental degradation, multinational companies are behaving more responsibly towards the environment, often at the expense of higher profits, in order to achieve sustainable growth and to build a better world. Many governments are also joining in the effort to become 'greener' in the area of clean energy. Cooperative networks incorporating a multi-level solution to some problems have been found to be quite effective. Examples include locally-generated energy solutions that present a great opportunity for innovation and that supplement state-driven initiatives. In the economic sphere, the growth of micro-finance solutions is emerging as an effective mechanism for offering small loans for self-employment and small scale entrepreneurship without. These are some of the many instances which illustrate the growth in networks incorporating micro-solutions, as well as macro-resources.

Many analysts see conflict and competition rendered obsolete by integrative globalizing forces and have pointed to the examples of the states of modern Europe, and the North American continent. The emphasis on cooperative associations, rather than on confrontational positions, characterizes relations between these neighbors. Karl Deutsch described these as 'pluralistic security communities', distinguished by the absence of hostile plans and strategies and by acceptance of common interests and values in their interactions (Deutsch, *et al.* 1957). Thus, border cooperation, trade and commercial relations pursued through common agreements, relative freedom of movement between countries, and shared currency, as in Europe, set these examples apart. What prevents such regional partnerships from proliferating throughout the international system? The answers lie in examining normative values and concepts and in determining the scope and levels of input into the decision-making process. Expanding this approach to look at global conflict in the contemporary world, we could argue with some credibility that parties that are not involved in formulating these normative rules, or that do not share a normative tradition have no stake in subscribing to the code of action that they prescribe. Even if states formally subscribe to such conventions, there is no assurance that they can ensure that individuals and groups within their respective states will follow the prescribed behavior. For example, terrorists and terrorist groups operating in asymmetric war conditions ignore such rules. Such conventions, therefore, can only function when all parties subscribe to them and when sanctions can be imposed on those states, groups, and individuals that break the rules. Where states are concerned, it is increasingly evident that the formal pledge to uphold an international convention is often only symbolic, and therefore subject to violation.

The proliferation of weapons of mass destruction – chemical, biological, radiological, and nuclear – is a concern that is increasingly promising to change our way of thinking about the international order in even more fundamental ways. Many states are focusing on the perceived decline in America's protective power as North Korea, Pakistan, Iran and other states enter the nuclear age. As the diffusion of nuclear knowledge and technology becomes progressively more difficult to contain, it is quite reasonable to expect that more and more states will want to develop their own nuclear capabilities. The rapid progress of computation and simulation techniques will enable states to develop devices without being detected by prevailing surveillance mechanisms. The international regimes in place to prevent nuclear proliferation have proven to be ineffective in discouraging the spread of this technology. This exposes the weakness of regimes that are not subscribed to by all actors and which are practically unenforceable, except through voluntary action. As noted above, the entrance of non-state actors whose behavior is not subject to existing safeguards into this field is to be anticipated. The premise of deterrence theory does not hold in an environment where ideology and suicidal tendencies combine to overwhelm rationality. The assumptions on which we have based international relations theory to this point have to take into consideration the apocalyptic pronouncements of emerging power players who publicly profess to the inevitability of an Armageddon (Poole, 2006).

Some analysts suggest that engagement through constructive dialogue and economic incentives is the best way to control the development of nuclear weapons. The hope is that reason and self-interest will prevail. As nations increasingly confront the challenge of developing common security policies in response to global challenges, it becomes obvious that multilateral consultation is the only way to go. This is reflected in the growth of a broad range of international organizations and institutions engaged in dealing with transnational issues. The direction of national policy will increasingly have to incorporate a shift towards cooperative international strategy as the process of globalization continues to bring about a convergence of interests and interconnectedness produces global consequences. Advances in information technology and wider availability of data flows have enabled us to see the importance of cooperation as humankind faces challenges that pertain to the survival of the entire planet, rather than specific groups or civilizations, as has been the case in previous centuries (Krishna-Hensel, 2006, 1).

The scholars contributing to this volume have approached the challenge of interpreting the globalizing world from a variety of perspectives. The chapters explore the role of major players, the great powers, international organizations and institutions, as well as regional and individual state actors as they respond to the imperatives of a globalizing world. The authors have made a significant contribution to our understanding of the emerging international order through a discussion of regional and transnational paradigms. Many of the chapters reflect a sensitivity to the unique challenges confronting theorists as they factor in the impact of scale and speed on the changing international system. A common thread that runs through the volume is the recognition that there is a multiplicity of actors on the world stage contributing at one level or another to the process of collective decision-making. These studies, therefore, anticipate further transformation of global society and the increasing reliance on voluntary compliance among the participants of the new international order.

Cooperative strategies and institutions offer the most effective solution to the challenges of the contemporary international system. They also offer the best opportunities for achieving the fundamental objective of sustainable development for a world where inequalties have been amplified by the forces underpinning globalization. Cooperation has been an important approach in the development of early societies when cooperative hunting evolved as an efficient survival mechanism for groups of hunters. The same principle applies as humanity confronts the challenges of a rapidly changing world. Contemporary global organizations and institutions are proliferating at an impressive pace and incorporate diverse public and private participation. Collaborative networks, functioning in some instances in cooperation with local and regional agencies, are emerging as a solution for the future.

Our attention, however, once again returns to the significance of norms of behavior within the international community. For these collaborative networks to serve as effective mechanisms to facilitate cooperation in response to global challenges and opportunities, there must be a normative commitment on the part of all participants to work together in a spirit of compromise and consensus. Moreover, there must be a commitment to the common good of the whole of humankind that may require sacrifices by individual members of the community in order to promote that common good. In the final analysis, given the challenges and opportunities that confront the members of the international community in the twenty-first century, this normative commitment to the common good of all peoples is the only approach that promises the prospect of global survival, future security, and prosperity for all peoples.

References

Deutsch, Karl *et al.* (1957) *Political Community and the North Atlantic Area* (Princeton, N.J: Princeton University Press).

Executive Board of the UNDP and the UNPF (2000), *Second Global Cooperation Framework*, 2001–2003 (New York: United Nations).

Falk, Richard (1999), *Predatory Globalization* (Cambridge, UK: Polity Press).

Giddens, Anthony (1990), *The Consequences of Modernity* (Stanford, CA: Stanford University Press).

Habermas, Jürgen (2001), *The Postnational Constellation: Political Essays* (Cambridge, MA: MIT Press).

Harvey, David (1989), *The Condition of Postmodernity* (Oxford: Blackwell).

Held, David (1995), *Democracy and the Global Order: From the Modern State to Cosmopolitan Governance* (Stanford, CA: Stanford University Press).

Held, David, McGrew, Anthony, Goldblatt, David and Perraton, Jonathan (1999), *Global Transformations: Politics, Economics and Culture* (Stanford, CA: Stanford University Press).

Keohane, Robert O. and Nye, Joseph S., Jr. (1998), 'Power and Interdependence in the Information Age', *Foreign Affairs* 77/5 (September/October), pp. 81–94.

Kluckhohn, Clyde (1949), *Mirror for Man* (New York: Premier Books).

Krishna-Hensel, Sai Felicia (2006), *Global Cooperation: Challenges and Opportunities in the Twenty-First Century* (Aldershot: Ashgate Publishing).

Modelski, George (1972), *Principles of World Politics* (New York: Free Press).

Morgenthau, Hans (1954), *Politics Among Nations: The Struggle for Power and Peace* (New York: Knopf).

Poole, Patrick, 'Ahmadinejad's Apocalyptic Faith', *FrontPageMagazine.com.* (August 17, 2006), http://www.frontpagemag.com/Articles/ReadArticle.asp?ID=23916 accessed December 2006.

Raymond, Gregory (1997), 'Problems and Prospects in the Study of International Norms', *Mershon International Studies Review*, 41, pp. 205–245.

Rawls, John (1993), *Political Liberalism* (New York: Columbia University Press).

Robertson, R. (1992), *Globalization: Social Theory and Global Culture* (London: Sage).

Ruggie, John Gerard (1993), 'Territoriality and Beyond: Problematizing Modernity in International Relations', *International Organization* 47, pp. 139–74.

Scheuerman, William E. (2004), *Liberal Democracy and the Social Acceleration of Time* (Baltimore: Johns Hopkins Press).

Scholte, Jan Aart (2000), *Globalization: A Critical Introduction* (New York: St. Martin's Press).

Young, Oran, R. (1989), *International Cooperation: Building Regimes for Natural Resources and the Environment* (Ithaca and London: Cornell University Press).

Toffler, Alvin (1987), *The Third Wave* (New York: Random House Value Publishing).

Index